For the Victims…

Innocent Children of God, their Families and Friends….

This endeavor is dedicated to you in hope and in faith
That new life emerges in those touched
and inspired through this writing.

A Gift Of Love

To my Wife Sheryl;

My gift from God, my angel, for you are one of God's very own. You have taught me about faith, patience, and love. You are my best friend. From your first letter I knew what God was allowing to occur between us and in us was a spirit filled gift. I am grateful to God to have you as my wife and blessed to walk with you in ministry. As God prepares the way, I think of your life and the person I love, (Proverbs 2:3-6) " Let love and faithfulness never leave you; bind them around your neck, write them on the tablet of your heart. Then you will win favor and a good name in the sight of God and man. Trust in the Lord with all your heart and lean not on your own understanding; in all your ways acknowledge him, and he will make your paths straight." My dear, you are a precious gift in my life, and I know why all this is possible. Your love of Christ is a reflection of your faithfulness.

To my dear friends;

Lynda Mazzella

Your gift of Love, Patience, and enduring Faith in Christ, is a testimony to your walk with our Lord. Witnessing your guiding hand to nurture this text, while applying God's Word, I was touched by your humbled attitude and servant's heart. I am reminded in (Mathew 23:11-12) "The greatest among you will be your servant. For whoever exalts himself will be humbled, and whoever humbles himself will be exalted." I am grateful and thankful to God, to have worked with you, and to call you friend. God Bless you for your faith, that through your openness, your sharing, lives will be touched and families reconciled unto the Lord.

Pastor David Mazzella

Your faithfulness, support, encouragement to uplift the ministry and serve the will of God is a gift. I thank you and give praise to God that I have the opportunity to be a part of your life. I am grateful that you opened your heart, your home, and your time. Your Passion for Christ and the church, is spoken of in (Ephesians 4:11-13) "It was he who gave some to be apostles, some to be prophets, some to be evangelists, and some to be pastors and teachers, to prepare God's people for works of service, so that the body of Christ may be built up until we all reach unity in the faith and in the knowledge of the Son of God and become mature, attaining to the whole measure of the fullness of Christ."

Redeeming Grace

Terry King

With Lynda Mazzella

Saving Grace Ministries

Amherst, NY

Acknowledgements

I owe a debt of gratitude to Mr. Paul Gray, CC., Gowanda Correctional Facility, Gowanda, NY, who introduced me to R.E.T., Rational Emotive Therapy and the treatment process.

To Mr. Earl Merritt, CC., Cayuga Correctional Facility, Moravia, NY, who inspired me to seek my God and helped me to renew my faith.

To Sue King, my mother and friend, whose influence has impacted my life from infancy to my rebirth as a maturing man. She never lost faith in me and always remains as an inspiration.

To all the men I have met through this journey...men of diverse histories, sharing, caring, loving, showing forgiveness, and living lives of meaning and purpose. May God fulfill your dreams, thoughts and goals according to His will. We are reborn as children of God alive in faith, hope, and love all because of His transforming grace.

In memory of Roy C. Maines, Esq. (1939-1999) friend of Saving Grace Ministries, who dedicated his life to giving men a second chance through the Christian discipleship program of Kairos Prison Fellowship. His legacy lives on through the many lives in whom he made a difference.

~ Contents ~

~ Beginnings ~

Chapter One

I will never forget the cold hollow echo of steel against steel as the doors of my prison cell slammed and locked behind me. There is not a lonelier sound in the whole world.

While the fast-paced wheeling dealing world I had left behind went on without me, my life had come to a complete halt. Former friends, now competitors, jockeyed to grab the positions I once controlled. My friendships had been mutually based on need/want fulfillment. I was no longer in a position to benefit anyone. For the first time in a long time I was really alone. It was a sobering realization.

What had brought me to this place? I had nothing but time alone to ponder my life, its influences, and the consequences of my choices. I didn't know it then, but with all my heart, I know today that what satan meant for evil God meant for good. My name is Terry and this is my story.

Let me start at the beginning….

I am the son of Andrew Louis King, a proud man of Hungarian ancestry. He was born March 11, 1918, the son of John Kiroly and Rose Molnar Kiroly, a nice Hungarian couple, or "so I am told."

How did the son of John Kiroly become a King? It's a rather simple explanation. John and Rose had a second son named William. I called him "Uncle Bill." When Uncle Bill and my Dad (Andrew) enlisted in the service they decided to change their last names. Uncle Bill chose "Miller," the English translation of Molnar, and Dad chose "King," the English translation of Kiroly. (What's wrong with Kiroly? I kind of like it.) I don't know how their parents felt about it, but it's the way things were at the time, or "so I am told."

What was their motivation? I am not sure what generated the discomfort that this specific generation had with their names and heritage, but name changing seemed to be in vogue at that time. It seems many of us tend to do things as others do...follow the crowd.

Have you ever given any thought to your beginnings, the influencing factors that have affected your life's course? It's interesting, as we each study our family's beliefs and moral heritage we can begin to understand how we became who we are through influences and learned behavior.

Before our behavior patterns were established, we learned values and accepted beliefs by what we were told and what we observed. But do we simply accept who we are by what we are told without the value of conscious choices?

My hope is that as you read on, you will challenge yourself to define your beliefs, to know your life's beginnings, and to reach an understanding of what changes in your life may be needed so that you too may live a life of purpose and fulfillment.

My Grandparents, John and Rose Kiroly, lived in Wimber, Pennsylvania. Oh, my memories of Wimber! I remember our family trips as a kid. Packed in the family car for hours and hours, off we went to the Aunts' or to Grandma's, to have our ears pulled, cheeks pinched, and then just as the conversation got interesting be told, "This is an adult conversation. Go play, little kid, go play." And play we did. We had a sense of belonging, love and security. (For the most part, they are good memories.)

Take a moment and look back upon your happier childhood memories. Does any particular one stick out? How about bad memories? Are there incidents that just subconsciously keep revolving around and around in your mind, unsettled?

My paternal grandmother, Rose, was restless or "so I am told." Eventually she divorced John Kiroly. Rose Molnar less Kiroly, set off for New York City with her own dreams, goals, and aspirations. Oh, the sweet life. The 30's were tough, being the Depression years, but she was filled with a sense of adventure and anticipation.

She met a fellow named Mr. Frank Amigo of Spanish decent. Aunt Sue and Uncle Frank, two wonderful people, are the result of this union.

Isn't it neat to really look back on the dichotomy of our families and think of its development?

Uncle Frank, an extrovert by nature, is a world traveler. He is an ex-CIA agent, now residing in Maryland and New Mexico. A gifted artisan, he creates beautiful pottery. He is thus far our most famous family member having designed a Christmas bulb selected for a White House Christmas Tree. This bulb, crafted by Uncle Frank, now resides in the Smithsonian Institute.

Aunt Sue is versatile, eclectic, resourceful and an inspiration to independent living. Sue (or Rosalind) talented, perhaps a genius, most definitely travels along the road to the beat of a different drummer. Her art, antique crafted jewelry, is absolutely stunning. But! Never ask her about the IRS. (Family joke.)

Aunt Sue instilled within me a value. No, she never "instructed me" per se, but she taught me by example. She always did her best artistically in each item she made striving for perfection. There are issues in life that I always thought were important. I would question her motivation, but...well...she wins. She has the life I always wanted.

What about my father? Andrew King left home as a young man. He quit school, I believe, and headed off to Scalps-Level, Pennsylvania to work the labor gang in a coal mine. (Scalps-Level? Where on earth? Well, I checked and it is located right next door to Wimber.) At age 17, moved "by the times," Andrew left for the city that never sleeps...New York, New York. He attempted to live for a short period with his mother and Frank Amigo, but the city or the living circumstances just did not fit him.

He once again moved and began another journey in life. Off to Detroit! (Hungarian Gypsies, always on the move.)

Andrew was young, but was he naïve, innocent? I do not think so! He had to grow up too fast. He was running numbers, gambling and, well, let's just say that this innocent child was hired to distribute union organizer flyers at the Briggs Manufacturing Corporation, which later was to become part of the Chrysler Corporation of America.

Did you ever watch an old movie or newsreels of the late 30's when industry, the power of America, was undergoing a transformation? Workers were fed up with working 12 hours per day for very little wages, with very few health related or safety concerns in place. So the Unions did become the workingman's voice, but oh, the violence that ensued. I remember my father telling the Detroit story over and over so many times I could quote it verbatim. (I'm not making fun. These stories are part of our family history, our legacy, influencing all we have come to believe.)

What stories have been passed down to you? How have they influenced your way of thinking?

As my father would tell me these stories, hearing his voice, watching his face, I will always remember not only what he said, but also what he did not say. It was the adventure, the thrill of living on the edge, and the camaraderie...that welcome feeling of fitting in, of belonging.

How many of us go through life searching for a place to fit in where we feel comfortable...our place to belong? But where do you want to belong? What price are you willing to pay?

A lot had begun in my life and I am not even here yet. Amazing, how family stories become legacies of life, influencing our way of thinking! Do you question all that you were told as fact? I have used the phrase "so I am told," because that is a fact. I was not there, yet, I fully believe that these stories being passed from generation to generation are true. We assume them to be true. But, is it possible that the "truth" may be slanted according to the bias of the one telling the story? Should we believe all that we have been told? Can we always believe the family source? It is okay to challenge, question, or defend these stories of family history.

Andrew moved in with an aunt in Detroit. (I always wondered if his aunt pinched his cheeks too!) This aunt, a sister of John Kiroly, extended herself to make a home for Andrew. But for some reason, Andrew left the aunt's house in Detroit and moved into the home of a Hungarian family.

Andrew was young, gregarious, worldly-wise and on the move. He began frequenting a certain Hungarian Restaurant in the neighborhood, where he met and befriended a man named Mr. Ed Petricko, a circumstance which will play an important role in sculpting his life's course.

Looking back on your own life, can you identify times, places and people who influenced the course of your life?

Ed introduced his new friend Andrew to his sister, a fine beautiful young lady, named Susan Ann Petricko. Beautiful, oh yes! For I have seen her pictures. She was innocence and beauty. But who is she? Where did she come from? Well, let's go back and investigate.

Anna Murray my maternal great grandmother was born during the mid-to-late 1800's, in Czechoslovakia, which, at the time was Austria–Hungary. At the same time her future husband, Paul Petricko, was being raised in the same country. My maternal great grandfather, Paul, married Anna Murray and this union resulted in the birth of four children Paul, John, Mary and Michael. Even in the late 1800's life was tough compared to what we consider life's necessities today.

Anna and Paul's son John, born 1891, possessed some Gypsy blood in him as well. John was the restless one. Like many people of the times, he decided it was time to come to America to seek his fortune.

The old country was suffering from the devastation imposed upon it as a result of World War I. The basic needs of life…food, clothing, housing, were scarce or nonexistent. America seemed to offer hope for a better life. He had heard that this was a Land where dreams come true.

On the same ship, coming to America in 1914 was Susie Tkacs, born in Austria-Hungary in 1895. Her family had sent Susie to America to seek a better life, not only for herself but also for the rest of her family. She was to find employment, save money and then send for them. It was quite a responsibility for a nineteen-year-old girl. With practically no formal education, leaving one's family, possibly forever, traveling alone to a foreign country, unable to speak the language, with no money and absolutely nothing except two suitcases containing all of your worldly possessions, is astoundingly courageous!

This woman, Susie, was my Baba. Baba, Slovak for "grandma," is an honored name. (You see, not all elderly women or grandmothers are Babas. She earned the honored title.)

Redeeming Grace

As I sat alone in my cell, I thought of Baba, standing alone on the deck of that ship, entombed by the chilling darkness as night settled in around her. As she stood there cold, lonely, and certainly apprehensive, to whom did she turn for guidance, faith, and comfort? How did she find the courage she needed? Baba was a devout Catholic. She drew strength from her deep faith in God.

Although I knew of her faith in God, it would not be until many years later that I would embrace it as my own. But throughout my formative years, she was there, a strong positive influence and example.

Take a look at your own heritage...not just your cultural heritage, but also the foundation of your real beginning, moral values, legacies of life. As my story unfolds, I hope you will stop for a moment and reflect on your own.

Destiny! Paul Petricko and Susie Tkacs were each seeking a better life for themselves and all generations to follow. It took only ten days, traveling by ship across the Atlantic, to alter the course of our entire family history. They chose to transcend a lifestyle, perhaps to fulfill dreams. But was that their intention, or were they simply making courageous choices as necessity required, experiencing life one day at a time?

I remember watching the Bi-Centennial Celebration of 1976 and the magnificent flotillas in the Hudson River channel. The stunning views of the Statue of Liberty evoke so many emotions. I must admit that each time I see that Lady I feel proudly secure, full of hope and gratitude for my legacy of life.

I often wonder what was going through their minds, as John and Susie, (at that time strangers to each other) standing on board the ship among the other immigrants, approached this truly magnificent symbol of freedom. Did they hope for a completely new life? Yes. But still, they were each bringing their old ways of life with them. See, John and Susie were leaving oppression, but they were not leaving their meaning of life behind. They would never give up the traditions that defined their beliefs, values and purpose.

When you are oppressed, but still maintain your instinct for survival, supported by a heritage of Christian values, then your purpose in life will succeed. First we must define our purpose in life. Why are we here? Do you sense your purpose or are you simply going through the motions of living, being lead by the forces of life, yet totally unsure of its direction? See, our lives do have meaning each and every day. The choices we make in life should be made to keep us moving in the direction toward achieving our goal. Our lives become the sum total of our life choices. Do we stay the same, remain on the same course or change for a better meaning of life?

No matter how incredible the odds, God will help us. He is present and interested in our lives.

Surviving the voyage, tired and weary, the journey was far from over. There was the ordeal of processing through Ellis Island. "Let me see your papers." "Go here!" "Stand there!" "Tuberculosis check, over there!" "You stay. You go!" Imagine the confusion of all this, not understanding one word of English. Not One! It was only their sense of purpose that gave them the courage to persevere.

Today we have a generation emerging as little more than adult children, with no direction, no values, no sense of accomplishment, just going through the motions of life. Many of us have no idea what it means to sacrifice or persevere under pressure.

Life is a precious gift for those individuals who are fortunate enough to discover and know their life's purpose. For many life is little more that a meaningless existence. Tough statement! Yes. But, when we confront that which "just isn't right" in our lives, well, it needn't be comfortable. Are you the person you want to be? If not, why not? Have you identified the values of the family into which you were born? Do you really know what your forefathers stood for, what they were willing to devote their lives to, what they were willing to die for?

After processing through Ellis Island John, Susan, and other immigrants from Austria-Hungary boarded a train to Braddock, Pennsylvania. Why Braddock? They knew that in Braddock they would find people of their own kind who would help them regain their balance. There were people living in Braddock who shared a common heritage, values, ethics and similar beliefs.

How do we assimilate into a society? Herding, I'm told. Group consciousness. This concept "your own kind" has intrigued me for many years, perhaps since puberty when my eager little eyes began to view the world around me with enthusiastic interest. Many of us attach racial barriers to this concept, separating White, Black, Latino, Asian, and so forth. But in reality, isn't it a reflection of our beliefs, values, ethics and moral affiliations?

16

Weren't Susie and John searching for a supporting cast to re-enforce all the learned behavior, religious and family traditions they held so dear?

In prison I met men from all walks of life with backgrounds that would petrify even the bravest of heart. But what I've learned is that somewhere along the way they too were taught, introduced to a value system (perceived as good or bad), acquired learned behavior which taught them to seek out their own kind…to maintain a lifestyle…balance.

Homeostasis is an intriguing word. I have come to appreciate its meaning as a coming together, picking up the pieces of one's life and regaining one's balance. Certainly my life, perhaps your life as well, has experienced over and over again the struggle for homeostasis, to find, retain, and maintain life's balance.

Look at your life and its beginnings. Challenge your thoughts to honestly appraise your forefathers and "their own kind." With whom did they assimilate? Were they leaders or followers? Do you find in the history of your family's life a reflection of your own?

~ Building Family Values ~

Chapter Two

What was it about Braddock, Pennsylvania, or any other city in America where people settle? What does it really mean, "to settle?" Is it putting down roots, owning a lovely house, with a white picket fence, two children, a dog and a nice automobile...a "happily-ever-after" kind of life?

We cannot ignore the fact that trials and tribulations are a part of life. The drunken fights, the unruly neighbors, the child prone to drinking or drugs, social influences, breaking societal boundaries. Can we earn the "picket fence" lifestyle and still live outside society's accepted framework of understanding and balance? Many people try.

Although they traveled down life's adventurous road together, John and Susan did not meet until they arrived in Braddock.

They married, and as they had already discovered, life was not without heartache even in America. Of the three children born to them, Johnny lived only 18 months, and Mary died at birth leaving Michael as the only remaining Braddock legacy. (Uncle Mike grew up to become a war hero. A debt of gratitude is owed this man.)

Eventually Susie and John with their son Michael, migrated to a city dear to my heart, Newton Falls, Ohio. It was a quiet town in Middle

America. The Newton Steel Mill offered jobs where families could work and live the American Dream. They had a dream, American I'm not sure, but a dream. They lived their realities. But from what I am told, life was not all that happy. Alcohol, abusiveness, arguments were a way of life, an inherent (or learned) propensity to demand life's "wants" and acquire life "needs."

During the period 1918-1925, Susie and John had three more children... Edward, Susan Ann (my mother, born May 1, 1923), and Margaret.

The children were raised on a 78-acres farm, located in Palmyra, Ohio, approximately seven miles from Newton Falls. (The farm is now owned by the Federal Government and is made part of the Kirwin Dam Project.)

Mom told such wonderful stories of the farm. It was a tough, hard life but they were self-sufficient. The children of Susie and John were taught to value the land, to cherish their beliefs, and to achieve their purpose in life. Theirs was a lifestyle filled with determination.

To the best of his knowledge and experience, John Petricko lived his life to the fullest. His sons and daughters are his legacy of life. For his life, his teachings and beliefs live on through Mike, Ed, Sue, and Margaret, and now through Rick, Carol and Terry, Paul, Cheryl, Michael, Johnny, Gloria, Bobby, Ed, Ronnie and their children's children.

Susan Ann, was taught her lessons by Baba, Ed, Michael and the Palmyra School, (a neat little school of the 1930's style.) During the summers of her junior and senior school years, Mom left Palmyra to stay with her brothers, Edward and Michael, in Detroit. They were always a close loving family. Even today there are strong attachments of love, understanding and shared-values.

Families share life experiences. When we have lived an experience (good, bad, challenging, whatever it might be) we carry that memory for life. We may consciously try to escape from our past, because the pain is too great to deal with it, but we never can run away. We may try to hide...but we cannot hide forever. Family gatherings...Michael, Ed, Susie, Margaret separately and collectively, are lessons of life's history. They are lessons to be cherished for they reflect our birth of values, beliefs and foundations.

As Sue spent her summers in Detroit with her older brothers, she took a part-time job as a housekeeper in the home of a Hungarian family. Well, guess who lived next door? Remember the adventurous young man from Scalps-Level, to Detroit via New York. Yes! Andrew Louis King had taken residence at the home of a Hungarian family living right next door to the family where Sue Ann was working. "The boy next door!" Destiny perhaps.

Stories from Mom allude to the fact that it was this year,1940, that she "briefly" met Andrew L. King. I have to laugh because even today, some 56 years later, Mom in her innocent way, self-consciously qualifies this happening by inserting the word "briefly." The bottom line is they met. A romance developed. (And no wonder…Sue was an absolutely beautiful young woman.)

As summer ended Sue returned to Ohio to the farm and her simple way of life. But was her life so simple? As I am told, life on the farm was far from easy. It was challenging and demanding for a teenage girl or anyone for that matter. With Baba, (with her European Slovak customs, and tough-as-nails "can do," spirit) and her father, John (an alcoholic, hard working, demanding and physical man,) what was her home life really like? Was it abusive? Perhaps yes, by today's definition. At the very least we would have to conclude that it was physically, mentally and emotionally difficult.

I never met either of my grandfathers, but I knew them. I knew them through their legacy of life, the teachings of life that were passed along the way.

Think about your family. What intrinsic values held by your parents and grandparents, passed down to you, have become the family norm by which you now live. Have you accepted these values or are you searching for your own?

An unsettled feeling motivated Sue to return to her brothers in Detroit the summer of her senior year. But what was she searching for that she could not find on the farm? Adventure? Romance? Her destiny? She found employment at a Hungarian Restaurant. Well, who do you think frequented this Hungarian Restaurant? Andrew L. King. Their relationship began to develop.

When she returned home, they continued to correspond, sharing their life's adventures, expressing wants, needs but more importantly, sharing their beliefs and values. Along the way they fell in love, and as Mom often states, "Well...you know the rest of the story."

Perhaps I do know the rest of the story. I also know that life wasn't easy for Mom. Life was a struggle to achieve. She always, always sacrificed her wants to fulfill someone else's wants, which they perceived as needs.

Mom and Dad married on the farm. Many stories have been told about this wedding. Drunkenness seems to have played a major role in the events of the day. Actually alcohol, by whatever means necessary, played a role in the life of my Dad, my uncles and certainly my Grandpas respectively.

Mr. Paul Gray introduced me to a Chinese proverb: "We inherit our father's demons." Now please do not take this wrong. I am not blaming Dad, but I did inherit his demons. The difference with me is that I have identified my demons and can now change that in my life that I have challenged.

To the best of my knowledge, my father never had the privilege of identifying his demons. I'll never forget the night my father died. He and I had a spiritual and emotional awakening. That moment of spiritual bonding, forgiveness and surrender to God is what gives life its meaning.

I wish I could say that experience was the turning point of my life, but unfortunately, at the time, I was just unwilling to acknowledge those demons. But today I will share a story for those who will listen.

After my parents were married, my father joined the Marines. Adventure, civic pride, the war machine...whatever his motivation, Andrew found himself married, wife with child, going off to war. He served in the Pacific Theater of operations, Pearl Harbor, and Midway Island. A young Corporal, his area of expertise was electronic repair and telephone installation. I admire my father. He enlisted in the service to serve his country and he did, proudly.

My sister Carol, a Marine child, born April 26, 1946 in Detroit, Michigan, was an early King family traveler. Dad carried along his family to Camp Lejune in the Carolinas.

What was it like to be twenty-something, thousands of miles from home with wife and child? What were his thoughts, ambitions, and dreams? His addictions and vices were already affecting his life. As life will unfold for Andrew he will be blessed in many ways, yet it seems that his addictions will win out. But do they? For remember, as long as life continues, there is hope for change.

Redeeming Grace

It was a trying and frightening time for Mom, the consummate pleaser, living with Dad, who by this time had made excessive drinking his way of life. He found that alcohol helped him temporarily forget all the things that he didn't like about the world...and himself. From his inebriated perception, he was more confident, outgoing, suave and debonair. Mom's perception was a bit different.

Mom tells stories of Dad, Dad told stories of Mom, "rational" stories, depending on one's perspective.

I remember a story in which Andrew, the boisterous, outgoing, socializer came home to Sue, drunk, with his Marine Corps buddies in tow. He had promised them a spectacular spaghetti dinner. Only one minor problem! Well, more than one problem was occurring here. But the one I remembered through the years was that Mom had no idea how to cook pasta sauce. Though she probably wanted to kill him, Sue, the constant pleaser, prevailed! Resourcefulness is a family legacy born of necessity. (Baba taught Mom how to be resourceful, Mom taught me, and hopefully, my sons Joshua and Justin will follow suite.) So you ask, what was the outcome of the debacle?

Sue turned to her gracious neighbor, an older Italian woman, who came to her aid and cooked the sauce for her. The meal was a success, Dad was well pleased with himself and several drunken Marines went off gratified, thinking, "That Andrew, what a guy!"

Was this acceptable behavior for Andrew? I think not. But then again do we always act socially responsible? No. Andrew really did love his wife and family deeply. He just didn't know how to show it.

As I began an honest inventory of my life, I had to ask myself, "Who had I become? Life is an amazing process. I am not referring to our birth or physical growth, but the process of life choices. Not only fundamental beliefs, but also negative lifestyles and inappropriate antisocial behavior are often perpetuated from generation to generation, even though that practice may be despised.

I saw what alcohol did to my father, uncles and grandfathers, and how their drinking caused so much pain in our family. Yet I copied that behavior without considering that my life could be different. I knew excessive drinking was not the norm of society, but it was the norm of my family. I followed the example without question.

I hope as we progress on this journey that you will take some time to reflect on your life's heritage, the transference of values, beliefs and moral teachings you have carried with you from your family. Remember that you are also an example to others who will follow you in this life and certainly beyond this brief moment in time.

What I have now come to learn is that these addictive behavior patterns do not have to continue.

"You were redeemed from the empty way of life handed down to you from your forefathers...with the precious blood of Christ..." (1Peter1:18,19).

"You see, just at the right time, when we were still powerless, Christ died for the ungodly. God demonstrates His own love for us in this: While we were sinners, Christ died for us"(Romans 5:6,8).

You see, with God's help, the cycle can be broken. Today I am a living testimony that this is true. I wish I had known this earlier on in my life.

I pray you will realize that God's power is available for you, now. Call on God. He can change your life today and the history of your family for every generation that will follow.

~ The Post-war Years ~

Chapter Three

Blessed with life having survived the war, Andrew took his family and "staked his claim," so to speak, in Detroit with Uncle Ed and Aunt Helen. Finding employment with Rockwell International, Andrew began his quest to seek fame and fortune. Dad was gregarious, a good talker and entertainer…a natural born salesman.

I am not sure that fame ever came in the way he would have liked. But he will never be forgotten, for his legacy lives on through his children, grandchildren, and beyond.

Then came the move to Newton Falls, Ohio. They were hard times for all. But Mom made our house a home. My memories of Newton Falls are memories of pleasure, peace, and a future filled with possibilities, as I searched for my life's meaning.

I am not sure about Dad. He was searching for something. Even at a very young age, I knew instinctively that a piece of Dad's dream was still missing. There was always some "unfinished business."

Newton Falls is a quaint, beautiful, Middle-American city. It is a place you can still leave your house and car unlocked, windows open and go about your business without worrying. It was a safe and secure environment in which to grow up. We lived in a section of town commonly referred to as the projects. The projects were duplexes and four-plexes built by the government for veterans and their families returning from the war effort. A great many cities across America built these projects. But in the 1950's Newton Falls was a racially and economically segregated village. The poor whites lived in the projects. The kids of the projects played in the projects and let's just say I'm sure it was frowned upon for the project children to play in the city park.

Blacks, (coloreds) couldn't live within the city or village boundaries. There was no written law as such but it was understood. None lived there while I grew up. Several families tried, as I remembered, with grave consequences.

The Village elders had a unique way of dealing with this racial harmony issue. They erected an area several blocks square, provided basic community services such as water, electric, and sewer. They called the area Braceville, and made sure the blacks all lived in their spacious woodlands community, exactly one-and-a-half miles from downtown Newton Falls.

The stores in Newton Falls were happy to accept their money, as there was no other place for them to shop. But that was all they would accept. Beyond that, they were not welcome.

Sue and Andrew, with cute little precocious Carol, lived in the projects. Photographs of Carol at that time reflect a happy child, secure and at peace. Working for Rockwell International, Andrew was on the road a lot, traveling the country chasing his dreams and drinking all along the way.

Mom told story after story about the projects. The neighbors, the Wortman's, Donny, Bo and Mom's best friend Ann, Josephine Baryak, friends in good times and bad. They were there to offer love, lend a hand, to comfort, and support. Most importantly, they shared similar values.

Did you ever consider for a moment how you choose your friends? Do they share your beliefs and values, or do they simply serve a purpose, aiding and preserving your own comfort.

May I challenge you to make an honest assessment? Make a list of your friends. Beside their names, reflect for just a moment. Is this a friend with whom I share common interests...no wants, no needs, just basic camaraderie? Or is this friend a provider, an enabler from whom I am always receiving, money, time, rides, etc.? Serious self-reflection!

Mom shared so many stories about her friends and life in the projects. As I listened, what came through to me more than what she said, was the emotions emanating from these stories. I was able to discern that these were happy times, filled with love, peace and contented dreams. Her honesty, innocence and laughter are a reflection of her life. My mother, my friend.

I remember the story of the snowstorm of 1952. Uncle Ed and Aunt Helen, visiting from Detroit, were snowbound for a week. Cars were buried in six feet of snow. Uncle Ed had to walk several miles for milk. I know that "snow stories," like "fish stories" tend to grow with the each retelling, but thanks to the old Brownie Camera (those of you old enough to remember them), I have seen pictures. (Pretty neat thing that Brownie camera. Mom still has it tucked away.)

Times of family "togetherness" are opportunities to share our family legacy. Through the medium of stories, we meet ancestors we never knew, through the memories and experiences of those who did. It can be fun, discovering we have inherited a skill, talent or physical features from a distant relative. But sometimes, memories are painful. In my own family I've heard, "Oh, I can't remember that far back." Is it that they cannot, or will not? What is it that we want to bury? Sometimes it's necessary to make peace with our past to live in peace with our present.

I remember that as a child, once a month or there about, I would go with Mom to Baba's house and Mom would read letters from the old country. These letters were always so sad. Mom would read in Slovak and Baba would cry, then Mom would cry. I was young (somewhere between five and nine) and certainly impressionable. Even in the Slovak language pain and heartache can be understood. I would watch them both and wonder, "why don't they just come here. It's so free and so peaceful." At that age it all seemed so simple. See, at Baba's, back at the orchard, under the plum tree, or back at the waterfalls, one could always find peace. Life seemed so simple to me then. The innocence of our youth, where does it go?

But even Baba's peaceful home could not heal her heartache, knowing her family was suffering back in the old country with Tito or Leonid Breshnev and the imminent invasion of Czechoslovakia.

As history repeats, the eastern bloc countries have experienced human devastation for centuries. Religious fanaticism? Land? No! It's power and greed. Someone confusing wants with needs!

There was a constant source of contention in our family between my Dad and Baba. She did not support this union between her daughter and my Dad. Baba, strong willed and domineering, could see only one issue where Andrew was concerned. He was of Hungarian decent. This one issue would repeatedly play a part in Andrew's life where Baba is concerned.

Remember where Baba came from? As I am told, this woman did witness the human degradation, starvation, and the direct ravages of war. In her sense of frustration, Baba knew two things: one was that her family was oppressed and destroyed by the invading forces during World War I, and two: those invading warriors who were responsible for mostly destroying her country and her family forcing her to flee her homeland, were the Hungarians.

According to Baba, Andrew (whose family was of Hungarian descent) was single handedly responsible for her countries indignation and the travesties of war. I remember the hostility, her tirades, the constant bickering directed towards Dad.   Even at an early age, I knew it was taking its toll. Andrew, placing his pride and family heritage aside, took this verbal assault.

Did Andrew have to take her abuse? No, certainly not. Yet when he was sober, he would check his emotional responses to protect his family. However, when he had been drinking, his repressed rage would raise its ugly head. When he was drunk he would fight back and oh, what arguing ensued. I can assure you that many many arguments developed as a result of Baba and Dad's ideological differences. Irrational thinking, medicated by alcohol, proved to be a family time bomb exploding over and over again.

As you take your reflective travels through your life's legacy, can you begin to see irrational behaviors or consequences in your family that have come as a result of irrational thinking?

With regard to Andrew and Baba's constant conflict over his heritage, she blamed Andrew and held him accountable for acts of violence in which he could never possibly have participated and over which he had no control.

The teaching for me is that, though I do not condone or agree with all Baba believed in or did during her lifetime, still, she remains an inspiration to me for the good I saw in her. We can love and admire people without being blind to their faults.

It is important that we are able to discern rational beliefs and values from irrational beliefs and actions. If I were to go through life rationalizing, memorializing Baba's irrational beliefs and adopting them as my own, it would simply perpetuate the hatred, bigotry and unnecessary emotional responses so wrong in life.

Where do our prejudices and biases begin? Challenge your beliefs and values. Are they rational or irrational? For many of us this step is a most painful process. We are being asked to shed some of those things to which we have grown accustomed, to identify issues which we know "just aren't right."

By 1954, television came of age. I remember our little black and white Philco. Because of this triumph in communication, the world was getting smaller. But Andrew and Sue's family was getting larger.

My Brother Richard Louis was born June 9, 1954, in Warren, Ohio and raised a Buckeye. Rick, as we refer to him (although to my Wimber aunts he was always addressed more formally as Richard) was strong willed and determined. He was born in the projects but was never of the projects. Mom made our home a place of peace, when Dad wasn't there. But when Dad was home, Rick often felt the brunt of Dad's drunken rages. I wasn't there, but I do remember the stories. Rick, to his credit, would take the abuse but never perceived himself as a victim. Instead, he would focus his energies in his sports, academics, wherever his concentration was needed to forge ahead. His driving ambition earned him scholarships and the opportunity to succeed in life.

Mom baked, cooked, cleaned and nurtured her children. If Carol and Rick's early years were anything like mine, there would be wonderfully fun times with a doting Dad and yet fearful times of a raging man full of grief, anxiety and petty jealousies.

Carol maintains that Rick and I were spoiled children. From her perspective, perhaps she was right. We were given a lot of "things" as we were able to afford them, but the emotional support we longed for was not always there. Mom provided a comforting balance between Dad and his calm fatherly role, and a buffer for his bitter, angry, adult-child rages.

Andrew had fears he never learned to express. His foundation was fragile. His life's dream, tenuous. Perhaps he was disappointed in himself, but he could never admit that. Instead, he would blame others, make excuses, and medicate to escape from his own feelings. And when he did, he was not accountable. Or was he?

The truth is, we are all accountable for our own actions. We make choices. We can admit when things "just aren't right" and strive to make things better, or we can deny our inner conflicts and spend our lives vainly trying to just avoid pain.

As I reflect upon my life, for me it was "like father like son." Andrew (and I) simply made decisions to avoid pain. I'd just ignore my feelings, hide the rage, accept my insecurities and make life choices simply to avoid the pain of who I had really become. Yet with medication, I, like Andrew and many other people in society, made decisions seeking for pleasure.

How do we find our balance? Will we always avoid pain?

What about Sue, the nurturer, the peacekeeper. Did Sue go through life peacefully with no trials and tribulations? Were her decisions made to seek a measure of pleasure or to avoid pain?

I have come to truly love my parents, each in a profoundly different way. Andrew and Sue did not have a perfect union, but the commitment made to each other held that union together for many years.

But you may wonder why people such as Andrew and Sue stay together, hoping, dreaming, planning, seeking pleasure while avoiding pain. The answer lies within their values and beliefs. Each of them inherited through teaching and by example a predisposed way of thinking, a moral and ethical foundation on which to build their lives. These teachings, real, concrete and tangible, provided Sue and Andrew with the faith and inner spiritual strength to know that each day of their lives God was with them, and would bring blessings upon them. And bless them He did.

It is my hope that as you look upon your life and who you have become, you will begin to understand how a part of who you are today was formed long ago by your inherited legacy of life. For some, this may be a painful process. Some of us hide from our heritage. We simply choose to ignore what our parents or grandparents were or believed in. But whether good or bad, whatever our heritage, we still have the gift of choice.

~ As A Twig is Bent ~

Chapter Four

As the King family grew and prospered, Andrew decided it was time to move out of the Newton Falls projects to a brand new subdivision called Circle Drive. It was here, in 1957, that I was born.

My siblings, Carol and Rick, said I was spoiled. "Mom's favorite," "Dad's kid!" I did get my way a lot, although at the time I certainly didn't think so. Early on I learned that if I was nice, acted cute and polite then all my sister Carol's girlfriends would give me candy and plenty of attention. It worked. I never needed a babysitter. Wherever Carol went, Terry went. Carol had an influence on my life, allowing me to have fun, expressing my self as a child making wonderful childhood memories. (I still remember her delicious homemade hot dog sauce.)

But even as a young child, I remember clear boundaries were set. Even then, I tempted fate, and always tried to push the limit.

Do you remember your parents' established boundaries? What specifically stands out? Did they spend time with you showing love and sharing values? For many of us we seem to remember the happy times, naturally repressing the bad experiences, avoiding the pain.

As I meet people today I often hear the comment, "I wish my parents had been tougher." What are they really saying? Aren't they really wishing that their parents had shown more concern and personal interest?

We can blame our parents for their failures but are we not ultimately responsible for our own choices? Perhaps they were struggling with their own demons. Who knows what was happening in their lives at the time? Perhaps they never had the advantage of nurturing examples in their own lives. Though we can't change our memories, we can change our perspective. Those innermost dark secrets, which cause us more pain than at times we think we can handle, can be healed. We can find peace with our past. *"The LORD is close to the brokenhearted and saves those who are crushed in spirit"* (Psalms 34:18).

"Then they cried out to the LORD in their trouble, and he delivered them from their distress" (Psalm 107:6).

My mother was a nurturer. She fed, clothed, and cared for me, and taught me about life from her own experience. No, Mom was not a learned scholar, but she had confidence in her abilities as a mother. She knew right from wrong and was careful to teach us in practical ways. I always knew I was loved and that knowledge created a secure environment in which to grow. We were a family divided in many ways, but Mom was the glue that held us together. She always placed her children before herself, without question. The little things in life, such as nightly prayers and stories, were times to teach and nurture.

One winter when I was about two-and-a-half, Newton Falls was snowed in. Mom bundled us up in our snowsuits, hats, scarves, gloves and boots, and outside we went to enjoy the day. Rick, Mom and I built snow forts, had snowball fights, horseback rides, (on Mom's back, of course), laughing and enjoying innocent fun. Mom spent time with us, showing us how to experience life's simple pleasures. See, Mom would continually introduce us to life's simple ways, imparting values through her traditions, and giving us guidance.

From my Mom I learned the value of faith, loyalty and unconditional love, which she gave her children and continues to give to each of her grandchildren. She has earned the honored endearment "Baba."

Not too long ago, while going through a difficult time in my life, I received a letter from Mom. She wrote:

"You said how much I have helped you along the rough road. That's what Mothers are for. There is an old saying, 'When children are little they step on your toes, when they grow up they step on your heart.' Lots of times, that is very true but through it all, sometimes through your own tears and hurts, you still try to take away the pain and suffering of your children in what ever way you can." That describes my Mom.

Dad saw himself as a family man, but during my infancy and early childhood, Dad simply didn't show love. Period! He was a great provider, and he loved his family, I came to know that when he died. But what I knew of him was work, work, come home, drink, become intoxicated, argue, attack, and the cycle would continue. Dad was a dreamer, with an eighth-grade education and a strong work ethic. He had a beautiful wife and family. What was it in his life that he had to medicate? Andrew knew right from wrong but seemed to live his life trying to isolate himself from realities that challenged his comfort zone. He needed to be in control, yet often, could not control himself. Yes, I grew up, "like father, like son."

Our family was devoutly Roman Catholic. At least at an early age, nightly prayers were read, Holy Days observed, weekly trips to confessions and Mass every Sunday at 11:30 a.m., in Dad's pew (last pew on the right) at St. Joseph's church. We had religious statues and icons around the house. I'd say we were very religious. I am thankful that this spiritual foundation existed. But it wasn't until later on in life that this introduction to my spiritual legacy would become the beginning of a whole new way of life.

Sundays were special. Dad followed his Sunday traditions, "religiously." His Sunday morning coffee was served with two newspapers, "The Akron Beacon Journal" and the "Warren Tribune Chronicle." Unless it was a holiday, Mom attended Sunday Mass alone at 8:00 a.m. so she could stop at Talenka's Bakery, purchase Dad's favorite donuts, and be home by nine, to serve them with Dad's coffee. It was the same routine, week after week.

Redeeming Grace

In order to secure his pew for the 11:30 a.m. Mass, Dad and his meticulously scrubbed, starched, pressed and perfectly polished boys, marched into church at 11:00 a.m. Mom made sure we looked our best in our dress shirts, ties, suits, and of course, hats and top coats in winter. We always arrived in a clean brightly polished car. That was a necessity. Those things were important to Dad.

When Rick and I look back through the family album I can assure you that the dress policy extended just until our teen years when either Dad began to accept change or Rick and I rebelled. Probably the latter.

After church we would return home to Circle Drive and change our clothes immediately. Dad would sneak downstairs and a have beer or two before dinner. Carol would help Mom, and as I remember, Sunday dinner was always a fabulous meal. Mom always made it a formal affair since it was one of the few times we would all sit town together as a family.

The fear, of course, was Andrew's temper. Would he get through dinner without lashing out verbally or physically at Rick, Carol, Mom or me? More times than I care to recall, the lovingly prepared family dinner, intended for family bonding, became the center of violence and rage.

As much as I tried to forget, one lasting impression I have is Sunday after Sunday Dad would remind Rick, Carol and me of all that we could never and would never be in life. What we could be in life was simply left to us to figure out.

But make no mistake, as Andrew King's children, we were taught what we wouldn't say, how we wouldn't act, what we wouldn't wear, who we couldn't associate with, lest we embarrass the family.

For all Dad's faults, I believe his intentions were good. Today I am able to understand that.

Sunday afternoons Dad did his best to be a family man. Packing us in the family car, we would travel to Akron, Ohio to visit Dad's closest relatives, the Stoynoff clan, Dad's Uncle George, Aunt Liz, Aunt Vernie, Uncle Larry, Aunt Betty and Uncle Tom, and all the cousins. Like Baba, Uncle George brought legacies of life to this country from Hungary. A practicing Russian Orthodox, his faith in God, the church and his family became one. Uncle George's family came first before any other need in his life. He made time for the simplest pleasures, the stories, the dancing, fun Hungarian traditions.

Etched upon my soul are the many talks I had with Uncle George as I grew up. Years ago I took these teachings for granted. Today I take them to heart. Someday I will meet Uncle George again and thank him for the importance he played in my life.

I was blessed growing up near my Mom's family, knowing my Baba, aunts, uncles and cousins. Family values were passed along through our relationships over the years. Aunt Helen and Uncle Ed, (Dad's friend and Mom's brother) were chosen to be my Godparents upon my day of baptism.

I have always respected and admired them for the values and faith by which they live.

For as long as I can remember, Mom and her sister Margaret stayed in touch weekly, loving, supporting and encouraging one another. Aunt Margaret, Uncle Andy, cousins Paul and Cheryl, Aunt Ann, all were part of my childhood memories. Family gatherings meant wonderful dinners, ice skating, rides on the tractor, running wild by the river, so many fun times with my Mom's side of the family. The value of strong loving family ties is a priceless legacy.

I can't say the same about my Dad's family. But as I think about it though, Dad's contribution to our family support system was his willingness to drive over an hour each way every day, rather than uprooting us and moving closer to his work in Streetsboro, Ohio, home of the Chrysler Corporation. It's not that Newton Falls was so grand (although they do boast of having the only five-digit zip code in America with a the same number: "44444"). The city has its own charm, until you look up and see the blackened relics of the once productive steel mills, rusted giants standing as monuments to a former era. But I was happy and contented there. It was home. In this way Andrew did pass along his values, although they were never spoken.

I do have many good memories of my Dad. But I need to weigh the good with the bad. I never experienced a weekday father.

Andrew worked the afternoon shift, which meant he had to leave before two o'clock every afternoon. He left for work early enough to give himself time to stop at a bar on Route 5 in Ravenna. And yes, he always seemed to find the need to stop there on his way home. Perhaps this is where he found his peace.

Arriving home between one and two in the early morning hours, never allowed him time with his family. Throughout the week Mom had to be both Mom and Dad.

Saturday was Dad's day. Every two weeks he paid a visit to Ed's barbershop for a haircut and then home to relax, unless a project around the home needed his attention, like painting, mowing the lawn or other similar projects. But mostly what I remember was Dad's drinking. Duke Beer, Iron City, Black Label, Windsor Canadian Whiskey or Ten High, whatever order didn't matter but what did matter was a shot, a beer, a shot, a beer and then he'd be a father. I shouldn't be too hard on Dad. I saw the mistakes he was making, yet unfortunately, I followed in his footsteps.

Rick and I found solace in each other, playing, hiding, to avoid our father. Sometimes he would be Dad! Then other times, he was a man with such deep anger we would not want to know him. Mom spent the majority of her time keeping Dad at bay, attempting to involve him in family matters, while always monitoring his emotional balance.

Redeeming Grace

As I look upon these early years what is becoming very clear is that guided or misguided, the person I would become was already developing.

I see children giving birth to children today. Uneducated, unsupported, with crippling addictions, they have babies they don't know how to care for or value. Many of these children have never known what it means to be loved. Victims of rage or neglect, they grow into adults who do not trust their parents, so how can they trust themselves? What is their basis of faith? What values do they hold? What will they teach the generations who will follow?

Sue always had her family. Andrew was on his own from the time he was fourteen, really still a child. Yes, he had anger and resentments. But life had taught him to be tough. Life is not fair. Accept your fate. Hide the pain, be a man.

As I said, not all memories are bad. Dad, the weekend warrior, had a spirit of adventure! He planned family vacations like our summer trips to Cedar Point Amusement Park, outings to watch the Cleveland Indians or Cleveland Browns. There was summer training camp in Hiram, Ohio, Storyland Forrest in Leggionier, Pennsylvania, Geauga Lake Park, Conneaut Lake Park, The Canfields Fair, the Newton Falls summer carnivals, swimming at Mary's Lake, the list of local events goes on and on.

During the summer, we would visit Dad's family in New York and Hoboken, New Jersey. We would stay with Uncle Bill, Aunt Helen, cousins Patty and Bill. I remember the Hudson Street shipyards, the George Washington Bridge, the park, the stick ball games in the street and my favorite, trips to Manhattan. It was safer then and my cousins would watch out for me. Rick was never too far away. But I loved to wander, exploring alleys, warehouses, and the waterfront. The Statue of Liberty, the Lincoln Tunnel and the subways were fascinating.

Dad and Uncle Bill would spend hours and hours reminiscing and reliving the pains of their past, arguing, debating family events which neither of them could change or influence.

Aunt Sue resided on Hudson Street as well and lived approximately 14 blocks east from Uncle Bill. Aunt Sue, an artist and teacher, is a true inspiration to the way things ought to be. We would all go to Grandma Rose's for dinner and more cheek pinching.

Grandma Rose had two Chihuahuas, positively annoying little things, as well as a very large, smelly collie named Boris who drank water from the toilet bowl. I remember Grandma Rose moving around the apartment in her wheel chair yelling, "Boris, Boris." Boris would bark, Grandma Rose would yell, the two chihuahuas would yip and I would hide.

Sitting on Grandma's couch, usually next to Mom or cousin Patty, my feet would be far enough off the floor to entice the two little chihuahuas to play hide and seek with my ankles. Unfortunately each time they would find my ankles, they would bite them with their little razor sharp teeth. I hated those dogs.

Dinner at Grandma's was always memorable. Pot Roast and always store-bought gourmet desserts. If Aunt Sue said dinner was at six o'clock more than likely she would start preparing it at six o'clock. We wouldn't eat until eight or nine…pretty late for a little guy, but oh, so delicious and worth the wait! During the waiting time Grandma Rose would spoil us grandchildren something awful with chocolates, chocolate covered cherries, more chocolates and candies of all assortments and more stories.

At the tender age of six I knew that adults meant pleasure, satisfaction, providers of needs and wants, but I also knew them as a source of pain (I remember Dad's belt when he had been drinking. Who knew what would trigger his frustration and anger?) Thus, I began a simple process of separating those adults who provide pain from those who provide pleasure.

Beginning to place wants before needs was easy, especially at six and seven. I knew I could act like a sweet, cute, cuddly child, and play out this act with some adults and have my wants fulfilled. As I grew older, maturing, I soon realized that this manipulation to "get what I want" worked. If only I could get better at playing the game, the world was mine to own. Even at the age of six, that ambition was my escape!

~ Spreading My Wings ~

Chapter Five

My school career began in the first grade, a nice brisk walk three blocks from home! Mom took me to school with my new lunch pail filled with two sandwiches, cookies, fruit and three cents to buy milk. That first day Mom cried, but I was eager. Wow! What an adventure. I was ready to fly.

The elementary school was attached to the high school so Carol was not far away. Rick, my protector or so I thought, was starting fourth grade.

I soon found out that satisfying my wants was not as easy in Mrs. Sloan's first grade class as it was at home with Mom. My friend Alan Baryak (the son of Mom's friend) and I wanted to behave like children, fulfilling our wants. We soon learned Mrs. Sloan had other expectations. Forever etched in my memory is the heavy price I had to pay for disobeying Mrs. Sloan's expectations.

About an hour and a half into my first day of school I experienced my first (unfortunately not last) teacher administered corporal punishment! Mrs. Sloan paddled Alan and me in the hallway with the Principal, Mr. White, as a witness. Four whacks with a wooden paddle about 48 inches long probably 12 inches wide, designed with quarter inch holes for less air resistance and greater impact. (I may be exaggerating the size of the paddle a little, but in the eyes of a six-year old, wow!)

That afternoon I returned home to tell my mother all about my first day of school. However, I thought it prudent not to mention this traumatic part of my day. In fact, I never disclosed this humiliation to anyone for years. Unfortunately school paddlings did not stop in the first grade.

As shared before, I believe that the person that we are is formed and structured, experience-by-experience, like the foundation of a big brick house. The bricks provided by Mom, Dad, their parents before them, as well as those people whose input in our lives holds significance.

So much of our life is in place before we're even aware of it. The fundamental teachings, experiences, "cause and effect" lessons from observation...all these mile markers influence our lives.

Sometimes we deny painful events, not allowing ourselves to remember. But in realty, none of us have had a Camelot existence. (Even Camelot was not perfect.) Perhaps our childhood wasn't as comforting as we wished or perceived it to be. The unconscious reaction is to avoid, hide, shield, minimize, "Oh, that was so long ago, it doesn't matter." A more healthy approach is to admit to God and ourselves, that the hurts still exist. This is the first step toward healing.

Throughout the elementary school years, Catholic Sunday school was mandatory. I didn't like it, perhaps because it meant less playtime. Anyway,

I did not take it seriously. But what Sunday school did provide was a vehicle by which I avoided sitting in the church pew at 11:00 a.m. with Dad. I'd purposely wait until 11:15 a.m. and then proceed from the school to church.

First Communion is one of the sacraments of the church. Traditionally, it's a reason to get the family together for a celebration. We had a lot of celebrations. Dad loved these family events. They were on the weekend so he could attend and he put himself in charge of securing the beverages.

By the age of eight my life script was well defined, if only I would have paid attention. Reflecting back today upon this unsettled time, I was caught between the innocence of a time past and the cultural, industrial, ideological, spiritual revolution like no other time in our history.

The sixties were an unsettled time, a time of upheaval where changes were occurring rapidly in every echelon of our society. Dad had a difficult time with change. He liked to be in control, but he could not control the changes brought about by time.

The church was beginning to undergo a renaissance of sorts. The sixties reflected perhaps the greatest fundamental ideology change to occur over the course of Catholic Church history. Masses given in English were replacing the traditional Latin masses. The church altar was being modernized to reflect the changing attitudes. Dad was having a fit! Leave things as they are.

Change! Change for Dad was madness. He simply would not accept it. The generational changing of the guard left Dad unsettled and uncomfortable.

I remember Dad's tirades about work. Dad and Chrysler went back a long way. Chrysler, a flagship automaker, was in madness and chaos. He blamed the younger generation, men with no work ethic. But younger men than he were taking over. Now they were his bosses. He couldn't accept it, but because he had no choice, begrudgingly, he acquiesced. Perhaps part of Dad's anger was fear. He had only an eighth grade education. Working as a laborer and administrator, there were not many options open for him at this stage of life. Around him the world he knew was changing. Unsettling? You bet! And his way of dealing with painful issues was unsettling for all of us.

Approaching the age of nine meant little league tryouts. It was my dream to play ball, to wear a uniform, to fit in! Dad, the weekend warrior, never paid much attention to either Rick or me regarding sporting activities, but when he could, occasionally he would play catch or hit us fly balls.

The Circle Drive Boys' Club had been active in Little League. Rick played on the St. Joseph's team. He was a good player. I dreamed of playing for one of the better teams. Tryouts came and Mom allowed me to sign up. I was so excited. Mom just kept telling me, "Terry, just do your best, that's all you can do."

At this tender age, I was introduced to politics Newton Falls' style. I was drafted to the Union Local team for ages nine to twelve. I attended every practice. Mom allowed me to ride my bike by myself to the city park. I rarely got to play during practice. The coach had several of his sons on the team. The assistant coach had his sons on the team as well. Many of my friends told me I was a far better player. I was often told I had "heart." Nevertheless, one week before the start of the season I was cut. Yep! The coach said a mistake had been made. I was devastated.

Remember, this is little league baseball. No, mistakes like this just are not made. The coach just wanted to make room on his roster for his friend's son who also wanted to play. I had to turn in my uniform. It was humiliating.

But I was determined more than ever to try out again next year. I simply could not accept defeat. A value. Perhaps a quest for what is right. See, I had a goal. I also realized from Baba that when you want something badly enough, you must dedicate your very soul to attain it, within the proper rules.

One of many mistakes I made along the way was disregarding my teachings about living within the rules. I broke far too many, acquiring wants, living with irrational beliefs, along with delusional values. After all, others did it. It seemed to work for them.

I found out years later that Mom confronted the coach of the Union Local. She let him know that she was sincerely displeased with his actions.

Redeeming Grace

After several very dejected days, a neighbor came to see me. Mr. Tomaino was my friend George's Dad, and Coach for the Jaycees Little League Team. Well, to my surprise he came into the house and handed me a uniform and with a big smile said, "Terry, you're on my team. Practice is tonight." I felt ten feet tall. The events that unfolded regarding my little league experience are what lessons of life are all about.

Mom was involved behind the scenes. She must have told Baba. I remember one spring day at her house, Baba placed her arm around me and said "Teddy, practice, practice." (Baba never could say Terry. That's okay. I kind of liked how she pronounced my name anyway.)

So practice I did. Every day. I practically lived at the ball field until about age of twelve when girls and money started to peak my interest.

I played ball everyday. Mr. Tomaino had values and knew what was really important in life. He understood right from wrong. Even after a loss he treated his team to ice cream at the Dairy Queen. A tradition. He always did try to win, but not at any cost. See, he wanted all team members to play, to laugh, to try, to enjoy being kids.

So practice I did, until finally in 1968 at age eleven, I started as the team catcher. My greatest personal satisfaction as a child came July 4th, 1969, when I played in the big American League vs. National League playoff game. I was the pitcher for several innings and catcher the remainder of the game. Mr. Tomaino was our coach for the American League, and guess who was the coach for the National League? Yes, the coach that fired me...kicked me to the curb.

The last inning we were losing. There were two outs, and several runners on base. I was at bat with a three-two count. I prayed. Swing! Whoosh! Over the center field fence...over the flag pole...Home Run! We win!!!! Oh! That was sweet!

Nothing more need ever be said. But I do remember Mr. Union Local kicking a batting helmet into the dugout fence.

Some coaches and even some parents, it seems, are living their unfulfilled "field of dreams" through their children. Teach them, guide them, give them opportunities, but let kids be kids. Berating them for failure or pushing them to win at any cost is setting them up with distorted values that will affect them throughout their lifetime.

Are there values being built? Was it Divine intervention or Mom's? But where was Dad? As I said, he left those chores to Mom.

Think for just a moment back to your formative years. Do any incidents come to mind that affected you profoundly? Good or bad? What did you learn from them? What values did you take away from the experience? Are you able to discern these events from an adult perspective? Do you agree with this value today? If not, what are you willing to do to change it?

Baseball, football, basketball, marbles, wiffle ball, army, G.I. Joe, peeking at girls became our focus of play. Not to forget, bikes, skateboards, sleds, hockey, bows and arrows, cards, life, money, checkers, Chinese checkers, and my remote control tanker truck. Tents, forts, sleep outs, my dog Rusty…life was good.

But there was another mile marker that impacted my life. I was twelve years of age. It was 1969.

As the 60's unfolded, the nation was struggling with a repositioning of national boundaries, societal expectations. Integration. White vs. Black. Housing, equality, racial balance, affirmative action, Vietnam, the draft, the black soldier, Life, Liberty, the Pursuit of freedom.

I was being raised within the King family circle of rules. Expanded boundaries, governed by the village elders, supported by the community religious and political leaders to offer faith, support beliefs and create a value hierarchy. Bottom line, my parents were very much aware of the racial imbalance prevalent in this country during the 50's, 60's, and 70's, and still prevalent today. But my father had his own values regarding the race issue. He refused to accept any expression in his home or in his presence that inferred a derogatory comment or racial slur against another human being. The use of the term "nigger" or any verbal assault brought down the wrath of Andrew L. King. Sue King enforced the rule by washing our mouths out with soap. I'm not referring to a quick lick and a rinse, but more like…eating it, taking a bite, getting a good painfully disgusting mouthful, then washing it out. It was quite an effective deterrent.

So from a very early age Rick, Carol and Terry were taught that Black people, (Coloreds, as many Newton Fallites referred to them) were our equals. Even to this day I'm not sure what generated this most definitive valued position Dad took. I'm glad he did. Perhaps there were incidents of racial injustices perpetrated against Dad as a young Hungarian. I often remember Dad sharing stories about the white man's world, and the discrimination against the Europeans by the Aristocratic Blue Bloods.

Whatever the cause, I am grateful because at an early age in my life I realized, whatever our race or ethnic origin, we are one. We are all God's children.

As mentioned before, Newton Falls was segregated, relegating the Blacks to the designated rural living community of Braceville. Dad, Mom, and Carol pushed this assumed community rule.

One of my best friends in high school was a black boy named Johnny Herbert. Carol, as a maturing teenager had a friend, the daughter of the Professional Boxer Ernie Shavers, "the Acorn." Mom allowed Carol to have her young friend sleep over one evening. "As I am told" the neighbors were quite incensed? Their concern was that this might precipitate racial interaction. Can you believe it?

Redeeming Grace

Ernie Shavers was considered by the Newton Falls politically powerful to be "one of them," yet he was relegated to live in Braceville. He built his home in Newton Township, but was he ever a true Newton Fallite?

Mr. Shavers was a local hero, a professional boxer, a star fighter, challenger to Mohammed Ali. He fought out of the Army Navy Club in Warren, Ohio. I do remember his training. (I was also tempting fate, learning to be a boxer. I'm not sure I needed any lessons in this regard for even at an early age I had the fight game down pretty well.)

I knew, even at age ten, that racial disharmony was bad. Bad for Newton Falls, bad for our Nation. The nation was experiencing racial unrest with widespread civil disobedience breaking out into riots. President Kennedy, the Reformer, was dead. Mr. Johnson, a man with vision, yet a hungry man without values, assumed leadership. His wants were his needs.

One particular August evening, I mounted my little orange Huffy bike with high grip handle bars, knobby tires, my baseball glove slung from the handle bars, and left Circle Drive heading for ball practice at the racially segregated city park.

Our little league team was scheduled to play the late evening game so it must have been approximately ten minutes to seven. As I peddled my bike leisurely down Windom Road I came to the end of the road and stopped at the four-way intersection. The road to the right was Charlestown Road, an affluent housing section of Newton Falls. To the left was Ridge Road, which was the road to Braceville, one and a half miles away. Straight ahead at a slight left angle was Canal Street, Main Street USA, downtown Newton Falls, the rivers, the scenery, City Hall, the center of power and influence.

I stopped at this corner, as I had done hundreds of times before, and turned to my right. I was startled to see two men standing next to a white Chevrolet in the parking lot of the First Congregational Church. These two men wore hoods to shield their identity, white robes and vestments, full Ku Klux Klan regalia. It was a very scary sight. I watched as these men walked to the church. I could hardly believe my eyes.

So why were these men hiding behind masks? What were they afraid of? Who were they? Did I know them? Were they local fathers, husbands, church leaders, community elders perhaps?

Two years later a black music teacher and her family attempted to move to Newton F alls. One night a cross was erected in their front yard and ignited. It was a most malevolent warning.

This horror couldn't be happening in our safe little community, could it? The warning was not heeded and it wasn't long before their house was burned to the ground. I knew that life in Newton Falls would never be the same for me again.

Years earlier Dad had a statue standing guard upon our front porch. I think the term I often heard was "black Sambo." It was a little black man dressed in a petticoat, holding a lantern. I must have been four or five years old at the time. Dad painted the man white (a most feeble attempt at racial harmony.) But one day in the mid-sixties, our "black statue turned white," simply disappeared.

If only the memories of racial prejudice could disappear as easily.

Children have inquisitive minds, constantly soaking in messages from surrounding influences. What happens when they receive incongruent messages? Do they have the discernment necessary to sort through those things which "just aren't right?" More than likely not!

Amazing, isn't it, when we think back to our formative years, growing and developing our values. Not only are we taught certain behaviors but consider for the moment the enormous societal influences via newspapers, radio and television media. Are values being introduced or manipulated?

Many children have not been so fortunate as to be raised within a family structure with a mother, father, siblings, and extended family each contributing to his development and sense of belonging.

Many children have no one to whom they can turn for love, guidance, and security. Many children are raised by a succession of virtual strangers. Raised? Who instills values, beliefs and faith? Who become their role models? Confusing? Certainly is for many. Yet all the while societal expectations remain the same, no matter what our background.

What's so beautiful about this nation is that we are equal as a people. But unfortunately our life's foundations are not equal. So along the way we pick and choose our values and our path. While avoiding pain, we seek pleasure fulfilling life's wants as best we can, while ignoring life's needs.

So many of us turned to heroes for our role models. But what constitutes a hero? Men of solid character? Leaders? Or not?

Even at an early age remembering the death of John F. Kennedy, Robert Kennedy and Martin Luther King, I knew that great men or shall we say men of conviction, had left this world. Each man held values indelibly written throughout their life's script.

John Wayne was often referred to as a hero. The Pope, The Beatles, Walter Cronkite, Malcom X, Hughey Newton, the Black Panthers, John Glenn, Neil Armstrong, Sally Ride, Tupac Shakur, Marion Suge, and of course Michael Jordan.

As a child I, too, had heroes. Johnny Unitas, Len Dawson, NFL and AFL quarterbacks. Neil Armstrong, Pope John Paul II, and of course Ben Cartwright, patriarch of the Cartwright family of Bonanza fame. Interesting dichotomy of persons! As to female heroes, well, Julie Andrews, of The Sound of Music fame. Indira Gandhi, Mary Leachy, Diane Fossy, Margaret

Thatcher, Sister Teresa of India, all people leading their lives for the betterment of planet Earth.

The list can go on and on. But what is clear in all instances is that these people had a purpose to which they dedicated their lives. Their purpose was derived from a clear distinct system of values, supported by beliefs taught, learned and adopted by faith.

To what are you willing to dedicate your life?

"For we are God's workmanship, created in Christ Jesus to do good works, which God prepared in advance for us to do." (Ephesians 2:10 NIV)

~ One For The Money ~

Chapter Six

I always resented having to do my chores, more specifically my weekly devotion to Baba's grass. Beginning when I was about ten and into my teenage years, I had the duty of riding my bike across town approximately one and a half miles to Baba's house. Once there, I would cut her grass all the way down the hill to her magnificent waterfalls and to my rock! As I reflect back to those much simpler times I realize that teachings of life were being passed from Baba to me on each work assignment.

Initially I had to mow her lawn with a mechanical rotary mower, push, pull, push, pull, push, pull, for hours. Finally Uncle Andy acquired a small 18" mower with a gasoline engine. Suddenly, life got a whole lot easier.

What amazed me about Baba was her persistence to perfection, the demands she placed upon herself and others.

I can still picture her at age 76, standing with her Babushka wrapped around her head, a long dress, stockings rolled around her ankles, black shoe boots, and coke bottle thick glasses. Cataracts had left her close to blind but gosh, she sure had eagle eyes when it came to the lines my mower wheels left in the grass. When I finished a line of mowing, if the wheel line was crooked, well, that was simply unacceptable. It must be done over. To her, a job was not worth doing unless you did it right. So what if no one would ever see the wheel lines, except Baba. This was unacceptable. Period. She was committed to perfection.

Even at fourteen, I was learning a value, a behavior pattern passed down from Baba. Friends and collegues have often told me that I am far too demanding on myself and others.

But Baba never asked anything of me or anyone else that she would not demand of herself. She literally built her own home on Warren Road, "so I'm told."

Baba kept many of the old farm implements; hoes, shovels, yawls, ax, saws, plows, and seeders. One of the images that I'll always have is of Baba planting her garden. At age 72, using a horse collar pull plow, she plowed an area approximately 40 feet by 20 feet and planted her entire garden by hand, by herself. The garden was meticulous. As Baba aged, the garden kept getting smaller and smaller. But even at age 90 Baba still tilled the soil by herself.

After I would redo the lines to Baba's satisfaction she would reappear with a tiny three-ounce lime green plastic cup, containing warm red pop. She'd follow me through the yard just to reward me with one swallow of liquid refreshment. Baba would purchase one bottle of pop, red or grape and pour just enough to stretch one bottle for a month. Frugal? Yes! She remembered the time of the great depression when food sources were scarce. Each remaining edible item just may be your last, so conserve it.

As the present generation grows, the Great Depression is no more than a paragraph in our history books. We, who did not live through that kind of hardship and struggle, can never fully understand or appreciate its impact.

Baba was a leader, a doer. This woman never quit, and lived life with a purpose, as she perceived it to be, every day of her life.

Baba passed away March 23, 1986, but her memory, her example, teachings, values, and her faith live on. This woman influenced my life.

As I reached thirteen, Mom was working fulltime at the Ravenna Arsenal Ammunitions Plant. Personally I wasn't comfortable with Mom's need to work, but Rick was going to college and well, frankly, money was needed. Perhaps I would go too, but well, my parents might not be able to help me.

By the time I was fourteen I knew that if I wanted to fulfill more wants I would need to spend more time with adults, who had money that could be mine.

The early 1970's ideologies were converging and imploding. Kent State, the National Guard, students dead. Why? See, Vietnam was a war no one wanted, no one really understood, but it affected all Americans. My neighborhood friends, my brother, my cousins, feared the draft. There was even a point when I, too, was concerned that the war, death, drugs and destruction would envelop my life and threaten my life script.

As the King family grew, after school activities as well as weekend activities seemed to center at our home. Mom realized that we children needed more space to grow, explore, experience life away from Dad.

As I reflect back, the basement bedroom became my sanctuary, my home away from home. Of course I politicked for months with Mom, Carol, and Rick, in order to assure that I would get the basement bedroom. Again, Terry fulfilling more wants and more needs as every twelve-year-old should, or so I reasoned.

Safe zones are a good, comfortable place to hide away and feel at peace. Life brings with it the inevitability of change. Death, divorce, growing up, leaving home, college, choices that we must make, can all be overwhelming. We often need to step back and take a time out from the pressures and stresses of life, for a moment of reflection, to regain our strength and endurance, to reclaim our values, revive our beliefs and renew our faith.

Did you have such a place? Perhaps for you it was a porch, a special room, a backyard swing, a favorite chair, a star-watching rock, a special tree, a church, a favorite hang-out? Or was it a bar, a drug, or a drink? Our private sanctuary is meant to help us gain perspective and move forward, not to medicate the pain for a few minutes and emotionally retreat.

I'm not necessarily saying that if you enjoyed a safe haven you were running rather than confronting issues in your life. For many of us this place offered us a moment of temporary relief from all the pain.

Because Mom was working and I was the first to arrive home, it was my responsibility to start dinner for Sue and Rick. I didn't mind. I liked to cook. (In fact, still today, cooking is my passion.) Being home alone, in my basement sanctuary, with a well-stocked bar in the family room right outside my bedroom door, I began experimenting. It was fun. Life was good.

While my friends were now emulating sports heroes, I was absorbing adult information on how to acquire money. It became my obsession.

I enjoyed school. My grades were good, excellent in many subjects, but there was no challenge. I found academics absolutely boring. I liked adult attention and I liked to talk. Believe it or not, I learned a lot of life's lessons while in school but not from the suggested course material.

Upon arriving home one day, Mom informed me that the school principal had called and asked her to come to school for a special meeting. She immediately assumed I was in trouble. "Okay Terry, what did you do? Do you want to tell me anything?" I was scared. I thought, "Oh no! What happened?" My world was crumbling. Crumbling no! But my comfort zone was definitely about to change. Challenged, is the best way to put it.

The next day Mom met with the school Principal. Upon returning home that day, Mom was waiting for one of those mother-son talks.

It seems that the principal, guidance counselor and teachers wanted to meet with Mom to address Terry's academic performance. We had been given I.Q. tests and apparently the results were unexpected. The accumulative test scores indicated that the school possessed a genius among the students. According to the results I was now considered a gifted student. Math, engineering, and mechanical issues were identified as my strong points.

My troubles were just beginning. In a matter of a very short period of time adult attitudes towards me changed. I had always been content to achieve an average grade and no one seemed to have a problem with that. But things were different now.

My curriculum had changed and teachers immediately began to demand more of me than I was prepared to give back. A war of mental madness had begun. I remember a teacher stating emphatically, "Okay Mr. Smarty, no more foolishness. You're going to buckle down and master this material."

Oh how silly! This authority figure demanding childishly that this gifted student must now master all school assignments was ridiculous. I simply did not care what she thought.

No one ever asked me what I thought was important. I had no interest in the scholastic material presented to me. Now if I had a choice, the study of how to acquire money would captivate my attention. I had money to make, or shall I say, money to lose. My goals now changed. This knowledge now afforded me an arrogance to achieve at all costs. I was never afraid to work. Work was enjoyable. Truly. But most important, work generated money and money was what I needed.

My goal was to become a millionaire by the time I was forty. As my life unfolded this goal became my obsession without regard to the consequences.

I inventoried adults, Newton Fallites, in order to assimilate those who could assist or enable my moneymaking.

My algebra/calculus teacher, Mr. Gene Zorn, was an empowering intervention in my life. He was a very good teacher. Every day he brought the Wall Street Journal to class. I was eager to learn about stocks. I studied the market and learned it well. I talked Mom into allowing me to acquire stock in Gulf Oil Corp. I had earned money mowing grass for Mrs. Dresher. She paid me ten dollars a week to mow a large lot, plus plant flowers, rake leaves, or do whatever yard work she requested.

I learned how to save money and bought my first ten-speed bike. By the age of 15, one thing became clear. I needed money. No, I did not just want it, I needed it. My obsession had now become my life's mission.

Carol had moved out, Rick was a senior preparing for college. I had the house to myself. I remember people saying, "Oh Terry is so mature for his age. Such a nice young man." I knew how to play the game in order to get what I wanted.

The owner of a local Sparkle Market called me one day and offered me a job as a stock boy. Wow! White shirt, black pants. I loved it! Only two blocks from home, I worked every imaginable hour I could, for $1.65 an hour. Thirty to forty hours per week, wow, I could get a car. Save, save. I worked quite a few months progressing to evening stock clerk. Paychecks were fun. I could entertain, buy beer and experience life.

After working there over five months, cashing numerous paychecks, the boss asked me for the first time, how old I was. When I replied, "fifteen." she was irate! "You can't work here. Why didn't you tell me?" I replied, "You didn't ask."

So that was that! No longer a Sparkle Sparky! I was let go. Wow! No more money. But this was only a temporary set back. Within a week I went to work for another woman who paid cash, doing odd jobs. She liked the work I did. Her son owned an auto shop. Within a short time he asked me if I would like to come and work for him at $2.25 an hour.

Throughout the summer I started each day at 5:00 , finishing at 3:00 p.m. I learned to repair cars, paint, sand and polish.

At about this same time, I had chosen to make beer and wine an integral part of my life. Although marijuana was a popular cultural drug, along with LSD, I just couldn't do it. Experiment, that is! But with my friend Paul Banko, I would sneak up to town, three blocks from Circle Drive and go to the Gay Bar. The name would eventually change but the Bar was the happening place in Newton Falls. I went two or three nights per week. At age 15, I bought beer to go! I was starting to also enjoy (or so I thought) shots of whiskey.

One memorable Friday night I was at the bar drinking beer when the bartender approached me and said, "Look to your right!" Well, to my surprise guess who was seated right next to me? Andrew L. King! I wasn't allowed to be there, but he was supposed to be working! When he saw me he responded, "Well, finish up and go home. You didn't see me, I didn't see you." It was to be our little secret. Not for long. I'm not exactly sure when Mom found out but she eventually did.

Surprisingly enough, that same year I was listed in the book, Who's Who Among Young Americans. I traveled to Spain and Portugal with several Spanish students and my Spanish teacher, Mrs. Delvechio.

I think Dad had pretty much given up on me. Drinking, parties, money and girls all played a part. But along the same time Dad's drinking went to new heights and his violent outburst increased as well.

Drinking, working, and parties seemed the lifestyle I enjoyed most. My path of destructive behavior had already begun. The only person that didn't know it was me.

Scholastic work became secondary. I was accepted at Boston College with a partial scholarship. However I had no means to afford the difference even working part time.

By my junior year of high school my financial exploration had really taken off. So did the drinking and carousing. Exploring life, pushing boundaries. Entering my senior year of high school was a blessing. I was grateful to have made it. I knew that Boston College would not be in my future, but another college would be inevitable. But where?

I applied and was accepted at Youngstown State University, an engineering and music school. It meant staying close to home and my cousin Paul. Paul and I... what a business future we would enjoy.

As Dad approached retirement, he again saw his world changing. As we discussed prior, Dad always did have a problem with change, any kind of change. With Rick moving out and me going to college, Dad's weekends became lonely. He always wanted to know if we would be coming home, but we never knew what condition he would be in when we got there.

I remember vividly one weekend when I was home from college, Dad was drunk and argumentative. I went downstairs to my comfort zone but could no longer find peace. Dad was accusing Mom of many untruths and was becoming abusive. At that moment Dad and I had a confrontation of ideology. I had made up my mind that Dad would no longer attack, hurt or exhibit this behavior towards my mother or me. Thus I entered the fray. It became physical. Dad realized that his son was no longer a child.

I made a decision that night that I would never be like my father. Dad's behavior would never impact my life. Dad's values may have been good, but his behavior was bad. He only knew two ways to express himself, silence or yelling. No moderation. I realized later on that Dad did care, but we were caught in this ugly power struggle, a fight for supremacy. Nothing was ever the same from then on. After that Saturday night of rage, my values were challenged, my beliefs crumbled, and my faith was put on hold.

I was leaving home to prove him wrong. Or was I leaving to simply acquire more wants, using Dad's inconsistencies and my oppressive upbringing as my supporting justification? I was determined to do better than he thought I could do. I was determined to be successful. So, life became an obsession. And I do mean an obsession.

Through these maturing years, testing, challenging, we have all the answers or so many of us think. We vow never to grow up "like Dad!" "Gosh, I never want to follow in his footsteps." But we do.

Look how I messed up! Although I didn't realize it yet, I began to arbitrarily rearrange my value base, capriciously selecting my values, compromising them, avoiding them and justifying all the way to the top. "I will never be like Dad" became my obsession. Well, it isn't that I couldn't be just like Dad, I was like my Dad. I simply didn't know it just yet.

My college scholastic endeavors were okay. It seems that I did just enough to get by. A's and B's, some C's, that was just fine with me, as long as I passed the class.

I joined the fraternity Zeta Beta Ta, Jewish fraternity, but most of the brothers were not Jewish. The members of ZBT were my friends and all enjoyed the traditions of fraternities, drinking and fraternizing with women.

Redeeming Grace

I met a young girl early on during my freshmen year. We spent a considerable amount of time together. Dad was angry about it. (Although Dad and I had an estranged relationship, Mom continued to insist that he visit and that I come home periodically.) Dad was upset because he was afraid my relationship with this girl would interfere with my education. Actually it wasn't she that was interfering.

Although I was obsessed with money, my value hierarchy insisted that I work within acceptable societal boundaries for my money. I did meet men at the fraternity who profited off drugs. I detested that. I did try marijuana in college but I didn't like it or its effects. Whiskey or beer now, that's another story.

While I was going to school full-time, I worked for a security company, installing commercial security devices. Soon my income approached $300 a week. At the same time my infamous cousin Paul was developing his entrepreneurial skills as well. Paul and I always appeared to challenge the norm. Our lifestyle included expensive cars, dinner out nightly, cigars, bourbon and cognac, and women.

Paul was developing oil and gas limited partnerships, raising hundreds and thousands of dollars to drill and develop oil and gas wells. Wealthy affluent investors were intrigued, because during the years 1978 and 1979 natural gas and oil was at a premium. A well drilled in northeast Ohio could generate an 85% tax write-off on the investor capital, while realizing a three to four year return of capital.

So during this time of college, dating, fraternity, and work, my need for money meant investing time with Paul. Learning the ropes at nightclubs, soaking in the ambiance, learning about gourmet cuisine, drinking, and meeting men who were very, very rich, my dreams were coming true.

My job at Sonitrol Security introduced me to businessmen and men of influence. Soon I found myself managing a security detail at the Cleveland Coliseum. Primarily our responsibility was to provide security coverage for special events and concerts. My responsibility was to hire college guys, big tough men who would listen and be part of our security detail.

I became adept at negotiating early on. Initially I was offered a flat fee per event and a travel allowance. I realized that I could request an amount of money for each man hired. In other words, the owners needed me, to acquire their staff. I needed their money.

I found that school, work, the fraternity, the lifestyle Paul had aided me in adapting, and the entertainers I met through my new part-time job were truly very exciting. Meeting the Eagles, America, Crosby, Stills, h and Young, Frank Sinatra, Diana Ross, Chicago, and Rod Stewart, was certainly reinforcing a pattern of behavior I had come to enjoy.

Youthful enthusiasm led me to choose paths that fulfilled my needs. My need of adult interaction, learned as a toddler, continued to be reinforced by Paul. I admired his brand of success. Earning a handsome income, profiting from investing other people's money, Paul saw alcohol, nightclubs, and the fast life as a vehicle to raise money and meet influential people, doing business the American way.

I was intrigued. I had some decisions to make. My young girl friend had plans (or shall I say her family had plans). However, at the moment those plans were not my plans. As I spent more and more time with Paul, the more I adapted to this life style of expensive suits, diamonds, dinner, drinks, travel and women. I was alive, living life in the fast lane and I was only eighteen.

By my sophomore year my perception of college was profoundly different. While my college friends exhibited childlike behavior, or so I thought, I was torn between the benefits of a degree and the lifestyle I knew was immediately available. This lifestyle fulfilled my immediate needs and provided instant gratification. I had begun to roll over people. What better way to achieve the American Dream?

~ On My Way ~

Chapter Seven

As Paul progressed in business acquiring more and more money and the toys it could buy, I was afforded the opportunity to meet one of Paul's investors. Mr. Fred George had enormous influence on my life. He was a self-made millionaire builder, developer directly involved in anything and everything that made money. Fatherly and friendly, he was respected in Youngstown, Ohio and maintained absolute control over his empire, which included prostitution, numbers, and gambling. Fred befriended me and before I could say "no," I was spending four out of seven nights a week with him, drinking, gourmet dining, dancing, meeting life's glamorous people.

Now with the above as a lifestyle consideration, compared to my college friends and their fraternity parties, you can guess which path I chose.

Dad was livid. He was deathly afraid that I was connected to disreputable characters. He was right but I wouldn't listen. I was on a mission to prove him wrong. The more he protested, the more it fueled the engine for me to run full speed ahead.

By age nineteen, I had no more interest in college. Fred introduced me to partners of his in various business ventures. Before I knew it, I was a partner with Fred and Paul, along with several others, running an electronic security company.

Emulating Fred, doing business became my way of life, money and women became my passion. Dad was furious and Mom had all but given up on me. The business progressing, Fred suggested that Paul and I share an office. I had adjusted into this lifestyle as if I was born to it. Travel, nightlife, the best food and drinks, good cigars (Hoyo de Monterrey) were standard fare. I was earning over $500 a week, a new car and all expenses paid. Life was good.

As time went on a problem arose between Fred and Paul. Paul relied on Fred to fund his oil and natural gas wells. However, after financial review, Paul was accused of using corporate funds in a manner in which Fred did not approve. Being Paul's cousin, having been brought into this business family placed me in an untenable position. Fred was a powerful man, respected and feared and not one you willfully opposed.

As Fred began to regain control of his investment and daily operations, he turned to someone he had come to befriend. Me! He said under his tutelage, I was ready. Of course, I was thrilled. Paul felt betrayed. But what Paul realized over time was that by my being there close to Fred, he was protected.

By the time I was twenty, I moved into my own apartment, a bachelor's paradise.

Paul acquired a boat, another place to drink. On July 4th, 1977, with no practice, no lessons, we took it out. I was comfortably seated, right rear seat, glass of whiskey in hand, when Paul jumped a wake of a rather large pleasure craft. I fell backwards overboard, hitting my chin on the outboard engine, breaking my jaw. My feet almost caught in the propeller. Fortunately I'm a capable swimmer and was able to stay afloat long enough to be picked up by the boat. Well, another lesson of life! But who was listening?

At this same July 4th yacht club party, Paul invited several of his friends as well. He introduced me to young woman named Elaine, recently divorced. She liked my lifestyle and we met each other's immediate needs. She was seven years older than I, but it didn't seem to matter. She was eager to form a lasting relationship and settle down.

Poor Dad and Mom had had such high hopes for me to settle down to a simpler life…like that of a mechanic. My brother, Rick, on the other hand was committed to achieving, one step-at-a-time, slowly, correctly. He studied, graduated college, and began a teaching career. I thought little of Rick's attempt at life's accomplishments. My style was to skip the steps and start right at the top. I thought I had everything under control.

During this period of my life I had clearly established a demarcation line with Dad. I loved him but ignored his concerns and advice. I felt that he was a threat to my accomplishments. Dad knew what my early affiliation with Fred meant. Remember, as a teenager himself, he had ventured on his own to Detroit and worked for union organizers during the most violent time of the unions' existence. Today I understand his concerns, but not then.

Fred's lifestyle intrigued me. He was the focal point of his entire family's affairs. Everyone went to Fred...brothers, sisters, sons, nephews, and grandchildren. It was Fred's world. Time was money. Playtime was money. Everything you do involves influence to achieve your desired wants. Fulfill the needs of others to achieve your goals.

As the oil industry expanded Fred ventured into the machine shop industry in Massillon, Ohio. A partner of his, R.B., was responsible for designing an oil pump jack. I learned first-hand how America does business. Fred also just happened to be the chairman of the hospital board. I was working installing security equipment at a hospital in Massillon. We received the contract.

By now I was earning approximately $700 a week, dating Elaine and learning all I could about oil and gas equipment. More importantly, I was a friend of Fred's. Although forty years separated us, we each shared a common value.

Also during this period, Fred had provided the security company with a job referral in Monaca, Pennsylvania, close to the Pittsburgh International Airport. This was an investment counselor and another partner of Fred's in Fisher Big Wheels.

Mr. K.'s house was under construction. It was magnificent. There was a room for his indoor swimming pool with a stone waterfall, three-stories high, and hydraulic doors opening to an outdoor pool. He built stables for his Clydesdale. I was impressed. I talked a lot to this man about money, what he did and how he did it! I certainly was not afraid to ask questions. Seeing the opulence, planes, helicopters, trips at a whim, I knew I was running in the right circles.

At twenty-one, I had a new home in Warren, Ohio, was married, with our first child on the way. Life was moving very rapidly. Too rapidly. The marriage was tenuous at best. Mom, attempting to regain her child, tried always to reconcile Dad and me. Carol and Mom wanted to develop a relationship with Elaine, but Elaine's comfort zone was invaded. They were not welcome. The chasm widened between us causing more family grief.

I'm not sure when it actually occurred but after Josh's birth Dad and I reached an unofficial truce. Dad was a grandfather and he loved every moment of it. He doted on Josh's every whim. That was good because Dad's focus was away from me. In Dad I had found a convenient babysitter!

At this point I was earning more money than Dad. I know he had difficulty with that. Mom assured us that Dad's drinking had subsided because of medical concerns. But it wasn't true. Interestingly enough by now Dad and I were able to speak a little more openly about how he was drinking. I should have looked at myself. But then again, I was on top of the world. It wasn't a problem.

During this time I spent a considerable amount of time with Fred and determined, in conjunction with R.B., to investigate the feasibility of designing and manufacturing a unique product to support the booming oil and gas industry. The field separator, a steel, skid-mounted unit containing a 20-inch high-pressure vessel approximately 8 inches long with welded concave end plates, had inlets and outlets for special instrumentation and gauges, and was encased in an all weather enclosure. Upon completion and selection of accessories equipment, the final cost to a gas producer would approach $7,000. Not bad.

I had lots to do. Fred allowed me to find a shop to start production. It didn't matter where, but what did matter to Fred was a budget. This man taught me to plan precisely. Over several months, before we started our new venture, we defined a budget, confirmed engineering designs, costs of material, equipment and more specifically determined if there was a market for revenue. Our goal was to make money.

Within six months we had settled for a manufacturing shop in Newton Falls, Ohio, in an empty warehouse situated along the east branch of the Mahoning River, Baba's river. It was central for every one involved and only $500 a month to rent. Funny, but Newton Falls, like a magnet kept drawing me back, this time as a founder of another business.

Initially I had no employees. I learned to weld and installed 440 electrical service panels and all related plugs. As the business grew I prospered, having earnings over $36,000. Not bad for a twenty-one-year-old college dropout.

Mom told me once early on, "Terry, slow down. Tomorrow is another day." I didn't understand then, but I do today. She also said, "Terry you're like a bulldozer, you can't keep running over things, people and expect your desired results." Back then I didn't take heed. Deep down I really knew she was right, but I ignored her. If I accepted what she said as true, it meant removing myself from a comfort zone that I had arbitrarily and capriciously established. My wants came first!

There's nothing wrong with wanting to succeed. What's wrong was the method I used to achieve my end. With all the opportunities that seemingly fell at my feet, I constantly sought to build my own value system. Right or wrong, I was a young man on a mission. Only problem was, I didn't understand the rules or the consequences that would result.

In 1979, Fred informed me (not asked) that our founding plant and activities would be moved to his plant in Massillon, Ohio. The business was growing and we were marketing approximately three to four units per week, but Fred wanted ten to fifteen units. Always bigger.

R.B., the seasoned engineer, would supervise the production while I would take over the marketing and sales of the product. That meant a car, an expense account, traveling to new cities, meeting people, a wonderful income and now something new, a bonus for each unit sold. The prospects were exciting.

I truly enjoyed the newfound freedom. The travel, however, meant an exhausting schedule. Everyday I drove ninety minutes each way from Warren to Massillon and back. My initial travels to market our products meant traveling to many major cities in the east where the oil and gas fields of the United States were located, including my favorite city, New York.

I learned early on that in order to sell this product, I had to reach out to the actual user of the product, not the buyer. The point of this is that once I had the support of the operating field staff employees, the rest was easy. So I dressed in work clothes, learned the lingo of the field staff, and would be there at 6 a.m., to buy breakfasts, go to the wells, the rigs, becoming a valued part of these men's lives. I'd buy lunch and drinks. These seasoned and weathered men enjoyed a life tradition that I had absolutely no problem encouraging. We drank at every imaginable bar and establishment that offered alcohol.

So I was an engineer. But what I possessed at the time was something these people needed; a tangible product, a device that assisted them in making money. Isn't that what life is all about?

Having established my newfound support network I had to reach the men and women who were responsible for authorizing purchases. Identifying this person in an organization can be difficult at times. It's all about power and control and I was learning the game. I had to look important, dress important, smell important. Play the game. Find the lounge where the influential people relaxed and made money. After that, selling was simple.

But as sales grew, our business developed a problem. Some companies wouldn't pay us, at least not when they said they would. It was a major problem for us, and especially for Fred, because no one ever owed Fred. But these people didn't know Fred. R.B. and I had a problem.

In any event, I needed to find a money source, someone who could fund this development for over $1,000,000 a week. Through my research I discovered a firm, U.S. Resources out of Buffalo, New York, owned by a truly gregarious man, Joseph M. Ryan. Joe's main core business was real estate, large residential garden style apartments.

Joe and I were as drawn to one another like a magnet and enjoyed a business relationship which developed over time into a long-term friendship. Ironically we share a similar family heritage.

Personally, the first half of my life I didn't have many friends. Many acquaintances offered me friendship but I was interested only in what they could offer me and how I might benefit from the relationship. Thus the magnetic attraction to Joe existed because of similar values, a commonality of goals and dependence on a lifestyle. We were two individuals fulfilling more wants and ignoring more needs, willing to compromise values, redefine and prostitute beliefs in order to reach our lofty dreams.

Joe visited with me while I was in prison. I realized that Joe was human, struggling with issues in life "that just aren't right." I was glad to see his honesty come forward.

Paul, my infamous cousin, reentered my life socially and in business. Paul was pursuing another field…Corporate take-overs. He was involved with a local accountant from Warren, Ohio. For weeks he reappeared on the nightclub social scene, no longer fearful of Fred's wrath.

During this period Paul spoke continually about his recently acquired business contact. Paul arranged for a prominent company, A&S Equipment, to take over a plastic extruder whose core business is in the automotive line. Like many businesses, the re-organization of Chrysler (the bailout) left a large number of moderate-size employers either bankrupt or curtailed their business as a viable ongoing concern.

I learned this concept, "ongoing concern," from people in charge of running a business and in accounting. If a business runs out of cash and cannot pay its bills nor borrow money, perhaps because of its debt, then it is unable to continue operating. Typically, in a business curtailed as an ongoing concern, the owners just won't give up believing things will get better. But they never do. They hope a white knight will come and rescue them, but not one ever shows up. The owner lives in an illusion until someone else locks his doors, like the IRS or court simply says, "Enough is enough."

Paul wanted me to come work with him. Well, I was not comfortable working with R.B. and realized I wasn't "Family." Perhaps I was just searching again for that which I hadn't found. What was I searching for? Money? Recognition? Acceptance? Success? Hadn't I achieved a measure of all these things? What was the drive that kept pushing me on? Was I still trying to prove something to Dad?

Cal M. and I met at an appropriate time in my life. Cal offered me a Vice President position in charge of Engineering and Sales at a starting salary of $54,000, a sales incentive plan, a new Volvo and an expense account.

My decision was easy. I gave R. B. and Fred my two-weeks' notice. R.B. was angry. Fred? Well, you would have thought I violated Family law. R.B. insisted that Fred sue me. Fred and I eventually renewed our friendship.

ADS Oil and Gas was formed in Warren, Ohio. I bought a brand new house on Nob Hill in Niles, Ohio. Cal was insistent on the use of budgets, plans and job objectives. Management is only as good as the reasonableness of its plans. Are the plans attainable? Objectives must be measurable, specific. What about a time frame? What is the anticipated economic profile, positive or negative? Cal often would tell me "Terry, invest wisely for today is your tomorrow."

By age 22, I wasn't much interested in philosophy. I'd listen but not listen. I think I patronized him. Oh gosh, I'd patronize Cal and just about anyone else necessary in my plan to make money.

My second gift of life arrived January 16, 1981. My son Justin was born, a wonderful contented, happy baby. As all babies do, he knew instinctively how to acquire his wants and needs.

Josh and Justin are my shining stars. However, their early development years were conflicting with my want fulfillment years. I arbitrarily left much of the day-to-day parenting obligation to their mother. I thank her for the job she did while I was off chasing my life's dream.

By the year Justin was born, ADS had grown to approximately 40 employees. Our sales had increased to result in shipping approximately 12 separators per week with a complete support equipment line. U.S. Resources became the number one client of ADS. Our receivables from U.S. Resources climbed as well. My income had increased again to $65,000, with a car and expense account. Trips, travel, weekend excursions with the boys, life was good.

I was still trying to prove something to Dad but he was noncommittal. I think he was proud, but I'm not sure, he never said. We always had a problem with communication. Dad was jealous. He said as much. Again, Sunday visits and holidays more often than not resulted in arguments. Dad would drink a lot and when the pain was well medicated, utilize a skill he had acquired to help him cope with life. He would transfer his pain to whoever was in his sights.

Mom would often tell me to slow down, to think of the boys. She was really saying was, "Life is cycling again, right before my very eyes."

Well, my relationship with Joe continued. Joe was on a roll financially. Arlington Capital, the marketing arm, was simultaneously raising money for a public limited partnership to acquire very large residential garden style apartment complexes. Landmark properties, the real estate developer, was raising $20,000,000 in cash from investors, promising ownership interests in the property along with a continual stream of tax deductions. Joe was a master at using other people's money to assume the risk. The $20,000,000, when used as down payment funds, could be leveraged by coupling the cash with mortgage money, thus allowing the investor group to acquire a portfolio exceeding $60,000,000. Tax breaks for the rich, so the rich get richer. That's business the American way.

During the 70's, Warren and Youngstown, Ohio had taken a beating with the extensive closure of many of the steel plants. Wages were far too high and the competitive advantage was gone. The powerful steel workers union was not so powerful any longer.

Now the unions were threatening to do the same thing to A&S Equipment. Cal was blunt. "Terry, if the union is voted in I have no choice but to close ADS Oil and Gas. So, think about it this weekend and we will meet Monday and look at our options."

Monday didn't change anything. Our only option seemed to be to sell or liquidate. Attorneys were called in, and with our accountants we drafted a plan of action. Cal's goal was to protect A&S Equipment, avoid pain. My goal was to protect my income and avoid pain.

We continued marketing our products, as if nothing was changing, rallying the staff and troops, meanwhile looking for a buyer. The process took several months but the obvious buyer emerged.

I was still traveling to Buffalo weekly, U.S. Resource being by far our largest client. I disclosed to P. G., Joe's Vice President, that problems existed in Paradise. Before I knew it I was sitting in Joe's office formulating a game plan.

Joe had now acquired a separator that his field personnel liked. He discovered a way to resell the equipment from his equipment company to U.S. Resource and resell again to the marketing company. Thus, Joe was making money over and over and over. When I traveled to Buffalo, Joe would see that I was entertained lavishly.

As the weeks progressed, I found myself the middleman in a high stakes poker game. Still being paid by ADS and acting as negotiator for Joe, trying so hard to satisfy everyone's wants while maintaining Terry's needs, something had to break before I broke.

Before long I was working solely for Joe and this position provided me the opportunity to acquire all the wants I wanted. My salary was $65,000, with an expense account, Cadillac and moving allowance.

Joe Ryan represented the lifestyle to which Fred had introduced me, and happily, without the threat of family consequences. Dinners costing between six and seven hundred dollars were standard fare, part of the fringe benefits.

I remember my first week working with Joe. We went to the Buffalo Playboy Club. I was like a wide-eyed child in a candy store. Dinner was simply not normal. Joe was late, leaving four of his guests to drink. In his typical grandiose style he called ahead leaving word to give us anything we wanted. Joe finally arrived, stylishly one hour late.

Dinner was a carnival atmosphere. I had consumed probably eight drinks. The "bunny" waitress knew how to play to her audience, flattering, teasing, stroking Joe's ego. He ordered "two of everything." I was mesmerized! Bottle after bottle of fine wine, 16 different appetizers, complete steak dinners and a rack of lamb, and all for just five men.

Dessert was a sideshow! Joe needed to be the center of attention. The waitress, scantily covered in her unique bunny costume, knew quite well how to play to Joe. Dessert was Bananas Foster. Bananas sautéed, tableside, in butter, sugar, brown sugar, and brandy with Grand Marnier. Ignited with 151 rum. The warm bananas were ladled into parfait glasses while the remaining sauce was poured ever so gingerly over vanilla ice cream. The bananas were topped with fresh whipped cream.

After all that, Joe directed us to the bar in the nightclub for us to relax. More drinks. More entertainment. I guess I was expected to work the next day. What I did not know just yet was that this ritual was not out of the ordinary, but routine for Joe.

I had accomplished a want. I was living in two different worlds, the lifestyle I was striving to achieve and the real world I was avoiding.

By 1983 I was contemplating moving to Buffalo permanently. Elaine was unsure. But I knew the commute was getting to be too much. I wanted to be with the boys more. I have always loved every moment I could spend with them.

Joe had a summer party like nothing I have ever seen. The yard, house and garage had been converted into a carnival, with a stage, bands, barbeques, all kinds of rides for the kids including a merry-go-round and a Ferris wheel. He had horses and carriages, and a garage packed with video game machines, cotton candy, a peanut vendor and on and on it went. A complete carnival in his back yard! The food was incredible. Tables of shrimp, clams, oysters, roast beef, lamb, and of course every kind of dessert. But most importantly, the bar was stocked with every imaginable beverage one could wish for. Of course, there was a full selection of cigars.

Josh and Justin, four and two-and-a-half, were mesmerized. They asked, "Dad, can we get a house like this?" I thought, "Well, I assume so. It was simply a process of acquiring more."

I will never forget going to lunch the following Tuesday with J. R's corporate accountant. He informed me that this one-day extravaganza cost over $25,000. Well, I was sold. I made up my mind right then and there that I wanted what they had. Power and control became the center of influence. I had convinced myself that I needed this lifestyle at all costs. I was continually being introduced to influential people who re-enforced this obsession. I was writing my own life script and, for me, God was not in the picture.

What about your life? Has your life unfolded as you dreamed or planned? Has your faith, teachings, beliefs and values influenced your choices or are you developing your set of values along the way. Is God in the picture? Believe me, He is there, whether we acknowledge Him or not.

"O LORD, you have searched me and you know me. You know when I sit and when I rise; you perceive my thoughts from afar. You discern my going out and my lying down; you are familiar with all my ways. Before a word is on my tongue you know it completely, O LORD. You hem me in-- behind and before; you have laid your hand upon me. Such knowledge is too wonderful for me, too lofty for me to attain. Where can I go from your Spirit? Where can I flee from your presence? If I go up to the heavens, you

are there; if I make my bed in the depths, you are there. If I rise on the wings of the dawn, if I settle on the far side of the sea, even there your hand will guide me, your right hand will hold me fast. If I say, 'Surely the darkness will hide me and the light become night around me,' even the darkness will not be dark to you; the night will shine like the day, for darkness is as light to you" (Psalm 139:1-12).

He loves us too much to let us go without getting our attention. I wasn't paying attention. I ignored the interventions He sent along the way. I was stubborn and self-willed. But God is patient. I had to go farther down in the depths before I took the time to look up.

~ My Father's Son ~

Chapter Eight

Joe began to pull me into the office to meet with investors, entertain brokers, dealers, real moneymen who brought Joe pleasure. Was I satisfied? So many of my values had been discarded. Well, no not discarded but certainly ignored. Because once I saw what income level the sales agents were at, immediately I had a new need. Needs and wants were all the same to me. I could not distinguish.

The average broker dealer working for Joe made an average of over $250,000 a year. I looked upon my meager income $70,000 plus bonus, plus travel expenses, weekly use of a Bell Jet Ranger helicopter (costing over $350 an operating hour, to save me time shuttling back and forth from Buffalo to Pennsylvania,) a Cadillac, expense account and of course my bonding with Joe. After business, Joe and I always seemed to find our way to a bar or bars in order to seek entertainment and share life's plans.

Although my immediate supervisor was an ex-CIA military man, Skip Dennis, Joe's style of management was to bypass Skip and go directly to the source. Skip held what I called a perfunctory position.

Joe was raising millions of dollars per month. The investors were very concerned that he had spread himself too thin. So Skip was hired as President, P.G. fired, and I was promoted.

My life could certainly be called successful. I traveled all over the country, owned a large beautiful home, and could acquire just about any toy I wanted. Dad and Mom came to visit. My relationship with Dad was clearly changing for the better. In 1983, Dad was told by his doctor that he must stop drinking. However, even having half of his stomach removed did not stop him. By 1984 Dad retired. He bought a new tractor for me and he received a brand new Ford Bronco XLT compliments of Joe and U.S. Energy.

Dad would come to Buffalo. The visits were nice, but I could tell something with Dad "just wasn't right." Dad knew his death was near. Mom described him as a man seemingly beaten by life. It had not turned out as he had dreamed.

He had worked all his life. Now his routine was broken. He had no hobbies except one, drinking. He would wake up about 9:00 a.m., drink eight to ten cups of coffee by noon, and then he would literally sit for hours and hours on the breezeway step guarding the house. He vegetated. And he drank more and more. What Dad would not do was talk. Whatever his feelings, emotions and expectations were, he simply wouldn't share them. I realize today that Dad did have values. He just didn't know how to communicate. He was never taught. But his family did come first, we knew that. He just couldn't express himself. Dad's retirement was very hard on Mom. He found his identity in his work at Chrysler Corporation. Without that comfort zone, he isolated himself from life idling away his hours on his front porch. But Dad's porch became Mom's prison. Dad was very jealous and control was a must.

I offered to have Dad stay in Buffalo for a month, to help me around the house and perhaps give him a chance to focus, to feel productive. He certainly needed to regain his balance.

At this point everything revolved around my business priorities. I began to mirror people I assimilated with, as justification for my actions. Coming home late or not at all was my prerogative. Family activities? My decision. Children's events, children's wants were relegated to the weekend. To my children I had become my father's son.

Look what happened here. I wanted to be in control. I clearly believed with more money, more toys, more trips, peace would come and I would be happy. Everyone would be happy. The problem was, however, everyone around me was not happy. Yes, I had clearly become my father's son and I was passing these demons to my boys and I didn't even know it.

During this period of time a neighbor entered my business life, Dr. Vong, a Vietnamese immigrant who clearly understood the American way of life. One thing was clear, Dr. Vong and his wife Mia never lost sight of their cultural identity. In their struggle leaving a homeland devastated by war, the effects of the Vietnam conflict, coming to America, they were dedicated to finding their purpose. Both became doctors while along the way their wants were being fulfilled. But their first priority was simply to fulfill each other's needs first.

Dr. Vong and I initially became acquainted "over the fence" talking as neighbors while our children played together. Gradually I begin to share more of my dreams, goals and ambitions. As the summer turned to fall, my relationship with Dr. Vong transferred from an "over-the-fence" relationship to a friendship. Buffalo Bills football games, Sabre's hockey games, golfing and lots and lots of activities with our boys, I found myself as Dr. Vong's friend slowly being allowed within his circle of influence.

One day Dr. Vong and I were socializing at the bar of a local country club. Next to us was a Supreme Court Judge along with another very successful man, a pillar of the community.

In conversation he asked where I worked. I said, "U.S. Resources, J.M. Ryan and Company." The Judge said, "Is that the company owned by Julie and Joe Ryan?" Then the discussion was on.

Dr. Vong was smart. He said, "Terry, Joe always makes money for managing his projects no matter what happens or what cash is generated." The salesmen make money one time only. Joe makes money every month.

The next question Dr. Vong asked was "Are you happy, there?" I was confused. Not knowing what to say, I said, "no." Mia was most opinionated, stating emphatically that many of her colleagues were most unhappy with J.R.'s performance.

What I learned was fascinating. Over several months I became most knowledgeable in business accounting and how income is hidden, sheltered or transferred for personal gain. Exciting stuff.

What became clear to me was exactly what Dr. Vong and Mia had said one year earlier. The Oil and Gas partnerships were so over priced and heavy with management fees that the investor was unlikely to receive his money back, let alone make a profit! The only benefit he received was the tax incentives.

How very much like my life. I had invested heavily in this lifestyle, giving it all I had, sacrificing those things that were most important. What was the return? Temporary gratification?

Through our discussions Dr. Vong proposed that he and I become fifty/fifty partners and establish a new corporation. My obvious question was how much would I contribute and how much would I make.

By 1985 King Oil and Gas Corporation was established with me as the President. We intended to duplicate what Joe had done only we would return capitol to our investors. I was excited. We funded the company with $10,000 and in less than six-months time found that we had funded our first three well drilling programs, with $480,000 in our corporate account and a

$50,000 line of bank credit, a salary of $85,000 a year, plus every imaginable benefit, a Gold card, a new Lincoln Town Car and a new letter of acceptance to the Orchard Park Country Club.

Over the course of the next two years King Oil and Gas began expanding and drilling wells in Pennsylvania, New York and had on staff two geologists, field staff and a secretary. We acquired new offices and at one point over $1,200,000 in cash in the bank intended for well development.

On paper, my income had risen to $270,000 a year. I should have been happy. But what is clear today, with all the material toys, a town house at a ski lodge, a new speedboat, I still had not found happiness. Peace and serenity did not exist. But what was I searching for?

How have you invested your time? Do you invest in people, loving, building and helping them develop their God-given potential? Or do you use them for what they can do for you and then toss them aside? What about eternal investments? Comparing the brevity of this life to all eternity, it should be obvious where we should invest the most.

"Do not store up for yourselves treasures on earth, where moth and rust destroy, and where thieves break in and steal. But store up for yourselves treasures in heaven, where moth and rust do not destroy, and where thieves do not break in and steal. For where your treasure is, there your heart will be also." (Matthew 6:19-21)

During the beginning of the second year of King Oil and Gas and the renaissance of Terry, on March 23, 1986, my Baba, Suzanne Tkacs Petricko born in the village of Zbince, Austria, Hungary, died at the age of 91. She had been my inspiration.

It was a time to mourn, reflect on the purpose of life. Did she balance her life? Yes! Baba's life, even in its simplicity had meaning and purpose, to herself and those around her. She touched lives by her example and her teachings. Her faith, her beliefs, and her values were passed on as her legacy of life to her heirs, her children's children. She balanced spirituality, emotional wellness and physical well being.

Mourning our family Matriarch brought our family together in a bond of sadness mixed with joy. The family gathered at Mom and Dad's house. Sons Ed and Mike from California, sisters Margaret and Sue, all the grandchildren, cousins, nephews, nieces, we were one. Mom was so concerned because of all the drinking that was occurring as we socialized. But what was really occurring all the while was that the family was going through a process of homeostasis, trying to find a new balance with a vital "Mainstay" missing.

By the second day of grieving, I noticed a subtle change in the stories. As the herd sat around the bar reminiscing, the stories changed from sad to good, funny stories. We laughed, recalling memories. Then came the expression of feelings, teachings, the retelling of stories from one generation to another. The purpose of these stories was to preserve a legacy for each subsequent generation. Uncle Mike wasn't done creating his own legacies. Some things just never change. The day before the funeral Uncle Mike and Uncle Ed, having been raised there 50 years earlier, wanted to return to their roots and search for meaning.

My cousin Paul, along with a supply of cigars, drove them to town to the Veterans of Foreign Wars' Club. Uncle Mike had earned a Purple Heart for his war service. Well, by the time I arrived at the bar, Dad, Rick, Paul, the Uncles and a very large herd had gathered to again rekindle friendships, tell stories and remember. One thing was clear. As we remembered, each one of us sought our own comfort zone, medicating our pain as we mourned our loss, processing through this rite of passage.

The people of the village of Newton Falls, her church, and her family, paid their last respects to this woman. I remember the large turn out for her calling hours, the church adulations, rosary and evening prayers. I was thankful that no one had decided to have her body on display in Mom's home like Uncle Andy's was at Baba's. I still have haunting memories of that experience.

In the end Baba was laid to rest. Her legacy of life passed down to all the generations that are to come.

King Oil and Gas was growing and I was acquiring more toys. By 1987, I made the decision to buy a new boat, much larger than the first. It was a deal not to be passed up. The prior owner, a business agent for a local union controlled by the Mob, had turned states evidence. My friend, at the time, Rocky, a local mob enforcer, told me I could get the yacht cheap. Well, it was appraised for $110,000. I purchased it for $78,000. What a deal.

Now I had a large, grandiose home on the water, a place for me and for Rocky to acquire more wants and fulfill more pleasures.

I remember having the boat screened for bugs (electronic listening devices). Not only was the prior owner a member of mafia now in the witness protection program, but my friend and boat dock neighbor was now the suspected Mafia leader.

Rocky and I spent quite a bit of time together sharing many stories. He invited me to become a partner in a business. Remembering my other "Family" involvement, I decided not to take him up on his offer. I'd much rather have Rocky as a friend than an enemy.

But today upon reflection I understand why I assimilated to people in the underworld. They made things happen! They represented power and ultimate control. Involving Rocky and his soldiers in my life was my choice. His wife and children were like family.

As the year progressed, Dad became more depressed and despondent over retirement. Mom insisted that they visit us in Buffalo every three to four months. It gave Dad something to look forward to. He tried to hide it, but his drinking was at an all time high. Dad had found his comfort zone. Medically, his physician had made it clear that with diabetes, high blood pressure, half a stomach, and ulcerated esophagus, he must stop drinking or die. Dad made his choice. The consequences were unfolding right before our eyes.

My childhood friend from Circle Drive, Roby Lee, had grown up as well. He had taken over a chain of pizza shops and was doing well. He believed it was time to open his own restaurant, but he needed money! This information was disclosed in an "over the fence" conversation between his father and my Dad who had been friends (on and off) for over thirty years. Roby's father was very upset that none of the wealthy village elders would assist Rob with capital and/or equipment. Dad suggested that maybe his son, Terry would be interested.

When my Dad told me about it, I listened, something I rarely did. Roby's father was interested in acquiring venture capital. Roby was seeking to fulfill a dream. Dad wanted a restaurant just like the one he and Roby's Dad used to frequent before and after work, their home away from home. I think Dad was proud of my success. Because of him, I wanted to make this work.

I'll never forget the day I got Mom's call. I knew something was wrong from the hesitation in her voice. "Terry, your Dad's in the hospital. Can you come home?" I was caught off guard. I knew that the inevitable would come some day. I tried not to think about it. This man I hated, yet loved, was my father and he was in need. I also knew that Mom, though strong and courageous, needed me too. I immediately left for Newton Falls. The drive gave me time to think. I was scared. What would Mom do? There were so many unresolved issues between Dad and me, I didn't want to lose him. There were things I needed to tell him. Perhaps for the first time in my life, I realized how fragile life is.

When I arrived in his room, Dad, though heavily medicated, held himself up and with a look of childlike innocence, reached up to accept my hug. Then he kissed and embraced me. There were tears in his eyes. I knew he was afraid. That moment, the look from within the very deepest part of Dad's soul told me a story. Dad's life had meaning and purpose for himself, others and yes, for me. So many of us never stop to find, know, or appreciate those meanings until faced with death

He explained what the doctors had told him. He had a heart attack but was stable. An angiogram was scheduled for later on in the week. Dad and I talked for a little while. We laughed, cried, and I knew this man had faced life head on and did his best. In that sense, he had won. His favorite friend, Father Kisch the parish priest, had been by to visit.

Interestingly, as I talked to Father Kisch later at the funeral, and numerous times thereafter, Dad's conversations with him were mostly asking questions, listening, and in his own way confirming his faith and expressing his love. Dad was sending a message. He knew his time was near. I think Mom realized this most of all.

I left Dad that night, spiritually aware that old wounds were beginning to heal. I couldn't say our differences were resolved, not completely anyway, not just yet.

Carol, Rick and I returned to Mom's house and sat up half the night just talking together. Mom and Rick seemed convinced that Dad would weather this attack. Carol was not so sure. She took me aside. "Terry it's really bad. What are you going to do?"

Mom was insistent that I return to Buffalo, "Your kids need you. If something else changes, we'll call you."

I followed her advice, but first stopped to see Dad the next morning before I left. He was doing better, more rested. But he had changed in a profound way. There was a peace about him, a spiritual calm that had not been there before. I thought things were going to be okay.

Returning to Buffalo, I called his cardiologist. The Doctor was very frank. Dad had abused his body. For some 50 years he smoked three packs of Camels' cigarettes a day. He was a heavy chronic drinker and routinely consumed a diet heavy in saturated fats. It had taken its toll. The prognosis was not good. I asked the doctor if I should go back to Newton Falls. He was very definite. "Terry, your Dad needs you now, right now!" I left my office returned home and gathered clothes for several days.

The boys simply asked, "Is Grandpa going to be okay?" I knew the answer but didn't know how to tell them. Yet, they needed to know.

Leaving by myself, I began to realize that time was of the essence. I drove quickly, soberly, aware of a need. Perhaps for the very first time in my life, the needs of someone else were being met before my own. I felt comforted to know that Dad and I had spoken, but there were a few more things that still needed to be said.

Several hours later I arrived at the intensive care unit of the hospital. Mom, Rick and Carol were there. During the last several hours Dad had summoned all his children

As his friend, Father Kisch, later told me, "Your father needed to touch his bases, complete unfinished business, find his peace and serenity, before he could meet his God."

Someday, we will meet again, I believe, and I will take him a message. "The business is complete." Bold statement! What Andrew L. King knew at death was that he was loved. His life and legacy live on. His contribution to this world was beyond his comprehension. For Andrew touched many in a profound way.

He wanted to see us, one by one. First Mom. They talked alone. She cried and didn't know it then, but Dad was saying, "good-by!" Carol went in next, then Rick, then me. One by one we talked.

As long as I live I will never forget the feeling, the emotion of what happened at that moment in time. Entering Dad's room I had a feeling of oneness with this man I had so loathed, feared, resented, yet loved and wanted so to please. He smiled and talked to me. I listened. Listened to each word, to the meaning. Dad was teaching, passing down a legacy of life. He was worried how his little ones were taking his sickness. Even today, years later, I remember his final words. Honest, clear, spiritual, Andrew L. King sought forgiveness. He had lived his life promise.

As I left Dad that night, I tucked him in, kissed him good-by and said, "See you tomorrow." He smiled.

We returned to Mom's house late that night. We talked, we cried and laughed. Finally we quieted down to rest for whatever the next day would bring.

During the night Dad had several more heart attacks and never made it back. He died February 13, 1987.

What I realized is that Dad's life's purpose had been met. The real sadness for me and those around me, was that although I know the meaning of Dad's life, the spiritual teachings, all of which are gifts, it required ten years of my life to sort through my fears and finally say good-bye to this man. The solution to my fear of failure, insecurity, and need for approval that I brooded and wept for, was taught to me long ago. I just wouldn't listen.

A year after Baba's death, the family gathered together once again at the home of Andrew L. King. The bar was again central in the process of mourning. Uncle Ed, Uncle Mike, the cousins, the sadness, the drinking, the stories, the laughter, life remembering and perpetuating life. For a man who spent little time with his children, he certainly touched many lives, perhaps far more than I imagined.

Dad was laid to rest in the family cemetery plot. His little ones were moved by his death. Josh and Justin missed their grandfather. See, what I was missing was a significant point. By allowing my jealousies, resentments, anger, and sense of entitlement to overshadow my view of Dad's life I missed the real purpose for which his life had been lived. The children didn't miss the point. Their innocence, trust and acceptance allowed them to bond with this man in a loving meaningful relationship such as I never knew. They didn't care what he wasn't. They just loved who he was. I wish I had been listening.

Will you be loved after your death? Serious stuff to ponder. If you have any doubts, well, there is still time to get to work.

~ Chasing The Wind ~

Chapter Nine

Dad's death left a void in my life, kind of like unfinished business. My commitment to Dad was to finish business. The problem was, I was finishing the wrong business.

Expanding King Oil & Gas into the transportation of Natural Gas was a novel approach to the tightening market. The energy crisis of which Jimmy Carter had so convincingly persuaded the American public, never materialized. His warnings that this nation would run out of natural gas energy sources by the turn of the century were in fact utter nonsense based on bad statistical information (or another hidden agenda). All the while life savings, corporate futures were being invested on this man's credibility. Prices for natural gas fell dramatically as the 80's progressed.

Brokering gas became the concentration of activity. Drilling was slowing down considerably. There was no way to justify drilling new marginal wells. Wells were now selected based solely on homerun track records. Only the very best would be drilled.

Personally I believed that we could weather the pending storm. By 1987 I had drilled 48 wells and was responsible for managing the day-to-day operations.

During the summer of 1987, the boat with its fully stocked bar became my sanctuary, a place to escape within my comfort zone to fulfill more wants.

Elaine and the kids lived on board weekends and I used it all during the week to entertain and do business. For me the boat was a necessity of life. This craft cost me $14,000 a year to own and operate.

Josh and Justin loved the boat, the opportunity to travel and be together. At least they were with me. I saw myself as a better parent than my father had been. At least I was allowing my children to enter my circle of influences. Was I a better parent? Was I just pacifying their wants rather than taking care of their needs?

Partnerships make for interesting relationships. Diverse and interactive, each party is required to make choices, yet remain in agreement. Everything was good with Dr. Vong as long as I agreed. When I didn't agree with him, he would become angry and isolate himself.

I was being sued. Joe Ryan and his corporate attorneys sued to seek an injunction which would, in fact, stop me from raising money, finding investors, working in the business. After many thousands of dollars, the court rejected Joe's claims and refused to invoke a court order restricting me in any way.

Meanwhile, Dr. Vong acquired a town house in Ellicottville, New York for $100,000, not including furnishings and operating expenses. It was something else for King Oil and Gas to finance. Dr. Vong's country club friend owned the development. The chaos continued.

Enraptured by this life style, the amount of debt I had now incurred exceeded over $500,000 and had to be paid back. The pressure became real. My fixed living expenses had now reached if not exceeded $8,000 a month and were climbing. As long as the gas kept flowing I was in good shape, comfortable but with a false sense of security.

Dr. Vong was a man who could easily afford the expense of all these "toy" acquisitions. I could not. Yet, I silenced my inner voice of reason and would not take "no" for an answer. My dream, the American Dream was coming unraveled, only at the time, I didn't know.

My boating friends, socializing friends, mobsters were handy for the right events. They were chosen by me strictly to provide support to my irrational lifestyle and assist me in remaining in my comfort zone.

Roby continued to call me on a daily basis informing me of his project. He was young, impressionable, yet appeared stable. Initially, I was intrigued by Roby's concept. Even though we had no business plan as yet, I made a decision. Perhaps because it was a link to my Dad and the change that had been happening in our relationship before his death, or whether it was to compete with Dr. Vong, I decided to pursue Roby's Restaurant idea. Newton Falls, Ohio deserved a new modern family style restaurant.

Rational thinking? No. But then again, want fulfillment that becomes a need never is rational. Roby came to Buffalo and brought along his plans. We renewed our old friendship, the Circle Drive memories, and then got down to business. I insisted Rob concentrate on a business plan. This project soon became my project.

I was working at the office every day from 7:30 a.m. until anywhere from 5:30 to 7:00 p.m. I'd stop for Happy Hour, relax, and be home by 8:00 p.m. Nights at home became an overwhelming hub of activity. The progression of visitors started every night about eight o'clock and continued until one or two in the morning. The bar was getting used quite regularly.

Roby would occupy two or three hours, the sales team for Niagara Gas Transmission would arrive, my accountant also visited nightly. Five, six men carrying out Terry's demands, planning, computer profiles, telephone banking, getting things done. Eight, nine cars were constantly lined up in the driveway. People came to drink, to plan, to earn money.

Some people told me I was on top of the world. I was on the bottom, but clearly unable to see it. My life was out of control.

Employees, salesmen, brokers, moneymen, my children, enforcers... no one wanted to upset Terry. I represented their money source and as Joe was to me several years earlier, I represented their comfort zone.

Elaine wanted a new kitchen, I didn't want my life's comfort zone questioned nor disrupted. In other words she had no real idea what I was doing, we simply weren't communicating. It was my choice.

So the kitchen project was her new project. New cabinets evolved into a cathedral ceiling with skylights, custom oak cabinets, French doors, a palladium window, three-level deck, and a hot tub, with a final cost of $40,000.

The most important factor to me about the addition was the size of the kitchen 18' x 22', and the new bar installed between the kitchen and family room. It was perfect for me to start financial investment home presentations to our investors and partners.

Roby consistently asked, "Where will you get the money?" I simply said, "Don't worry! That's my job." What Roby didn't know nor understand was, I had made building the restaurant my want. There was simply no stopping me.

Absurd! Yes. Sick? Yes, very much so. Mom questioned, "Who wants this restaurant, Roby or you? I couldn't honestly answer. What did occur was that this decision was now a need and any justification was allowable.

My obsession with multiple projects, a consistent almost perverse obsession with control provided me a medium to avoid "that which just wasn't right" in me!

Aunt Sue, visiting one evening observed, "Terry you drink too much!" Wow! How dare she tell me this! What right does she have? She had challenged my comfort zone and I didn't want to hear it.

As your life progresses, perhaps even now, right now, as you honestly reflect upon your life, are you beginning to recognize warning signs? Events, confrontations, challenges to the lifestyle you're pursuing may be Divine interventions keeping you from the consequences that are inevitable, if you remain on your present course.

The fall and ensuing winter of 1987 was a warning sign. There was nothing subtle about it. Dr. Vong and I were like the clash of the Titans. I realized that though we were partners, I didn't need him nor would I afford him any answers. Partners had become competitors. It was an equation for failure.

Ironically, Roby had selected a restaurant location that was one block from Mom's and next to the Sparkle Grocery Store, where I had worked (illegally) as a teenager. As the summer progressed into the fall, Roby had provided me with sufficient facts to assemble and compile a performance budget and business plan. Rob and I went to the local bank.

The Bank extended a one-year $75,000 line of credit to Dr. Vong and me, who in turn loaned the money to Roby Lee's Incorporated. Based on our forecasts and way of doing business, we felt we could pay approximately 50% of the note in one year. Aggressive? Yes. But we had needs to meet.

The restaurant renovation became a complete fiasco. During renovations, our grand opening was scheduled for Christmas, 1987. At Thanksgiving I knew we were in trouble. Our rent was due, contractors were not being paid by our general contractor, Jimmy G., and the kitchen equipment had not been ordered.

The general contractor was indicted for fraud, forgery and a few other things. A bank vice president called me demanding $1,000 a month interest, or approximately $6,000. Subcontractors called constantly to see if Dr. Vong and I would pay and Roby made every excuse imaginable.

In the end Roby Lee's opened. Dr. Vong and I had to expose ourselves to an indebtedness of over $140,000, all loans and personally guarantee lease commitments regardless of the economic feasibility. Could Roby's survive?

My mother, a practical, discerning woman, attended the Grand Opening. Her observation was simple. Roby doesn't respect you and Dr. Vong as his partners. She was right. He had acquired a want, I had acquired a need, and Dr. Vong, well, he just acquired.

This was another mile marker, a subtle warning sign (although not too subtle) and had I been listening, in tune with what was really happening, I would have taken heed. Roby Lee's and all the associated chaos that ensued was a warning sign. Things just weren't right, yet I rationalized that I could make them right.

But reality was, that at this juncture, it was almost impossible for King Oil and Gas Well Corporation to raise new money. Our prior investors were disgruntled. Tax benefits had been earned and wells completed but the production was limited and the price had dropped substantially.

At this period of my life not only were things "just not right," they were a total disaster. Important issues in my life, my feelings and emotions, had to be set aside. I had no time to deal with that now. I had banks to pay, payrolls to meet and a huge debt to pay off.

I stopped going to church, started spending more time at the boat, medicating the pain and fulfilling more wants. See, in 1988, the solution was easy, just ignore the mess, medicate the pain and move on. But move on to what?

When things get out of control, or life issues a "warning sign," instead of dealing with it, an addict or an alcoholic simply turns to his medication. Numb the pain and after the pain is gone and the drug takes over you can mentally go to a safe zone, a comfort zone, anywhere you would like to go. The problems seem to go away...but only for the moment. The next morning, the next day our problems are worse, compounded. The "things that just aren't right," that need our attention, remain untouched.

From early childhood we are taught in our society to compete, to achieve. If we aren't taught it directly we learn it by observation, through television from cartoons to commercials, even from family and neighborhood interaction. The rules teach us to strive to be the best, be first, succeed at all costs because if you fail you're less of a person, a loser. There's no room for second best.

See Roby Lee's Restaurant started off a loser. Every single thing imaginable was against us, yet I decided defeat was not acceptable.

Although Dr. Vong and his wife made a substantial income, he too had positioned his family into sizeable debt. But he didn't tell his wife every business problem or success, at least until it was too late.

It was at this same time that Mia, Dr. Vong's wife, made up her mind she deserved a house, and not just any house but one in the neighborhood of $600,000. Dr. Vong had no choice. The house would be built.

Dr. Vong and I met with our consultants to appraise our financial exposure. Clearly some belt tightening must occur. Severe changes were required if we were going to survive.

Roby Lee's concerned Dr. Vong. He didn't believe Rob or I could pull this off. On the other hand, I was angry over Dr. Vong's Wendy's franchise and his accountant, Tom, who had sold him the investment and placed himself in a position to realize substantial financial gains. To me it was clearly a conflict of interest.

Tom misrepresented the project and its expectations. The money was gone, or at least the interim earnings were nonexistent. Yet Dr. Vong continued to pay him $10,000 a month to stabilize Dr. Vong's comfort zone. Tom was once my accountant until it became clear to me he wasn't concerned at all about my comfort zone.

King Oil and Gas Corporation was struggling. The gas prices dropped and our income stream was stretched. Only the basics could remain.

The chess match had begun. The pawns were in position to protect the comfort zone. The banks wanted to be paid. I needed money. Dr. Vong was several million dollars in debt.

Elaine and the children knew very little of my business activities. I said "good bye" in the morning if they were lucky (or if I was lucky), and they managed nicely living in their comfort zones. But all that was about to be invaded and changed.

I was a successful salesman. My historical sales closing rate was approximately seventy percent. I understand the national average is about twenty percent.

One of the basic tenets of good salesmanship is that "no means yes." When a client tells me "no," rather than discouraging me, I know statistically, it brings me closer to a "yes." If I need two appointments to sell one client, I need to make one hundred phone calls. The equation is one hundred phone calls, equal six to eight approvals for appointments. People cancel, people just are not home so two to three will be visited. So, one hundred calls, two appointments equal one sale.

What this says to me is that I need to be told "no" ninety-eight times in order to succeed. So, if I push real hard, disregard rules, make my own boundaries, get told "no" ninety-eight out of one hundred times I will be a success. Wow! What a concept. So the more I'm told no! The more I'm rejected, the more successful I'll be, as long as I stay in the game.

Sound absurd! Yes, it is. I spent many thousands of dollars studying marketing practices, communications, attending sales conferences learning to be told "no," and move on.

But what did I do to the ninety-eight "nos?" I ran right over them. Based on my life's learned behaviors, "no meant yes!" Yes to what ever I wanted, whenever and wherever I wanted. When my social, moral and ethical values were challenged and I was told "no," I could not accept that as an answer. What a delusional life I was leading. Confused, losing ground, losing faith, disregarding beliefs, manipulating values all in an effort to be told "yes," no matter what the cost.

I wanted Roby Lee's, no matter what the cost. Dr. Vong's accountant was telling me, "no." The banks were saying "no," but I wouldn't take "no" for an answer. Dr. Vong's wife wanted her house and wouldn't take no for an answer.

With all the debt and uncertainties a swap was made. I retained my personal partnership interests, and Dr. Vong retained the corporate income stream in exchange for the bank debt. I continued to sell, raise money and do exactly what I've always done. Be told no 98 times out of 100. Make sense?

Elaine was in shock. "How could you do this to us? How are you going to pay your bills?" Funny, when the money flowed and everyone's comfort zone was secure, it was our money. Now, it was my bills, my problems. Today I understand, but in 1987 it was about wants and needs. Whose needs were being met? What she was saying was, "How can I continue this lifestyle?" She had been humiliated. Little did she know I had things well under control.

As Joe Ryan has often said, "Terry, when ever life has knocked you down, you seem to have this ability to pick yourself up and brush yourself off and began again." Perhaps this was Baba's strength passed down to me. "No matter how bad things may seem today, tomorrow brings a new day to begin again and reach our dreams."

With my freedom regained, my liability protected, I had made my decision to be proactive rather than be reactive. Separating from Dr. Vong and becoming independent allowed me a feeling of relief, that life would be okay, at least for that day.

In 1988, ignoring the warning signs, I ran full speed ahead to resume my "want" fulfillment. The Reagan Era ending was a time of economic prosperity. Wages were rising, the wealthy searching for tax breaks, life was good.

Approximately one week after officially separating with Dr. Vong, I received a telephone call. Joe Ryan wanted to talk. Whatever his motivation, he was reaching out to help a friend. The next day Joe and I met at his estate on Windmill Point, Canada. We had a private dinner, a drink or two, dessert, more drinks, reminiscences, more drinks, heated arguments and more drinks. As the night wore on the pain was medicated. Joe and I were finding common ground.

Friendship? Perhaps, at least that's what I had always perceived. Years later Joe has declared that we are friends. Funny though, for friends, we always seemed to be in a chess match, pushing pawns, trying to out maneuver each other. We each needed the other. As long as I could sell, I would be his friend. As long as he could meet my needs, he was mine. Healthy? No…but a relationship based on our own realities.

After a very long evening and many drinks later, Joe led me to his sitting room with a view of the nighttime skyline of Buffalo. There was a fire burning in the fireplace, reflecting softly on the priceless antiques adorning the walls. Joe brought a bottle of Jack Daniels for himself and a bottle of VO for me. By one o'clock, I realized that over 2/3 of my bottle was gone and Joe had left the room for bed. He hadn't said "goodnight," he just left the room. Drunk, puzzled, I realized I couldn't drive home. (At least part of me was thinking rationally.) So I stayed. About 3 a.m. I woke up so sick I thought I was going to die. It must have been the lamb we had for dinner or perhaps some bad clams, something. Oh, the pain!

I awoke at 9:00 a.m. on Joe's couch, still so sick. Joe had left for the office. How could he do it? He had considerably more to drink than I had. I was amazed. Julie, his wife, had also left for appointments.

The housekeeper/gardener came in and asked, "Sir would you like breakfast?" Oh my, breakfast was by far the farthest thing from my mind. I was so sick. I drove home with the windows down. Arriving home about ten o'clock, there was a message on my answering machine. Joe told me to report to his office that afternoon. Somewhere between dinner and drinks Joe and I had reached a settlement of sorts on past differences and I had a new job. But I couldn't remember exactly what I was hired to do.

Having retained my Oil and Gas Well ownership interests assured me of a modest income, less the bank loan payments. Retaining my ownership in Roby Lee's and actually increasing my stock position meant that Roby Lee's cash flow was about to be severely critiqued. Terry was about to fulfill more wants. The family finances were about to take a significant upward swing.

I reported to Joe's office and was welcomed back by him and his staff. His wife Julie was most assertive making sure that I clearly understood the chain of command. She ran the marketing arm of Arlington Capital Corporation and as such I would report to her on a daily basis.

Joe started me off rather slowly at $1,000 a week plus expenses, hospitalization, a leased car, a nice office and a new sales career. I passed all state licensing tests and within two months was a licensed registered representative of Arlington Capital. My goal was to make $4,000 a week in six months. Based on past experience, I knew I could do it.

Julie insisted on keeping me quite busy doing seminars to promote Landmark Properties public limited partnerships, along with Mutual Fund sales being our side business. In 1989, I was responsible for marketing over $1,000,000 of Landmark limited offering subscriptions. Were Joe's needs being met? Yes! See, Joes needs were really Joe's wants. His want of money was clearly being met. My needs were also being met. Things couldn't be better.

A boating neighbor, Elaine's friend Ellen G., was a local tax preparer and income property promoter. She was always introducing income-generating ideas for me to think about. At the same time, my friend Rocky was also coming up with moneymaking schemes. Ellen, with her supposedly legally correct schemes, was promoting a money management ideology that drew quite a bit of attention from various local radio and television personalities.

Just for a moment I want to stop and explore this period of my life. This period for me was, in fact, a warning sign. Upon reflection, what was I searching for? What was so unsettling?

My boss, Julie Ryan, was a very jealous competitor. She realized that my boating acquaintances represented a large segment of untapped money. Considering that each owner expended $12,000 to $18,000 per year to maintain these crafts and that this cost, directly related to the yacht owner's disposable earnings, must mean that there was substantially more money where this came from. The lines of demarcation had been laid. I had my boating friends, Elaine had her dock acquaintances who in fact were direct opposites. The mob on one hand, the socially elite on the other, just didn't mix.

Julie insisted on meeting and befriending Ellen. Ellen had a TV show and notoriety. I simply represented Julie's means to an end. Julie initiated a contract between Arlington Capital Corporation and Terry King and the King's Ransom (the boat). Arlington would take broker dealers from all over the United States on a dinner cruise to view the American-Canadian skyline. The brokers and accountants raising cash for Arlington won incentives for each level of sales production. Awards, no, not trophies but affirmation, expensive dinner cruises, trips all over the world with all expenses paid.

So, each week I would captain the "King's Ransom," the Ryans would commandeer the boat. Bernie, their private chef and house manager, would deliver cases of whiskey, beer, Mum's Champagne and the cycle continued.

Now I was making money on the "King's Ransom," entertaining, meeting a want. Julie's goal wasn't to entertain these people. She couldn't have cared less. She focused on meeting Ellen, Ellen's producer, and the various television personalities that came to the docks. Over time Julie won. Ellen acquiesced, but she wanted me to appear on her show as a guest (not Julie) to discuss investments and tax planning. Julie wasn't happy. Joe didn't care. I was his number one salesman, so don't fix what isn't broken.

~ Out Of Control ~

Chapter Ten

The dichotomy of people and their ideologies that surrounded me were vastly different. There were men who could hurt you, a criminal element of society who wouldn't hesitate to hurt you if you got in their way. There were others living life as society dictated. Within society's norms was Ellen, preaching righteousness, confronting my lifestyle, praying for me. As I reflect on this time, I see that God was there offering me the opportunity to choose. Again, I wasn't listening.

Meanwhile, Joe acquired a full service stock brokerage firm, Jonathan Allen and Company, located in Amherst, New York. This was an obsession in the making.

Henry, employed there as a stockbroker, was most intrigued with Joe and Julie's enterprises. Henry had his own agenda. At about this same, a product developer, Mr. B., was soliciting Jonathan Allen to raise venture capital money. He was working on drug protocols with Dr. K., a pharmacologist at the world-renowned Roswell Park Memorial Cancer Institute. Mr. B. had created a company, Pharmguard, which owned a patent on a drug delivery system that supposedly was an attractive alternative for drug companies seeking a method of delivery that would assure client, public safety from contamination of product tampering.

Venture capital is money at risk. There's a high degree of probability that the money would never be returned. But if the venture succeeds, there would be plenty of money for all.

Hank, Mr. B. and the Jonathan Allen branch manager had met numerous times to explore the Pharmguard project. At the same time, investors were arriving at the Jonathan Allen office. One in particular (George) came almost daily. George would figure prominently in my life over the next several years, lawsuits, litigation, finger pointing. Bottom line, his wants were not fulfilled.

Hank began liquidating stocks for George, consolidating and reinvesting. Initially Hank intended to liquidate all of George's accounts and place his money, his cash legacy, in an option account at Jonathan Allen. Several of the Brokers were placing money in client accounts and reinvesting in options generating large commissions for the Broker and Sales Agent all the while impressing the client of huge daily gains while minimizing the losses. Legal? Maybe, but certainly unethical. I overheard a plan by Hank and Robert, and a most ambitious broker, P.J., to take all of this man's money and invest it, the capital, in options. The perception was that George's money was making huge profits. In reality, all of George's money would be gone, legally, within weeks.

I couldn't let that happen. I spoke to Julie and Joe who intervened and together designed a plan by Arlington to reposition George's money away from options and into safety. Julie, seeking to improve her comfort zone, insisted that this man was better off investing in Landmark and Mutual Funds, which we represented. Right or wrong, this man entered that office for one reason and one reason only that day, to increase his comfort zone, and gain more pleasure. What he did not factor into his equation was pain, and the loss of pleasure.

Hank's world was coming apart. I was recommending to Joe and his financial advisors that Arlington or J.M. Ryan should not consummate the acquisition of this firm. Too much pain. As this scene unfolds, I was not well received by the Jonathan Allen brokers. I threatened to stop or curtail the pleasure center. Joe eventually elected not to complete this acquisition. But the damage was done.

Mr. B. had been introduced to George. Hank had solicited money from George for use by Mr. B. to start up Pharmguard.

I was interested in Pharmguard but at this point was not aware of the financial devastation Mr. B. had created with Pharmguard. He had lied, misrepresented to me, and to his past investors, what had happened to his initial money that he solicited. The money was gone. He had financial difficulties, legal, ethical difficulties, and was divorcing.

I admit today that I became involved in Pharmguard for all the wrong reasons. Seeking power, control, affirmations from the business community, my goal was to improve my weekly income stream. Did I believe in the company's products or concepts to be developed? Yes, I did. Absolutely. I will forever affirm that the purpose of Pharmguard was just. Along with that so did many, many others who had lent, advanced Mr. B. money on the sole promise that they would make money. Pharmguard became Triad Manufacturing Corporation.

Moving our Arlington Capital offices back to 770 Statler Towers, closing the Jonathan Allen offices in Amherst, New York brought me right back to my comfort zone. Since 1982, the Statler Towers and my association with Joe represented a comfort zone to me. Julie was traveling all over the country giving financial planning seminars. Terry was following suite.

The bars, happy hours, the social circles became influential over the choices of my life. Meeting the boys, always searching for more affirmation, more want fulfillment, no matter how much I received, it was never enough.

Triad evolved into a nightmare for all involved. A very sad state of events unfolded. As 1989 turned to 1990 I found myself working full time for Arlington, President of Triad Manufacturing and working with Dr. K. from Roswell Park.

Considering that Joe and Julie expected a full week's work effort for a reasonable pay, I did increase my income to $1,500 a week. I stagnated at Arlington. Triad was very demanding. Of course, I wasn't complaining.

Initially the partners, Dr. K., and George voted that I should be paid $1,000 a week, plus expenses, to take the company forward.

Now consider for a moment that Roby's is progressing, the bank is being paid. I was receiving $500 a week, accounting fee. Actually late at night I was still preparing the weekly computer generated income statements.

What was evident was that financially $3,000 a week was arriving into my hands. Enough? No! Dr. K. introduced me to a newspaper publisher Mr. Miller. Before I knew it, Mr. Miller had engaged me as his personal financial advisor handling his funds for his racehorse management company. Nighttime meetings at the racetrack, morning breakfast meetings, returning home carrying $50,000 cash of Mr. Miller's money was a very exciting experience. Were my services free? He paid me $500 a week and a new 1989 Nissan 4 Runner.

My evolving schedule began at 6:00 a.m., ending at 1:00 a.m. seven days a week. Did I pay attention to personal needs? No, not spiritually, emotionally, psychologically or physically. I just kept pushing. It was easier to just pay someone to do what I should have been doing. I hired a secretary.

Actually, he was a retired attorney, Jack Boyce. Jack was in recovery and worked part-time at Brylin Hospital as an addiction treatment counselor. Jack was an investment client of Arlington. The problem was I did not know Jack had Alzheimer's disease. It was slow but progressive. I simply couldn't have known. His family questioned his business practices during this time of his life. Outwardly his work performance was satisfactory. Jack simply had not disclosed enough of his real self for me to know. But then again, was I listening?

I remember Joe calling me into his office, closing the door, pouring a drink and asking, "Terry can you handle all this? You need help. Have you put together a personal business plan?" Of course the answer was "no." I hadn't. Joe was right. His advice well founded. Only problem was, I wasn't listening. I was out of control.

Drinking, happy hours, dinners, parties, social functions, political fundraisers, the symphony, I had arrived. Roby wanted to expand. I was on an acquiring spree, living life to the fullest. Trips at a whim, spending money at will, I had absolutely no plan.

As if all of this was not enough, an employee of J.M. Ryan introduced me to his father-in-law who owned a machine shop located in Buffalo. After talking awhile, I determined that this man, seeking financing of receivables, was actually bankrupt. The business was over 100 years old, manufacturing machined parts used by fortune 100 companies in high tech end products. What an opportunity. My goal was a corporate take over. But I needed cash, quickly, and not my cash, (I had learned the secret of using other people's money from Joe). I needed partners.

Now consider, I was working full-time for Arlington Capital, full-time for Triad, part-time for Mr. Miller, owning and managing a racehorse, charter boat Captain, accountant for Roby Lee's and now concentrating on a corporate take over of M.J. Grass Machine Screw Company.

I convinced the present owner that, yes, I would seek partners to assist in refinancing this project. But first, I would need to be paid. And so I was receiving another weekly salary.

Time was very precious now. I was stopping there everyday at 9 a.m. At night I was involved raising money, conducting seminars, investor presentations, happy hours with bar investors. I met an attorney, Mr. L., (another alcoholic,) who was a personal friend of Mrs. Ryan. He along with a stockbroker, J. P., invested $70,000 in M.J. Grass. I was working hard to protect my wants.

Periodically, I stopped at a gourmet restaurant in South Buffalo, The Old Pony Post. Quaint, sophisticated, I found a comfortable place to drink, conduct my business and relax. When I discovered that the owner was having financial difficulty and intending to close the place, I couldn't let that happen. I convinced the owner to sell to me. I had no idea if it was a good investment or not. It was another comfort zone I didn't want jeopardized. Did I have the money? No. But I never let that stop me. I took on two partners, Mr. L. and J. P. Our initial plan was to remain as silent partners. So much for that plan. Before I knew it I was bartending and doing the accounting. It wasn't long before I realized that we had been had! Someone was stealing money. It was either the prior owner or the earnings from The Pony Post had been grossly misrepresented. A meeting was called resulting in the removal of the prior owner.

I had preserved my place to drink and conduct business, but at what cost? Each week I was cashing my paycheck from J.M.R. and putting it into the expenses of the restaurant. The Old Pony Post was losing over $1,000 a week. Rational thinking? No, it was an obsession. I swore I'd get to the bottom of this.

Bar tending until 2 a.m., visiting other bar competitors, returning home 4 a.m., expecting to be at Miller's farm at 7 a.m. for our breakfast meeting, I was on a collision course.

Reflecting upon this period, 1990, my life was totally out of control. I was engaged in so many projects that consumed my entire being. Problems existed at every turn. Madness. Chaos ruled. Yet, I maintained a perception that all was okay. I worked hard at presenting an image that everything was wonderful. Deep inside I was in emotional trauma, scared and hurting. All the while, I irrationally chose to perceive my real self as highly successful, a good father and a contributing member of society.

This perception was only partly true. I was a good father at times. When I felt it necessary. All other times I simply didn't feel. Feelings are such a vital component of life. Natural, real, uncompromising, they affect our decisions and behavior. It was easier not to deal with feelings. When I was overwhelmed that things "just weren't right" I would run away, start new projects and medicate the pain.

The insanity was that I didn't acquire The Pony Post to make money. Upon reflection, the Pony Post was a perverse way of acquiring a comfort zone. Home was madness, chaos, work, too many visitors and no privacy. The boat was an escape. But the bar and restaurant irrationally validated within my real self all that was so wrong with my life.

I remember meeting Elise, the woman who would become my second wife. The relationship never evolved from friendship or love, but a need of affirmation. She drank a lot, smoked a lot and socialized with all the corrupt people I knew.

Divorcing Elaine was a necessary step in my life. But, creating the relationship with Elise was not. Our relationship was harmful, one alcoholic helping another drink life away. Our marriage was a facade, a perception of life as being so right yet it was so very wrong.

Being honest with myself today, I'm ashamed that I allowed myself to be manipulated by greed, acquiring, deceiving and sleaziness of it all.

I could write volumes about incidents during this period of my life, the people I hurt, the decisions I regret now. This entire period of my life was a warning sign for an alcoholic. The disease was taking control.

A warning occurred in February of 1991. The restaurant was losing money at the rate of over $1,000 a week, Triad was imploding, M.J. Grass was not acquiring new contracts and I was feeling sorry for myself. What could I do but medicate the pain. Drinking the day away, tending bar at The Pony Post, Elise was drunk by ten o'clock. Elaine appeared at the bar and was drunk by midnight. I remember thinking, "what an awful mess." About 3 a.m., I drove my Cadillac Fleetwood Brougham, white leather ragtop, to my house in Orchard Park. Leaving the restaurant, fog covered the entire area like a blanket. I couldn't see one hundred feet ahead of me yet I insisted on driving home. I'm not sure how I managed. I was on the wrong road heading east approximately one-quarter mile from my home. The normal route is to drive due south from The Old Pony Post, but I drove in a circle. The road was fogged in and I couldn't see. I opened the driver's side door and followed the centerline of the road. The lights of an on coming car were coming straight for me. I swerved left and crashed into a ditch, straight up and into a solid object. I looked up. Water was spraying like a storm. I realized I struck a fire hydrant. I panicked. The engine was still running but making hideous noises, steam spraying, oil burning, I placed the car in reverse racing the engine. After several loud bangs the car returned in reverse to the main road. I drove ever so slowly home.

I opened the garage door, pulled in and viewed the damage. The car was a mess. The front bumper and hood looked like a V. Entering the house I began drinking again, medicating the pain. I had a problem to solve. More drinks. Got to figure this out. Oh, tomorrow I'll call a friend, pay cash, get it fixed. Problem solved.

Elaine woke up and asked why I was such a mess. I told her I hit a little pole. She accepted this and returned to bed. An hour later I noticed spotlights directed on the house, and many, many flashing lights from police cars surrounding the house. Two town divisions, Hamburg and Orchard Park, were there as well as the Sheriff's Department.

Opening the front door I knew I had a wee bit of a problem. Apparently, when I backed out and away from the fire hydrant my license plate had attached itself to what was left of the fire hydrant. I was caught!

"Mr. King, are you the owner of a 1990 Cadillac Fleetwood Brougham?" "Yes!" "May we see it please?" "Sure."

"Mr. King, were you in an accident tonight?" "Yes!"

"Where and when were you driving? Mr. King were you driving on Armor Duells road tonight?"

This was the question that would save me, at least that was my perception. But ironically I wasn't saved at all, at least not yet. It just reaffirmed what was so horribly wrong. I failed a field sobriety test and was taken to Orchard Park for booking on DUI. By 6:30 a.m. I was released to Elaine. It was a quiet ride home.

The next day I contacted one of my nefarious friends, Attorney Jim Steel. Three months and two hearings later with $500 worth of with complimentary dinner coupons slipped here and there, I walked out of court with all charges dismissed on one technicality. When asked by the Judge, "Mr. King, was your vehicle involved in an accident?" I answered, "Yes, your honor!" My lawyer, in his wide-lapel, pinstriped suit, sporting the usual white carnation in his buttonhole, approached the bench requesting, "Your honor, may we go to chambers?" Returning to the bench the judge dismissed all charges. The District Attorney did not object. I was astonished! Although my vehicle was involved in the accident, no question about that, what couldn't be proven was who was driving the car. I was never asked if I drove the car that night, and there were no witnesses. My life was in utter chaos, lost, helpless, but I was okay! This proved it. I thought I was invincible.

My drinking companions and I had a victory celebration of sorts, making toasts, affirming how truly sick we all were. The problem was, I either didn't know I was sick, or did, but refused to acknowledge it. I was not listening. I simply did not care.

My lawyer's life was soon to unravel, as well. A gambler, womanizer, social elite, he would be indicted for tax evasion and fraud and found guilty on all charges.

Yes, this incident was far more than a marker point, it was a warning sign. But I wouldn't stop, I had wants to acquire. Clearly there is nothing normal about this behavior. All the while I continued to assimilate around other alcoholics who understood my pain and affirmed me. "Terry it's okay, it happens to us all."

The life I had created, my life script was a prescription for failure. My life was headed for a total breakdown, only I wasn't listening. Even Elaine attempted to reach me. Although the message was correct, I resented the messenger for she represented a stop sign, a roadblock from the delusional reality I felt was my right of life.

After divorcing Elaine, a marker point was the temporary order of child support. I attempted to control all of the court proceedings, as if the court cared what I wanted.

Cash, income, my comfort zone was about to be invaded. Elise insistently dictated her demands. I medicated the pain, hid my feelings.

Elaine's attorney was a sharp adversary. He had an accountant appraise my expenses generating a profile of what kind of gross income was required in order to support my lifestyle.

The judge bought the argument, ordering me to pay $800 a week child support. How could this happen? There was no way I could handle that. Elise was livid! My world as I knew it was crumbling. I started drinking everyday earlier and earlier. Elise would meet me at noon for a drink or four, five or more. Then I would go to work at the restaurant.

What about Triad, M.J. Grass, Arlington, Miller's, Roby's? I was supposed to be working. I was working but only on what I wanted, not what any one else wanted.

I was asked by my best friend and by my family why I ever got involved with Elise. Upon reflection I admit that she affirmed all that was so wrong. I perceived that she could be of use to me in some way.

The Pony Post Bar became my office. All business affairs were conducted from my new home. Arriving by 8:00 a.m., attempting to unravel the previous days affairs, I would medicate the pain.

Elise and I moved into an apartment close to the Pony Post. She enjoyed being at the bar nightly, drinking and socializing with her friends. Acting as hostess, she attempted to patch up problems at the restaurant, such as Chefs quitting, vendors needing payment, driving here and there to pick up food supplies. I called it firefighting. Vendors bringing in supplies at six and seven in the evening would be paid cash from happy hour receipts. Elise drove to the liquor supplier to pay cash for liquor to replenish the stock.

My monthly expenses were over $12,000 yet I truly believed I could hang on. My life style and work career was distinctly over, yet people who gravitated around me for financial assistance would not let go.

A story of bizarre behavior was a Friday night before Easter 1990. The restaurant was full, which didn't necessarily mean we had paying customers. Elise's family and socialite friends often came to enjoy gourmet dining and drinks at my expense.

Elaine parked outside the restaurant counting patrons one-by-one, keeping track to report to the court. This particular night she decided to come in and drink. In her mind, this would all be hers in the near future, by order of the court.   Fearing a scene, I asked her to leave. She began to scream, belittling and berating me, making sure every patron heard what she had to say. Then she entered the main dining room filled with people and tipped over the hostess station.

Within thirty minutes the restaurant was empty. The band in the lounge played on. The employees wanted to be paid. I locked the doors and poured myself another drink. "Tomorrow is another day," I thought. I was running out of "tomorrows."

Joe Ryan and I never met formerly to end our second business relationship. It was accomplished without fanfare. The summer 1991, a letter from Joe's attorney stated, "Your sales license will not be renewed. Your relationship with Arlington is over, you are free to go on."

My only concern was that I would be receiving no more checks. Without them, The Pony Post couldn't survive.

The Triad investors started arriving at the Pony Post for answers. I had none to give. M.J. Grass was bankrupt, no money there. No money was coming from Miller, but he kept coming to the restaurant wanting me to be his partner in another restaurant. Oh the cycle continues.

My divorce from Elaine was finalized in May of 1991 and I entered a new contractual relationship with Elise.

The children, Josh and Justin, continued to be with me whenever possible. Josh was always spending weekends, working at the restaurant.

But what became obvious (but again I wasn't listening) was that Elise had made a distinct decision that she would control my relationship with the boys. The demands, the inferences, the verbal attacks, I could not take. It hurt the boys and me, only I wouldn't do a thing about it. My life was still about my want fulfillment. I had lost so much and I just couldn't afford to lose anymore. I was afraid.

Have you ever found yourself in a friendship or a relationship that you know is not right? You feel that this is an unsettling situation, yet all the while continue to accept things just the way they are because you are afraid to leave your comfort zone. At this point, my comfort zone was a facade and it had ceased to be comfortable.

I now know why I stayed in the relationship for the next several years. I was afraid to lose anymore. It wasn't about love or friendship. My world was crumbling and crashing down yet the irony was that I was attempting to rebuild my life on the rubble of my delusional lifestyle.

Roby was anxious to expand Roby Lee's, adding on a banquet room. He needed $60,000, but where would it come from? He began driving to Buffalo monthly. The cycle continued. Roby had paid down the original bank loan by over $45,000 on principal. Original equipment vendors were paid, he was overly confident.

Consolidating loans, refinancing the business meant a commitment of time to prepare the bank loan presentation package. We also needed to deal with Mrs. S., the landlord, convincing her that our want was her need. We needed her to spend $60,000 to expand our business-operating environment. In return, we would give her monthly rent and an increased volume of business traffic. See, Mrs. S. was sharp. Traffic meant shoppers, shoppers meant sales, sales meant profits, or at least the hope of profits.

I continued to protect my rebuilding stage marrying Elise. At times in our life we do things, act in certain ways that, as we say, "just can't be explained." Oh, I made choices that year, the wrong choices that brought with them painful consequences. The events I couldn't change. But what I believed about the events I allowed Elise to influence. Why? I didn't want to accept reality. Chapters of my life were closing all around me. Arlington closed, Triad closed, M.J. Grass closed, Miller's closed. Roby Lee's was growing, but The Old Pony Post was a real noose around my neck.

The summer and fall of 1991 I lived in a vacuum. I knew that my life as I had known it was over, but I wouldn't accept it. I medicated my sorrow as I attempted to refocus on rebuilding a life.

Josh and Justin were spending time with me, sharing their lives. But Elise, the influencing factor in my life said, "No! They interfere with me." We never discussed anything. We just argued constantly. There was only one way, her way.

Then by Thanksgiving 1991, I realized that The Pony Post era was over. Despite Elise's demands and verbal assaults, I knew this madness had to stop and I had to do it. But more importantly, the taxman said it must stop. Elise was angry and resentful that I had allowed this to happen.

The restaurant was closed. I rented a van and removed the remaining assets and hid them as a legacy for myself. Selling them off one-by-one allowed me a brief moment of sanity, but not sobriety. At least for one or two months I could escape from the rat race and recognize my children.

When we find ourselves in phases of our life where it is necessary to regroup and rebuild, it is necessary to first deal with issues that led to the demise of the old life script and then bring closure to those chapters of our past. Even as we close chapters, unless we learn from our experience, we are destined to repeat the same mistakes.

We may shed the old baggage but continue with the same life script, only to see similar consequences unfold because we simply haven't changed that which is most basic. Unless we develop new beliefs and a new value system, our behavior will not change.

As 1991 turned into 1992, I was so glad that the nightmare was over. Yet it wasn't over. I was only fooling myself and those still around me. I wanted the lifestyle and the image I had created to continue, while deep inside I knew life could never be the same. But what could it be? Did I even know? What I did know was that the pain of all that was so wrong was subsiding, but it wasn't normal. It was so far from normal.

Warning signs signaling a life script that "just isn't right." But what exactly happened along the way?

~ Calm Before The Storm ~

Chapter Eleven

Life is precious gift. To live it to the fullest is a give and take proposition. We find as much joy in giving of ourselves to others as we do in receiving life's blessings. But at this stage in my life, I didn't realize that. I wrote my own rules, pushing the boundaries and was willing to sacrifice anything to satisfy my wants and needs. But what was being sacrificed? Anything? Everything? Yes indeed.

As 1991 evolved into 1992, I found myself relieved that The Pony Post was closed. Elaine was clearly upset. Her comfort zone was in jeopardy. What she thought represented her economic security and social status was gone. At least that was my perception, but again, I wasn't listening so how could I even know. What I have learned is that when insecure people feel threatened we either attack or run. I was still on the run only I hadn't gone anywhere.

My drinking continued. I was not working and for the first time in a very long time, I felt I could relax and take a break from life. But this was not to be. Elise and her family were not having it. Her social reputation was about to be threatened. Elise's perception of her social status was influenced by her mother, the businesswoman, Women's Club president and social butterfly of the country club set. My indolence was unacceptable.

As I ended the progression of one problematic period of my life, I just exchanged one set of blatant mistakes for another. At no time did I ever attempt to look within. At the time, a friend of mine, Father Nugent, attempted to reach out to me. Somewhere from within I felt the impulse to go to church. Father Nugent and I spoke together after mass. He asked how everything was going. "Great! Couldn't be better," I lied. He asked very bluntly about my life, me, the losses, my home life. He reached out to offer help. But I had established a very firm wall of denial. I believed that I had the strength to weather this storm. Father Nugent knew differently. Mom did too. But I refused to listen. I was sick. My life was out of balance. Creating an irrational delusional perception of life is sick…and dangerous.

Once Father Nugent had asked, "Owning a restaurant must be a hard life with so much drinking. What are your thoughts?" I responded glibly, "Well, it's just part of the business. No problem." What nonsense. I had a serious drinking problem. Father Nugent was trying to introduce me to reality, but I didn't want to deal with the pain of reality. He wanted me to meet another priest who was an AA member. Oh my, this was too much.

Returning home that day I knew that my life was in complete shambles. My drinking had subsided, simply because funds were limited. I began selling off pieces of artwork and antiques. I had fun establishing a little cash kitty. The storm could be weathered after all.

The storm that couldn't be weathered was the one brewing at home. I knew life could be different. Josh and Justin were spending more time with me, weekends and several weekday evenings, doing simple things, just enjoying one another. For the first time in a long time I was sober...well abstaining from drinking at least. Today I know it was not sober time, for I had not changed.

The home situation deteriorated. Elise was drinking. With no more Pony Post Bar to frequent, home had become the entertainment center. So night after night after night, mother Ingrid and her socially elite, stayed and drank around the kitchen table.

After several weeks, I remember feeling very overwhelmed by this invasion, so I confronted Elise. Wow! The idea that she or I could have even the slightest drinking problem was incomprehensible to her. The suggestion that she might need to deal with her alcohol dependence was too much. "Handle your alcohol like a man. Just drink less." But not drink? She wouldn't hear of it. Of course she informed her mother of our conversation. Her mother was angry. She also denied there was a problem.

But I had enough to worry about attempting to deal with Triad, refining Roby's and closing The Pony Post. I was scared, but most of all knew that I would not be defeated, no matter what the cost. So I isolated myself. I made up my mind to live my life for me. For Elise, it was a power and control issue. Her mother pushed to take control. I let them push. I had a new agenda, though I just wasn't quite sure what it was.

I knew it was time to find a job and start a new life. Was it possible? Not just yet. Many of my life's events and past entanglements were not concluded. I couldn't just pretend they didn't exist. Yet I was determined to start a new life. I reduced my alcohol intake, but nothing had really changed. I couldn't face how I was truly feeling. My life was a mess. Yet if I faced reality, confronted Elise, I would have to deal with the pain of all that was so wrong. So I avoided pain, continued to seek instant gratification, even if it was only temporary.

For many of us, I'm sure, there have been moments in our lives, when "things just weren't right," that we used "denial" to avoid pain and ignore our true feelings. The human spirit seems outwardly to be able to handle only so much confrontation before we seek a reprieve. When pain confronts us we avoid it, deny it, turn to pleasure, something to temporarily gratify our need for relief. But this only perpetuates the cycle of madness and chaos. For some of us this instant gratification isn't enough. See, the pleasure doesn't stay long enough to keep the pain from coming back. To stop the pain, drugs and alcohol do just fine. Sadly, I drank not so much to seek pleasure, but to medicate the pain. I sought out others just like me who would affirm me and reassure me that things were all right. So running away, creating new opportunities, became my pattern of behavior in order to simply avoid reality of the mess I was in. For when I did return home the pain continued.

Finding employment didn't take long, just a few days. Actually once I made up my mind that I wanted to work again then the question for me, arrogantly, was "where do I want to work?" Rocky asked me to come and work for him.

The cycle continued as if I hadn't learned by now. The FBI was investigating him for Mob control of various Buffalo businesses, extortion and unresolved murders. And here I was willingly listening to his offer. I was not dealing in reality, not even considering the consequences. I thought I was in control. Upon reflection I realize that there were other influences dictating my actions. Attorney threats, vendor pleas, Elise's mandates, Elaine's dictums...I just wanted it all to go away.

Rocky had wanted me to open a telemarketing office with Vito R., Jay and Johnny of a local pizza company fame. Rocky was the chief enforcer for the largest area union. Mr. J. was the Don, controlling the entire legal and illegal operations.

The FBI has never yet proved the interrelationship. Sometimes the pieces of the puzzle are right before our eyes yet we just don't see them. Vito had three offices open with over 200 employees, a 24 hour a day operation. He had just purchased a $400,000 home for cash, drove a new Porsche and made sure his bosses were taken care of daily.

Recently, I read in the Buffalo Evening News that Vito is pleading to a 90 count federal indictment with over $1,000,000 in fines and penalties. The FBI claims that the operation earned over $30,000,000 a year. Where is all the money?

At the time, February 1992, Rocky was kind enough to share with me that according to his informants, the FBI was closing in and that Vito was under surveillance.

Rocky said he wanted to start a new office, clean, ethical. What a line of nonsense. Rocky's cash comfort zone was being curtailed and he needed to reorganize, to avoid pain, seek pleasure. Jay asked me to consider starting an office or perhaps going to work for him raising capital for real estate deals. Jay had enticed one of the sales representatives of J. M. R. to join his staff, Jerry C., who I had worked with before. Their scheme was to assemble real estate limited partnerships to finance construction of drug stores and inner-city shopping centers. Sales marketing packages, financial projects, and banking were my forte.

I began stopping at a North Buffalo Eatery Bar that this group had patronized during the last eight to ten years. Returning to my bar stool, reacquainting myself with my glass, Jimmy Mac's became my home away from home, a new comfort zone. I acquired a circle of acquaintances to affirm that things were okay. See, Jay had a reason to stay close to me. It had nothing to do with money or friendship but simply personal pleasure protection.

Elise's best friend Nanci was Jay's girlfriend, his toy. Jay was married with a family and a beautiful home, but Jay had other needs to secure and protect. Nanci worked part time. Her car, apartment, credit cards were all paid by Jay. A nice life, but with no future! But when you're living for today the future doesn't matter. So, Jay, Rocky and I met nightly at Jimmy Mac's, socializing, drinking, participating in a familiar pastime, reestablishing old behaviors.

Jay introduced me to his cousin Angelo, the local branch manager of Metropolitan Life. Angelo and I seemed to get along, business-wise, immediately. Two weeks later I found myself a full-time employee of Metropolitan Life, a Fortune 100 company, and beginning a whole new life.

Redeeming Grace

Returning to work downtown in the Ellicott Square Building was rewarding. The offices were in the business district and close to the nightspots at which I enjoyed being affirmed. Angelo liked to go out nightly. Actually Angelo and Jay are cousins. As such, Rocky, the union, the Family, their Uncle Dominic, owner of ten area restaurants and nightclubs were all clients of MetLife.

The sales staff was well assembled. Timmy D., Niagara Frontier transportation Authority Board member, Democratic fundraiser, cousin of Sam S., Democratic chairman, friend of Bill Clinton. Barney, ex-city of Buffalo economic development commissioner, and on and on it went. It seemed that every ex-public official or politically connected official now worked for Angelo or was being solicited to work at this office. Season tickets to the Buffalo Sabres and Bills games, and invitations to almost every political and social function going on in the City of Buffalo were now mine. I had found a new life, or so I thought. It was amazing, as Jay and others often said to me, "you always land on your feet." It appeared he was right.

Well, I soon discovered that Angelo and I had a lot in common. We both had the ability to sell. Although married with a home in Orchard Park, Angelo was dating his secretary, Karen. He once told me that having a woman companion on the side was his right of heritage. So like his father, his cousin, his Uncle Dominic and all before him, this right of manhood was a need. (In time, his delusion would be his undoing.)

Angelo managed the Family's money. (I do not mean his family's money.) The Family, the Union, Rocky, Angelo all worked for them. Dating Angelo, Karen was really managing Angelo, securing Rocky's comfort zone.

So once again, having taken a time-out from the realities of my life, I was back in the mainstream. As I reflect upon this period of my life, a period marked by moral, ethical trepidation, I see that nothing had changed all that much. I had simply traded one life script for another. People and places had changed, but that was all. Unknowingly, I had simply continued on in the behavior patterns adopted so many years before. But the problems were all still there and ignoring them simply allowed the festering to continue and build like a firestorm.

A new beginning simply does not commence until we have accepted the past, assumed responsibility and made amends where necessary. At this point I was not even able to assume responsibilities for my current affairs let alone assume or accept my past. I was trying to rebuild my life all the while my past was running side-by-side and soon to overcome the present. My feelings were still repressed, my thoughts still the same and my behavior was being reinforced by those I had assembled around who would affirm that I was all right.

Did you ever feel overwhelmed, I mean really overwhelmed? Have you ever had the courage to admit to yourself that your life is out of control, unmanageable, and that your present issues just cannot continue? What did you do?

Redeeming Grace

Every aspect of my life was tenuous and unresolved, from business turmoil to the unrelenting pressure applied at home. Working provided a release valve. Friends and acquaintances would often tell me I was a workaholic. No, I was an alcoholic who simply used work as a replacement to avoid that which wasn't right. Alcohol affirmed and medicated the pain of it all.

Six months into working for MetLife brought success. The parties, the nightlife, the action, the affiliations, I had it all.

Elaine was persistent, I must say. Month-by-month I tried the best I could to help her with Josh and Justin. Her attorney stated that it wasn't enough. He filed suit for his fee and a court order for child support to be payroll deducted.

I knew that I had a valid responsibility to her. The children always have been very important to both of us. Many times, I am sorry to say, I had sacrificed my relationship with them in order to satisfy immediate personal needs. But I wanted them to have their financial needs met.

Elise dug her heals where Josh and Justin were concerned. Unrelentingly demanding, she stated emphatically that if I lost the court case and had to pay Elaine any more money, then new boundaries would have to be established. The boys would no longer be welcome in her home. I ignored this threat. There was no way my boys would ever be excluded from my life or my home.

I began arriving home later and later. Her mother was there constantly. The later I came in, the later her mother stayed. That was okay because I was out conducting business, medicating pain. Elise was usually inebriated. It was time to move along. Our relationship had deteriorated to nonexistence. This hurt infuriated me.

Approximately during the same time period, Elaine had successfully returned to court. I was unwilling to defend the action and in fact conceded that a payment deducted from my payroll was acceptable. But I had no intention of paying for her attorney. No question about that.

Our day in court, represented by my inept lawyer, was a comedy. I lost, of course, and during the fiasco I also acquired a $15,000 judgment against me for her lawyer's fees. I was livid. But, ironically, at the same, I didn't really care. My attorney kept telling me, "Oh, don't worry I'll get that dismissed." Well, he never did. Two hundred fifty dollars each week was the court-ordered payroll deduction. I was at peace with that, knowing that the boys were being taken care of. Their welfare was a high concern. I realized that they needed me, my time, my love and my attention.

I remember returning to Orchard Park that night feeling a little comforted that at least Elaine would now retreat and leave me alone, allowing some closure to the past. What a misconception. Elise was incensed at the court's decision. She had been drinking and, as always, was very outspoken. I was given ultimatums concerning Josh and Justin or a separation of sorts. I left that night, for where, I was not sure.

I had suffered enough. I didn't think the pain could get any worse. It was only the beginning.

~ Storm Warnings Ignored ~

Chapter Twelve

Arriving home one Friday night, seeking affirmation from Angelo and Jay, I was greeted by the question as to the identity of a certain man who kept calling for me all evening. I had no idea who it could be. Drunk, tired, frustrated, I went to bed. I was about to have a rude awakening.

Around midnight I was roused from my stupor by very loud knocks on the door. It was two lieutenants from the Orchard Park police. "Mr. King, please come with us. You are wanted for questioning in Buffalo, about several bounced checks from your business."

When I had walked away from The Pony Post, the other two partners had been left to clean up the mess. When the taxman came he attached all corporate assets and bank accounts. That meant several vendors were unable to cash their final checks. I had signed the checks. Not being able to reach me infuriated them. Pointing fingers towards my other partners had only delayed the inevitable.

Several hours later I found myself at the Buffalo City Jail having been arrested for passing a bad check. I could not believe that this was happening.

It did happen, whether I wanted to believe it or not. I was entitled to one phone call and was told I would see the judge Saturday morning. I was released on my own recognizance, a term with which I would become acquainted.

I was certainly being introduced to the consequences of my behavior but I was arrogant, self-centered, and certainly not listening. I had reasoned, "Let the other partners pay. I've paid and paid enough!" I had been warned by my nefarious attorney to pay these checks off. My attitude was, "Why throw good money after bad." The teaching was very simple. Invest wisely today for today's investments determine one's future. How that foundation is established will provide the basis of tomorrows well being. Never appreciating this concept, believing that investments revolved around money was inconsequential. Investing in time, wisely balancing one's life, spiritually, emotionally, mentally, and physically affords a life script foundation which allows fulfillment of all other needs and wants of life to follow.

The pressures from home were shame, guilt, and frustration. "Don't pay, we need the money." "Don't you dare. Why should you? Let the other partners pay." Ignoring my feelings, I knew this needed to be corrected but was too busy medicating my pain. Actually, I had found a new comfort zone and new acquaintances to affirm that I was still a valuable contributing member of the human race. This was the foundation of my new life script. All the while my defensive wall of denial was crumbling. My past was catching up and I was being held accountable.

Initially, I was embarrassed by what occurred and angry with myself because I knew better. I was frustrated with myself for not taking a position at home. I ran away, seeking more comfort.

Redeeming Grace

I realize today that I had sacrificed the best of my past, my life teachings, values and faith, to create an illusion, a way of life as fragile as a house of cards. Pushing, pulling, manipulating, hustling, trying to balance it all on an unstable foundation, I sacrificed all the blessings I had inherited, to achieve something that just doesn't exist. I sacrificed my relationships with my immediate family, my children, my religion, my mental, emotional and physical health simply to create a persona, achieve a reputation that simply would never occur.

Realizing and acknowledging my past, the events, and the person I came to be has afforded me the opportunity to change. It isn't easy. Facing yourself, acknowledging the person you have become can be painful. It was for me. I didn't want to let go.

Were the consequences of my life inevitable or could they have been avoided? Many innocent people have been affected and hurt by my actions. Although I never meant to hurt anyone, I bought into the lie that I had to think of myself first. Protecting myself, heedless of the consequences to others, was my life script. Now I had an arrest record. Sad. But it was absolutely avoidable. Knowing the potential consequences, why had I been so obstinate to disregard the advice? Perhaps I wanted all this to crash.

Returning to Newton Falls provided an escape from all that was so painfully wrong on a daily basis. Visiting old drinking establishments, meeting old acquaintances, reassuring others, I informed the uninformed that I was in fact the founding source of Roby's Restaurant. Unintentionally or capriciously, Roby had failed to disclose to those around him that he had a partner.

Roby knew very little of my difficulties in Buffalo. To this day he still knows very little of these events. Mom still enjoys a weekly meal there and Carol still questions why I ever sold out. Life continues.

Working for Metropolitan Life, associating with Angelo offered me a safety net, a brief attempt to secure a new business career and future. As the year 1992 advanced, the life I had assumed, (not earned or built), continued pushing on. Angelo and I developed a social schedule. We would work vigorously from 8:00 a.m. to 8:00 p.m., drink from 8:00 p.m. to 11:00 p.m. before returning home. This patterned continued day after day.

Angelo and Timmy D. were very creative salesmen. Like Jay, using other people's money, they used other people to sell for them and then enjoyed the fruits of their labor. Isn't that the American way? Mr. Niagara Frontier Transportation Association Commissioner, number one democratic fundraiser, used several favors owed from union officials and his union affiliations. The sales gem of the industry is to secure the area's largest employer to sell your services through payroll deduction. The Blue Collar Union President, Mr. S., another client of Angelo's, friend of Mr. D.'s and Mr. B.'s, informed, (yes informed) Mr. "G.," the County Executive, that his union membership wanted this free benefit. Simply allow MetLife to market their full line of services to our members and enjoy the convenience of payroll deduction. Of course Mr. S. would also enjoy the rewards financially of other people's labor.

Jay, a true slick politician, was not to be outdone. Approaching Mark B., President of CSEA, (Civil Service Employees of America) representing all county local affiliated employees, Jay informed him that Mr. S.'s union employees were enjoying this benefit. Mr. B. better sign this deal for his members before they find out that the other union has a benefit his members don't.

The result was that within weeks, Jay had secured the entire county employee payroll deduction slot, a million dollar deal.

Angelo's responsibilities were to assure that Corporate MetLife would allow our Queen City office the exclusive right to sell to the 16,000-employee base. Met reluctantly agreed. See, Corporate wanted to send in their New York attack dogs. Angelo's real family, his true supervisors informed him this just wouldn't work. Negotiating the power play, Angelo secured his role in this deal by protecting his family. Timmy D. secured his income stream, and I found a new way of doing business. The sales commission was distributed 30% to Timmy and Angelo, 70% to the selling agent. Timmy would show his appreciation to the Family and all parties involved would be rewarded.

A normal sales agent is required to market approximately 65 to 70 policies per year. As Angelo's drinking partner, I was offered along with Angelo's sister, the largest employee base, Erie County Medical Center. I loved it. We had fun. Annamarie and I attacked the employee base and before we knew it, the administration had awarded us with employee ID cards. So as the summer and fall progressed, I enjoyed a sales count increase from 60 policies per year average to 270 policies. Wow! This was neat. Success meant accolades, commissions, trips, and free time.

My pattern was to go to the hospital at shift change, sit at a desk near the time clock and meet people as they entered and left their place of employment. Shift changes start at 5:30 to 8:00 a.m. Every 30 minutes a group punches out or in.

Then I decided to come in at breakfast time, evening, and midnight shift change. Remembering my training from my marketing days, I solicited department heads and offered them a deal. Each department head supervises approximately 15 to 25 people. I discovered they had mandatory weekly meetings. I would bring a sheet pizza, bucket of wings, and ask them to listen to a ten-minute spiel. That was it, no pain and a little gift for their time. Before I could schedule my week, I literally had managers paging me, leaving messages to schedule a presentation. This was fun. Life was good.

I found myself arriving at the office between 9:00 and 10:00 a.m., having been up since 4:00 a.m. My business done for the day, I would enjoy lunch, go to the hospital in the evening and relax. Well, not exactly. My hospital scheduling was perfect. I could now stop about 6:00 p.m. to enjoy Happy Hour, then home for a brief nap and then begin again. I did not want to go home. The office, the dynamics, the camaraderie, the competition fueled my needs. I needed no more.

An interesting point to this is that Angelo and I never really became friends. We each had needs (or wants) to fulfill. As Angelo's life evolved, socializing, womanizing, he would use his business relationships as an excuse as to where he would be each evening. As long as he reported he was with me or Rocky, or Uncle Dominic he was safe. His sister always knew his whereabouts and what he was doing. She just didn't know with whom. What I did know was that three nights per week we would meet for two or three hours at our regular spot then Angelo was on his way to fulfill another want.

Working the county contract was a perfect foundation for time excuses. Whether the excuse was, "Oh, we worked late at the Water Authority, County Jail, or Hospital," we had our excuses to stay out all night, go where ever we wanted with no questions asked. We became quite a tag team.

Trips to Toronto, New York, where ever, whenever. For me, life at home was over. Angelo still wanted the best of both worlds, without any regard for anyone else.

What hurts the most today is the awareness that so much could have been prevented, had I listened. Elise and I simply didn't communicate. I wanted out. No, I needed out from under the pressure and hostility. I needed to regain my balance, my sobriety, to accept me for who I am, not for what someone else perceived they could make me. I could play this game no longer. I could not be remade, molded or subjugated. Her tactics were to apply more pressure, establish boundaries with my children, without communicating with me. She would denigrate Mom and her values, values I held dear. I couldn't allow this, but somehow I did. By ignoring the real issues, the real pain I was in, I allowed this to happen.

So during this rebuilding period I simply attempted to live a lifestyle that made no rhyme or reason. Debt obligations continued to ensconce me. Taxes from The Pony Post, Triad, unpaid vendors, legal fees, were just too much to shoulder, so I ignored them. The old manipulative Terry seemed to be slowly coming back to life. The MetLife salary wasn't enough. More money was needed for my plan to leave. But leave for where?

Take a moment and examine yourself and warning signs in your life, those unsettling moments when things seemed more than "just not right" but more like overwhelming, with no way of escape. Maybe it's a relationship, a loss, a job, an unfortunate or tragic event in your life. Sometimes things happen in life that are just so overpowering, they leave you numb. Unable to face things, we isolate, compromise, justify, and defend our reasons for not confronting our problems. Often we continue in a life script that can only bring us down.

Many times I've heard people say, "Well, that's just the way life is." "Do what you may, some things will never change." That's very true. We can't change anyone or anything. The only person I can change is me. The only person you can change is you.

So, while others may consciously or subconsciously accept that things must remain the same, hopelessness rules their life. The opportunities of life are lost in time.

We live in a materialistic society. Justifying ourselves as to why all the overtime hours are being worked, we delude ourselves that new "things" will give us a better quality of life. It's easy to misplace our values. Far too often we have a tendency to substitute our monetary gifts for the giving of ourselves, physically, emotionally, spiritually, to our families. If challenged or confronted, we assume the role of the victim, "I'm doing this for my family and others." "Can't you see, I gave up so much of my life for you and the children, just so you can have a better life."

Ever hear this? I have. I was a direct party to this type of behavior. The irony is that while I was assuming this victim role, justifying all the sacrifices I was making, life was still about me. I had sacrificed all right…my values, my faith, my relationships. But I would not act or take responsibility to confront my ills and change.

It's easy to blame others, "Look how she treats me, after all I've done," The establishment: "My boss is so tough on me." "Society keeps me down, I can't get ahead." Blame, transfer responsibility, living the role of the victim all the while the real purpose of one's life is being lost to greed, alcohol, addictions, power, control and self-centeredness. We become caught in a life script that delivers continual consequences that sacrifice the person we can be.

When we acknowledge who we have become, it can be painful. Emotions may come to the surface that we have denied ourselves the right to feel. We may have to confront thoughts about ourselves that we have irrationally preserved for a very long time.

By our life choices, are we fulfilling the negative predictions of someone in our past? Maybe, for the very first time, we need to take a long look at the things we have sacrificed in life, just to imitate the life script of someone else or follow a life script we know "just isn't right."

A true, honest appraisal of our lives leads us to ask ourselves the question, "Why?" Why have I allowed someone else to control who I am? Why did I sacrifice my beliefs and values, teachings of life, my emotional, mental and physical balance, in order to do what? Please others? Live the American dream? Why have I been willing to sacrifice my God-given potential, my relationship with my children, my family, my right of life to live a rich, rewarding peaceful life?

As I would sit and reflect upon my life, I would become angry with myself because I realized that the changes I talk about today could have occurred years ago had I listened. The warning signs were there, yet I didn't change. The anger comes from knowing that even then I knew things "just weren't right."

But why would I change? I was the victim was I not? Am I not owed? Isn't it my right to feel as I do? No one wants to help me."

But today, I must recognize that the person responsible is I. We are the only one that can effect change from within. Someone once said something to the effect that, "Life is 10% what happens to us, 90% the attitude we choose." If we change our way of thinking, our lives become significantly different.

~ Corruption In High Places ~

Chapter Thirteen

Through 1992 into 1993, my career with Angelo was progressing. I had made up my mind that I needed a fresh new start. At the time I thought it was kind of like a spiritual awakening. I wanted to take back control of my life. I went to work with a mission and a vengeance.

Working the county contract was a most rewarding and educational experience. Timmy D. would invite me to all of the political fundraisers. Angelo would show up as well as well as the rest of the members. I became obsessed with this sales concept and decided that if Timmy could get a contract like the county then I could too! So, now I had to find a large group contract and enjoy my own income stream while others would sell for me. This new want (which I perceive as a need) would solve all of my problems. I'd be financially solvent again. And with money, lots of money, I was sure all the pain of all my problems would just go away.

I didn't stop working the county contract but my sales effort dropped. I had found my pot of gold. Through my drinking partner, the Judge, I met his friend, the Superintendent of the Buffalo Public Schools. Through him I had access to seven thousand teachers, three thousand administrators, four thousand blue-collar workers. I would take care of the Judge financially and he would take care of his family. The Judge would meet me everyday at 5:00 p.m. at our local watering hole. He knew every politician in town.

I informed Angelo of my plan and he was excited. I secured confirmation from MetLife that this was my deal, a million dollar deal. When Timmy D. was informed of my actions, he expressed the opinion that he would be entitled to a portion of the money. He felt the unions needed to have approvals and he took the position that he represented the unions. Family, that is. I was not willing to hear it.

Over the course of six months, acquiring the Buffalo City Teachers contract became my obsession. The Judge, married, successful, was influential. He used our relationship to justify his whereabouts. He had numerous female acquaintances meeting him nightly, (his nieces as he so glibly called them.) Like Angelo, the Judge, lived only to satisfy his wants justifying his childlike behavior. As time will prove, the Judge's success and reputation will be challenged. Although he was taken to trial for DWI, a city court judge just cannot be convicted. We met at the bar to celebrate. More shots, more drinks. He decided it was time to reopen his own nightclub in the heart of the city, The Little Harlem.

The Judge had a very successful nightclub ten years earlier, as we were told, but a questionable fire burnt it to the ground. There was an investigation but the Judge was cleared and received a huge insurance settlement.

(Eventually his financial affairs would come under FBI investigation.)

Back when he and I were working on our teacher contract he was refinancing a 70-unit apartment complex he owned with his son on

Elmwood Avenue, two blocks from our drinking comfort station. Apparently he had received over a $2,000,000 loan from H.U.D. to renovate the property. Simultaneously he received a $1,000,000 State Economic Development loan for the same project. Without notifying the state or H.U.D. he applied for and received a $750,000 Urban Renewal loan from the City of Buffalo to provide necessary repairs for the same complex. As of five years later, less than one-third of the repairs were completed, the property was in foreclosure and the money had all disappeared

I must admit, upon reflection, that I, too, was constantly searching for the big deal, success at all costs. My life activities began to revolve around my obsession with acquiring this contract. More political parties, more time spent with the Judge. Happy Hours were simply not enough. Evenings, Friday nights, Saturday afternoons, I was willing sacrifice whatever it took to secure my newly defined need.

At the same time, Danny, a Met Life colleague of mine, and I explored another moneymaking scheme. This one I could do while working full time. At least that was my perception. Danny, a fine young black man raised in the inner city, was a struggling sales agent who wanted to pursue a construction business performing repairs on inner city projects. He and I developed a real friendship without any expectations from one another. Danny frequented a number of drinking establishments that were quite different than mine. I started meeting Danny on his turf. Later in the day I would meet the Judge, eventually not caring at all whether I ever went home or not.

There were news, radio and television personalities who owned inner-city property but couldn't find anyone to go into the danger zones to work. Well, Danny and I would. Danny introduced me to his cousins, excellent, but out-of-work painters, plumbers, and general handymen. Before I knew it, Danny was introducing me to the Baptist minister, and I was soliciting work from my inner-city clients to whom I had sold insurance. We were off and running a construction repair business that was paying off.

So less than one year after my empire had crashed (well at least to the point of rebuilding) I had managed to take a brief time out, enter a new career and replicate my entire life script as if time never passed. It was the same madness, chaos, fulfilling wants instead of fulfilling needs. Moving out from Orchard Park, I took up residence with an old friend and her husband in North Buffalo   I was still running. From what? I knew, but it was easier to just not face reality. I started to face it in 1993.

The Judge was busy securing his life script entitlements. He was actively involved in the election of the New York State Comptroller, actively raising thousands and thousands of dollars for this man's campaign. He needed his friend to be elected. So did I. The Judge needed the State Comptrollers office to approve his loan request. I needed the State Controller to endorse the MetLife contract with the teachers. Actually the

Judge and I had his approval to take over all State Municipal Workers. Retirement would come early.

Then the Judge decided that we must get close to the Governor's office. Mr. M.C. was our ticket. Accordingly, he planned an elaborate fundraiser for Mr. M.C. Angelo sold tickets to the Family. We contributed, securing the teacher contract. Mr. M.C. arrived in Buffalo with his entourage. The Judge arranged a private meeting the night of the fundraiser. Angelo, the Judge, Mr. M.C., and I met in the home study to discuss business the American way. Mr. M.C. was a man of his word. The next week I was before the union president representing the entire Buffalo Teacher Federation. I had already received written administrative approval through the superintendent that simply gave contractual approval contingent on union acceptance and approval. Mr. R. approved, felt the benefit was excellent for his membership. Off I went, now to secure Mr. S.'s people, the Blue Collar workers.

Without the help of Timmy D., I acquired Mr. S.'s approval. By October of 1993 I was now a free man with a new career and a million dollar contract. My drinking, well, it was a part of everyday life. So many things were wrong with my life, yet I ignored them. I was successful, and as long as I kept busy and was able to medicate the pain, I was once again beginning to get comfortable with me.

During the fall of 1993 several of the Judge's friends, acquaintances of mine, introduced me to the concept of running for a political office. They said, "Look you're a Buffalo resident now, a new political name. You're electable." "What office?" I asked. The Buffalo School Board, of course. What better way of protecting one's interests?

Was this a conflict of interest? Yes, but we didn't care. The Judge promised to check it out anyway. In fact, upon reflection, it amazes me how everyone I knew, someway or another, continually attempted to protect his comfort zone. The Judge's interest was to protect his future potential income stream. So was mine. The Judge even went one step further. He negotiated with Angelo in an attempt to get his wife employed by MetLife so he could legally enjoy the financial fruits of his labor. If his wife were employed he would have a check and balance in place, a check to verify his income and a balance to justify his means. Ironically, she had no real business interest.

When presented with the concept she balked, asking, "Am I just being used? Or do you and Angelo really think I can sell?" Well she was being used, no question about that. My need, along with Angelo's, was to keep the Judge happy. It was necessary for a successful relationship with City Hall and with the teachers.

Could Vanessa sell? We didn't care. She was a retired Buffalo school teacher and assistant principal. Being the salesmen that we were, we both realized her presence, her contacts, her credentials were much more valuable to us than her sales abilities. So yes, we could use her!

Passing the New York State Insurance exam became a trying experience for all. Week after week Vanessa sat for the practice exam failing numerous times. Frustrated, she simply told the three of us to find a new source of funding, financing, and manipulation.

The Judge, frustrated and angry that his plan had failed, resorted to other methods. This process now became a family affair. Daughter, son, the urgency became evident to license a family member. The problem, however, was that his family had no interest in his schemes, fortunately for them.

By the fall of 1993, I was practicing my life script and getting better at it all along the way. I was now putting in my perfunctory time at MetLife and the county, showing up for various group presentations, working at the downtown office, tracking Danny to check on jobs, chasing the Judge or pushing him, what ever the case may be, and setting the foundation at each of the eighty-nine public school facilities. I was also planning my campaign for a seat on the City of Buffalo School Board.

I was still receiving daily calls from attorneys, investors who wouldn't let me forget Triad, M.J. Grass, The Pony Post, and of course Arlington Capital, but I truly believed everything was okay.

Life has an interesting way of bringing people and events that are interventions in one's life. Something happens, or a person enters your life that impresses you in such a way that you feel emotions in the very depth of your soul.

The date, October 29, 1993, is a day that began a process of intervention. Working my normal work schedule, chasing my dream, drinking, sacrificing all my most important needs, I met the Judge for Happy Hour at our regular meeting spot. Earlier in the evening I had met an old friend of mine, Claire. She was a teacher, very involved in the Buffalo public school system. I knew Claire from years back. I felt that was enough justification to solicit her assistance to get me closer to the money, teachers and her school's principal, whose approval was necessary for me to go onsite and sell. Claire enjoyed my idea. I explained my plan. I would come to her school, sit in the teachers lounge, bring gifts, pizza and chicken wings. The teachers will be attentive for at least fifteen minutes.

So Claire, along with another friend Tina, who is also a Buffalo schoolteacher, and I met at a downtown bar to discuss social issues and drink. I listened to their individual love stories, interpersonal relationships, trials and tribulations, not really sure that I cared. What I did care about was securing her assistance. After spending about two hours with her I was assured that she would help me. We made a plan to meet later on that evening at our favorite watering hole. From there I met the Judge.

Later that evening, having identified all the world's problems, reviewed all the secret plans the Judge and I shared, Claire and Tina arrived. They informed me that they were meeting several of their friends.

One friend in particular made quite an impression. We were introduced and were instantly attracted to one another. Her name was Jane. This woman actually communicated. We talked, sharing stories, giving each other glimpses into our personal lives. I felt there was something very special about this lady. She was a refreshing inspiring individual with no pretense, no facade, just open and friendly. I wanted to see her again.

We met two days later at a suburban restaurant. She was there when I arrived. We talked for hours. For the first time in my whole life I wanted to share myself someone I was able to trust. Jane soon became my very best friend, then, love blossomed. She trusted me, shared her life but I was unable to be honest. I was ashamed, burdened by so many issues of my past and present, I didn't know how. I was not honest about my situation with Elise. The official end had not occurred. As far as I was concerned it was just a technicality, but that was my delusional refusal to deal with painful reality.

Here I was again attempting to build a new life without placing closure on the past or the present. But we are held accountable for all of our actions, to our Creator, ourselves, the rest of humanity. I was willing to sacrifice all the good, the love of life, loved ones and their Divine purpose in my life, for selfish irrational living. Insanity.

As 1993 came to a close, Jane and I developed our relationship built on a strong friendship. She discovered the truth as to my present personal life and my past business dealings. Closure of the past was beginning.

Contacting an attorney, I began the process of filing a notice of divorce. Proactively dealing with business issues, I started to legally separate myself from Triad. I felt that Jane and I had a future. The boys and I were working on our relationship. It was time to start anew.

The holidays were the happiest time I'd ever had. Jane and I spent the time together, decorating a tiny tree for her apartment, visiting with her mother, just enjoying one another and the boys. Life was relaxing, comforting and peaceful. Although I was rebuilding for many of the right reasons, the foundation had not yet stabilized.

As 1993 turned into 1994 I was beginning to take back control over various aspects of my life. Although this is what I truly believed, it was obvious that I was still falling. Building this life with Jane, planning our future, I continued to touch upon the past and present. Trying to appease Elaine and Elise for the wrong reasons, and compromising with people involved with past business ventures, said to me clearly and distinctly that I still couldn't confront the past. Trying to appease, pacify, justify, isolate and play the victim provided me with all the rationale necessary to continue life just as I had scripted it.

I continued to medicate. Drinking numbed the pain, provided a comfort zone where for the moment I felt everything was just fine. Finding this comfort zone, allowed me to feel affirmed. Selecting new acquaintances that supported my ideology, surrounding myself with other victims in order to feel victimized, it was an ugly time of self-pity and helplessness. If only I'd have been honest! I was sacrificing the greatest gifts in my life, but I didn't see it. Blinded by fear, I kept running in desperation.

In February of 1994 I found myself running for a political office that I truly could not have cared less about. Running for the Buffalo City Public School Board turned out to be a disaster. Jane questioned my rationale for even agreeing to run. So did I, but then again, the machine was rolling and I had to keep up to stay on board. See, my Happy Hour colleagues were the individuals that set up the election committee, each party having his own agenda.

In February my left knee started swelling and locking due to loose cartilage. I began experiencing difficulty walking, falling easily. Then I fell on an icy stairwell at a restaurant and actually tore the cartilage. Surgery was in order. I couldn't walk without a cane.

Campaigning door to door was far more than I could handle. It was just too painful. On St. Patrick's Day, 1994, I knew it was over. Jane, Josh, Justin and I attempted to pass out flyers, but I couldn't walk a block. So, where did I go? The first Irish Bar I could find. I had to medicate the pain. I was so happy to drop out of the race. Jane had never wanted me to pursue this endeavor, but my grandiosity and self-centeredness prevailed. My knee injury forced me to swallow a large dose of reality, if only for the moment.

~ A House Without A Foundation ~

Chapter Fourteen

In February of 1994 Angelo and I decided to form a partnership. Along these same lines so did Jane and I. She wanted a commitment and for the first time in my life, I too wanted this foundation. We agreed to marry but first, I needed to work on resolving some issues from the past.

Although separated from Elise and the notice of divorce filed, the action had not progressed to a point of closure. But heck, I'd deal with that later. I was getting good at building things. Unfortunately I'd neglect to stabilize the basic integrity of the foundation.

Brant, New York was to become a new comfort zone of sorts. Located approximately 30 miles from downtown Buffalo and approximately 21 miles from Jane's Hamburg, New York apartment, it represented an escape.

Through family affiliations, Angelo acquired ownership rights to a late 1800 or early 1900 school building, converted sometime in the mid 1950's to a four-unit apartment complex. Although he enjoyed receiving the rental income, he didn't enjoy spending money on repairs to the property. He viewed long-term expenditures as unnecessary. Just place a patch, do minimum work and collect the profits. Sounds rudimentary and simple. But it became far from simple. Month by month Angelo disclosed that Brant was a headache. Late rents, horrible collection processes, high maintenance with even a few tenants reporting him to the Erie County Health Department for supposed code violations. Angelo's wife Nanci, personal business manager for Angelo's selected interests, was fed up with Brant.

Remembering that I had a limited history of construction experience, Angelo invited me to go with him to look over the situation. Angelo didn't believe a word his wife said. All the way there he minimized the situation, laughing off her concerns. "Women are such worriers. Just watch what I do!"

The building was historic and picturesque, an ancient two-story red brick schoolhouse complete with roof top observation post. The surrounding property was beautiful, approximately two acres of land abutting the Seneca Indian Reservations. Isolated, several miles from anything, it was really quite striking.

But pulling into the driveway should have served as sufficient warning for what we were in for. The front yard was littered with three junk cars, one on blocks with no tires, oil drums, rims, 25 tires and an assortment of miscellaneous debris. We stepped around a huge pile of garbage and dirty diapers decomposing by the front entrance. The foyer door was broken off its hinges, the carpet saturated in animal urine, with dogs and cats coming and going at will! At the top of the stairs we found eight rabbits in cages, crickets, and rats in boxes along with crates of live chickens. Seems Angelo had his own animal menagerie and he didn't know it. Well, he knew it now and wanted no part of it.

Only one tenant was home. As we entered the apartment we were nearly overcome with the stench. In this two-bedroom apartment lived three dogs, six cats, a husband and wife with numerous kids, and several elderly people. I had never seen such filth and degradation. Mattresses were spread around the living room floor. An older man, connected to an oxygen tank and an IV drip, was sleeping in only his underwear on a bare mattress. He woke up while we were there and lit a cigarette. Angelo and I looked at each other in disbelief.

Going to the next neighboring unit we found more of the same squalor but other surprises as well. Seems the tenant raised exotic snakes, not just any snakes but huge, enormous ones. We were in shock. I saw a snake over 20 feet long approximately 8" in diameter. The caged rabbits, rats, and chickens we met in the hallway were fresh game for these snakes as well as iguana's, lizards and a whole host of other reptiles.

On the ride back home, Angelo was in silence for approximately ten to twelve miles. I was laughing too hard to be serious. Finally the realization of what was happening sunk in. Brant was a place of madness and chaos and it was all Angelo's. He was stuck with the property. It was heavily mortgaged with no market value. What could he do? Initially Angelo wanted me to inventory the structural repairs necessary to bring it up to code. The list went on and on. It seemed endless. But before anything could be done, we advised him that it was necessary to evict the menagerie and I'm not just speaking of the animals.

Redeeming Grace

I had an idea. Angelo knew Jane and I were looking for an apartment, a place to begin. For me, 30 miles from Buffalo was far enough away from the past, maybe even the present, for a new start. I returned to Brant, this time with my eyes wide open to the possibilities. Climbing, inspecting, searching, I drew up a proposal. Angelo would evict all tenants, I would have apartment #4, rent free, and free reign to renovate the rest of the building at will. Angelo would pay me a fair labor rate in cash or equity. He agreed to my proposal and started eviction processes.

I had the vision of an apartment with ceilings sixteen-feet high, and windows ten-feet tall, with an open loft two-and-a-half stories high. It would be something spectacular. My goal was to have our apartment completed by the first or the middle of May, sooner if possible, and then progress to the other units. I thought the plan had foundation.

About the first week of March, awaiting the eviction of the tenants, I began cleaning out the exterior of Brant removing garbage and debris. By the middle of March, with my bad knee, walking with a cane in one hand and tools in the other, I entered the apartment that I claimed. What a filthy mess. Everything had to go, carpet, doors, floors, paneling, even the walls and ceiling. Everything would be replaced. A spiral staircase would be built leading to a bedroom loft with walk-in closets. I envisioned an apartment right out of Architectural Digest. It would be our dream come true.

So, working full time for MetLife, full-time on the school contracts, part-time with Danny, chasing all of my dreams, spending all my Happy Hours with the Judge, I started Brant.

The question remained. When would I do all this? Was I running away? Or was I truly committed to a new start. I had fallen in love with the lifestyle Jane and I envisioned. Josh, Justin and I were beginning to spend personal time together. I was actually going to their school and extra-curricular activities and enjoying every moment.

What was occurring? Was my life finally starting to regain its balance? Yes and no. Some of the people around me knew that my life was still out of balance. Others did not. I spoke to Rita, Jane's mother, at length, confiding my feelings; only I still wasn't totally honest. I purposely left out important facts about my past concerning closure. Why talk about pain? Just ignore it and it will go away. But that was delusional thinking. It wasn't that simple.

I discovered that in Rita I had a friend. Our relationship too had evolved. Though she was protective of her daughter, she welcomed me with open arms. I also knew how my family felt about Jane. Josh and Justin were also very vocal. She was more than accepted, she was welcomed.

On March 26, 1994 Jane and I planned a trip to Toronto to see The Phantom of the Opera. We went shopping and stopped at a quaint bar and grill for drinks. I had made reservations at a French restaurant, a favorite of mine. Arrangements were made in advance for a second floor atrium table with a view of a center garden. Soft, mellow music from a baby grand piano set the mood for the evening. Dinner, drinks, wine, everything was perfect. Jane knew this was a special occasion. The ring was hidden on a plate and presented quite unassumingly. She found the ring, I proposed, she accepted. It seemed that our dreams for the future were well on their way to becoming reality.

Returning from Toronto I felt deep down in my soul that I had a chance in this life. The foundation was stabilizing. At least that was my perception.

Jane and I were officially engaged. Elise heard the news and called me to verify if it was true. She did not hesitate to tell me her opinion. I agreed to meet her to finalize closure. I needed to do this. I wanted no more pain.

Jane had planned to drive with her mother to Charlotte, North Carolina. While she was away I planned to spend each night working on the apartment. I needed to get this done. I went to work, to Brant, beginning to build our dreams.

"But everyone who hears these words of mine and does not put them into practice is like a foolish man who built his house on sand. The rain came down, the streams rose, and the winds blew and beat against that house, and it fell with a great crash" (Matthew 7:26-27).

~ And Great Was The Fall ~

Chapter Fifteen

On April 6, 1994 my chaotic life script began as every other. I worked for MetLife, touched base with all my business partners and went to Brant to work on what I thought was a new foundation. I was invincible. I could handle the workload. Anyway, it was only temporary. When this apartment was finished, I could relax.

My knee injury was worsened by a fall from a ladder. About eight o'clock, attempting to make the pain more tolerable I took a pain tablet, 500 milligrams of codeine and drank a six-pack of beer. Not a good thing to mix? Why not? Who could it hurt? I was in pain. See I'm the victim am I not, so I'm entitled. But even with all that, the pain would not subside so about ten o'clock I took another 500 milligrams of codeine. A few glasses of homemade wine helped me work the night away. I had a mission to accomplish and nothing, not even common sense, was going to stand in my way.

About 11:40 p.m. I decided to call it a night. It had been a very long day and I was exhausted. To make matters worse, by this time I was well medicated. Leaving Brant that night the weather was bad, foggy and cold. An ice storm had hit Buffalo during the evening leaving everything dangerously slippery. "But I don't have far to go" I reasoned. "Jane's apartment is only a few miles away. I can make it that far and spend the night there." I got into my truck, pulled out of the driveway and headed down the road.

Life is about choices. Each day we have opportunities to make choices that affect our lives and the lives of others. Don't we have the right to choose to do what we want? It's a free country. Yes. But our choices, like ripples in a pond, have far reaching affects. Some are of little consequence but others bring with them consequences that last for eternity.

On April 6, 1994 I made the wrong choice. I chose to drive drunk. This decision haunts me. If I could live the night over, knowing the outcome, I would choose to do things differently. But none of us have that privilege. That's why it is so important for us to think before we act, to take responsibility for our choices beyond the possible consequences to ourselves.

Halfway to Jane's apartment, I passed out. I woke up in Erie County Medical Center hooked up to IV's, monitors and conscious of a great deal of pain. However, my physical pain soon became nothing compared to the emotional agony of learning the outcome of my accident.

When I passed out, my truck crossed the centerline of the road striking a car occupied by two young adults. One young man, Jeff Brown, was in critical condition. I was informed that I would be arrested for DWI and Vehicular Assault.

I was in shock. The hospital contacted my next of kin and in New York State that meant Elise. More confusion. I so badly wanted to find Jane. I needed her support.

As I sat in the hospital, being visited by my attorney friend Allen, the impact of the accident began to take hold. Angelo came the next day. At the time neither of us knew the severity of Jeff's injuries. Elise came back to visit. It was wrong. I missed Jane.

Returning from Charlotte, Jane was petrified. Call after call to the house went unanswered. Where could I have possibly gone? I'm not sure exactly what events unfolded next, or how she found out what happened, but she came to the hospital. I'll never forget the look in her eyes, the fear, the loss, and disappointment. I couldn't face her. My life had hit bottom. Why had I made such a devastatingly foolish choice?

I still couldn't accept the reality of the situation. My attorney, very cold, calloused and direct said, "Terry you'd better pray he doesn't die." The implication was that it would be bad for me if he did.

What has happened in our society to compassion, to feeling for our fellow human beings? A young boy's life was hanging in the balance. His parents and family were in so much pain, suffering for their child. With all my heart I prayed he wouldn't die, but not to protect myself. I was filled with remorse for all that had happened. Life is precious. I was confused, afraid, searching for answers.

Several days later I was released from the hospital. Jane took me home to her mother's, our safety zone. I was scared, confused trying to hold on to what was left of life. To this day I cannot fully understand my thought process but I know I was in shock. A sixth sense told me the worst had not yet occurred. I wanted to run away and hide.

Elise was calling, asking me to return to Orchard Park. "I'll help you straighten out this mess, then you can deal with the divorce." More ultimatums were dictated. I waited, met with my attorney and soon I returned to work to my life script.

As the days turned to weeks I could no longer face Jane or her mom. I had deeply sacrificed a trust. Each evening looking at this innocent person I knew I had caused her enough hurt. I had broken her heart too many times. Although I really didn't want to, I left her. I ran away like a child who can't face the damage he has done. I needed to punish myself, cause myself more pain. Certainly pleasure was far away. I was so ashamed, so guilty.

I met my new attorney, Joe, who supposedly was Elise's friend. He informed me that Jeff Brown was in a coma, with major brain trauma and perhaps would never regain consciousness. Joe told me I would go to jail. "We must work out a defense."

My world as I knew it came to an end that afternoon. I walked to the Cathedral and prayed, crying out to God the best way I knew. I walked for hours.

Returning to the office I informed Angelo. Angelo, minimizing suggested, "Let's go out and talk." To this day I still remember him asking, "Do you want a drink?" This insanity continued to engulf my life.

I had a problem and there was no place to hide. I could run no more.

Returning to Elise's was a scenario I had practiced many times, continuous arguing, screaming, and the total chaotic life. Elise was the rescuer, codependent needing to be the parent, lecturing, demanding. I let it all unravel.

From Mom, to Carol, Rick, Josh, Justin, Jane, and Rita I had hurt so many people and destroyed so much of what I valued. The Brown family and the King family were in shock, hurting, mourning, because of my choice.

Thirty-one days after the accident, Jeff Brown passed away. When I heard the news I couldn't believe it was true. I went back to church and prayed to the God I knew as a child. I prayed for guidance. Why? Why did this have to happen?

The truth is, it didn't have to happen. It was avoidable had I listened to the warnings and changed "that which wasn't right" in my life. I knew that I had a drinking problem. I just didn't want to face it. It helped me perpetuate the lie of my delusional lifestyle. It medicated the pain and emptiness. But life isn't all about me. There were those who had reached out to help me, if only I had responded. The choices I made in my life had led me to this crisis, this tragedy. Choice by choice I wrote my own life script.

Because of my choices a family will mourn the death of their son and carry that sorrow and loss with them for the rest of their lives. A young woman will remember the horror of the crash and the loss of someone she loved because of one choice...a choice that I made.

Jeff Brown's death profoundly impacted many families and affected many lives. His life had meaning and purpose that lives beyond his brief life on this earth. Everyone who knew him and loved him carries with them (and extends to others) the influence of their relationship with him and the contribution he made to their lives.

His memory will live on through the efforts made by his family and friends to help spare others the pain and loss they have suffered.

Accepting responsibility for someone's death is an overpowering task. My faith, my beliefs and my values were placed to the ultimate test. Life is precious and sacred. It belongs to God Who is the Giver of Life.

I can never go back and change the past...oh, if only I could. But none of us can undo what has been done. I can take responsibility for my actions and I have. I have determined, by the grace of God, that his death will never be in vain.

I know now that He has a purpose for each of our lives and if we seek Him, He will guide us to achieve the fulfillment of that purpose. I am dedicated to reaching others with a message. If by my sobriety and the testimony of my life I can help others to see that old cycles can be broken, and lives can be changed, perhaps others might be spared this kind of heartache in the future. We are not without hope or help or recourse.

In May of 1994 I was initially arraigned in the Town of Evans Court with over 300 people, along with the media, in attendance. I was released on $300 bail.

I returned to Orchard Park that night. Although I didn't realize it at the time, I was just beginning to come to terms with God's purpose for my life.

~ Confronting Demons ~

Chapter Sixteen

When circumstances in life challenge us to "confront our demons," one of the greatest gifts we can give ourselves is honesty. Learning to be honest is not an easy task. Confronting my demons meant leaving my comfort zones and taking responsibility. Throughout so much of my life I continued to structure, build, start cycles of life without addressing the real internal issues that caused me so much darn pain. Many people thought that after Jeff Brown's death, I would some how miraculously change. Well, it was not so simple.

Reflecting back upon this period, I realize that many of the people with whom I associated were just as sick as I was. We tend to surround ourselves with people like ourselves. See, if my friends faced the reality that something about me "just wasn't right" then perhaps they would see the truth about themselves. This just could not happen...at any cost. So they supported me to protect their own comfort zones. Over and over I heard, "Oh, it's such an unfortunate accident." "It could happen to anyone." "These things happen." Sadly, I believed this too.

Afraid and lonely, I needed help, help for my alcoholism and help to deal with the responsibility of taking of a life. I was hurting. Deep inside, I knew that my actions had caused these tragic events to unfold. Many people were hurt, suffering, mourning, confused, asking God, "Why?"

The week after Jeff's passing, Angelo cared only about one issue, "Can you finish the house at Brant?" I felt numb. With all the legal machinations and maneuvering that I was processing, I was barely going through the motions of living. As the summer of 1994 unfolded I tried desperately to hold on, but my friends and acquaintances drifted away. Friends they were not. Enablers, rescuers, abusers yes, but certainly not friends. I did not realize it at the time.

My colleagues at MetLife were like vultures, anxious to protect their interests. The Buffalo Public School contract had just recently been completed as of May 1994 and this meant substantial commissions for the sales agents, which ultimately meant increased personal income for the men and women involved. Angelo's second primary concern was to make sure MetLife would not terminate me due to the arrest.

Although at this point I had not been indicted for a felony charge, my Attorney informed me socially, in front of Angelo and the Judge, that if indicted by a grand Jury I would more than likely go to prison. Prison! I was in shock. Until now this possibility had never entered my mind. But how could I not know the social consequences? It was too painful to consider. It was inconceivable. This couldn't be happening to me.

The Brown's were burying Jeff and I was burying the pain. Avoiding reality, being stroked, just reinforced my behavior. I was okay, nothing needed to change. I could not have been more wrong. I felt that the person who truly understood the shame, the guilt and the pain I was in, was Jane. Oh, how I wanted to call out to her. She tried to reach out to me, but not wanting to hurt her anymore, I withdrew. With the knowledge that I could or would go to State Prison, I decided that removing Jane from the cycle of pain and anguish would be best for her. The sad thing is, she didn't understand my motives. She was hurting too, only again, I saw things only from my perspective.

The Judge and I met with Don, an acquaintance from the boating days. He was a client of Ellen's and at times, a drinking partner of mine. Don, a well-known television personality, is the local anchor, for the six o'clock news for a local Buffalo station. My legal advisor felt that we needed a key contact so that we could limit exposure, minimizing public opinion, sentiment, and outcry. Could Don stop the TV coverage from his station at least? Don agreed that it was in my best interest that the media be minimized. Although he represented one TV station, he couldn't influence the others. He warned me, "Terry if you're indicted, 'Mother's Against Drunk Driving' is a very emotional group. They will attack you." And attack they did! As the story was broadcasted, it hurt Josh and Justin terribly. They were so confused as to what was happening to their father.

But today I fully appreciate the message of M.A.D.D., S.A.D.D. and their efforts. Tragedies such as this are most assuredly avoidable for those who are willing to listen. The message is clear, "Don't drink and drive."

The problem certainly isn't just about driving and goes beyond "drinking" to the reason behind it. The problem is about the issues in life to which we keep referring "that just aren't right." They affect our feelings, thoughts, emotions and our behavior. See, these issues and our response to them, need not continue. They can be changed if only we are willing. Our life script can be different if we are willing to honestly confront our demons, face the reality of who we have become, and summon the courage to reach out for help. Life can afford us blessings if we change. But first we have to face ourselves and be honest!

At this point of my life I was not being honest. I was allowing others to control my destiny. I let others dictate the representation of my feelings and emotions I so desperately want to express and share… with Jane, Josh, Justin, Mom, and, yes, with the Browns.

My attorneys explored the development of the case. Would there be an indictment? Could it be stopped? Could we talk to the District Attorney? If indicted, which Supreme Court Justice would be appointed to the case? Who knows the judge? Does the Judge know me? What happens to the school contract? All this posturing, defending and legal maneuvering was so far removed from the equation and totally void of emotion. It was so wrong.

I was feeling a myriad of emotions. Should I make a statement? I so wanted to reach out to Mr. and Mrs. Brown. At that time, as well as years later, I had wanted to reach out to them, apologize, mourn, express my sorrow, assume and take responsibility. Instead, I was reactive, again, rebuilding, manipulating, following the advice of others. The greatest mistake was that Terry was not willing to live life for Terry. I allowed others to deflect the pain, shield me from reality, and hide me from harm. Pay them, support them, no matter what the cost, make the pain go away.

The reality is that these individuals didn't really care one bit about Jeff's death, my pain, or the devastating loss that Mr. and Mrs. Brown were suffering. It was all about how the turn of events would affect them. Things were so out of sync. Not just out of control, out of sync. See, when issues are out of control, as in homeostasis, we see clearly the pieces of the circle that's missing. As I wobbled and vacillated, I knew my life was out of balance. But I did not know just yet what was missing, or how to put it back in sync.

About three weeks after the funeral I met the Judge at "The Little Harlem." He gave me the number of a friend of his, a psychologist.

Meeting Dr. O. was an interesting experience. He was a psychologist, alcohol addiction counselor, and the Judge's Sunday morning tennis partner. We met for several hours, exploring feelings and emotions, discussing social responsibilities, alcohol use, and money. Yes, money. He made it vividly clear that it would require lots of money...cash...for treatment and to acquire his professional testimony, which would make the difference whether or not I went to jail.

What was he saying? At that moment in my life, during that two-hour meeting, I began listening, really listening perhaps for the first time in many years. I asked Dr. O. to further explain what he meant, not just what he said. For as I listened, what I really heard was a blatant message. For the right price, an expert opinion can be adjusted to fit your needs. He made it clear that his profession was to work with probation, assess defendants and recommend sentences, even perhaps alternative sentences. He enumerated examples, clients he had represented from the Buffalo Bills, Cleveland Brown, Cincinnati Reds, as well as a large number of very prominent business men.

He described several cases similar to mine. It was resolved that if these individuals remained in treatment, he would go to court and actively testify that society was best served if these individuals received alternative sentences, home confinement, six months to five years probation, and monthly alcohol counseling. "Once we're done," he said, "just come once a month, visit one hour a month with my assistant and that's that. Those sessions are paid by insurance. My initial fee and court-supported defense documents well, that's another matter. You're a friend of the Judges? Right? Let's negotiate."

Bottom line, for the right price, I could get his time and attention. I asked what kind of money we were talking about. He responded, "Well, insurance pays the base, you pay the difference. Perhaps $5,000 is a fair start." I almost dropped my jaw. It costs $5,000 to form an opinion? Would $5,000 keep me from going to jail? (I was listening. I was all ears!) He said we would start at $5,000. There would be more expenses. He couldn't tell me exactly how much more, it depended on how much time was involved. It could be several more similar payments. In other words pay $5,000 to $10,000, perhaps $15,000 and hope to stay out of jail. What would this money buy…treatment for my demons, my alcoholism? Or was this money simply paying him to confabulate a medical opinion adjusted slightly, depending on whose "comfort zone" needed protecting?

I left the psychiatrist's office that night dumbfounded. Returning to Orchard Park I was more confused than ever.

Elise was not the help she purported to be. Her opinion that this entire situation should be handled as a business matter was again a direct contravention to what I felt. Behind my back she had taken steps to protect her financial interests. I knew she couldn't be trusted. I soon realized that I was in a worse position than ever before. Argue, fight, our relationship was intolerable.

Elaine demanded money. "What will happen to the boys? You had better get yourself out of this mess. What am I to do?" is all she would say. Ironically what I didn't know was that these two individuals continued to talk and developed a relationship. I was the odd man out.

Business was over. I was a broken man. I isolated myself from life in June and July, trying to insulate myself from the agony of confronting. I needed money and lots of it.

The Browns had now developed their own agenda. They hired a private investigator to find out all about Terry King. "What kind of man is this? Who is he? Is he the devil? Does he care? Why hasn't he made contact with us? Doesn't he have any feelings? If so where are they?"

Their attorney Ben Feingold, the uncle of the young lady passenger, had his own agenda: "Terry King will pay dearly for what he has done and monetarily as well."

My faith then was not what it is today, but deep down inside I knew a value system. I knew what was morally right and wrong. I had killed someone. It was an overwhelming feeling of responsibility I didn't know how to express. See, everything I felt was being verbalized, positioned by others for their own gain. Morally and ethically I knew what needed to be done. I needed to change. But how does one begin the process?

I wanted so to reach out for Jane, Josh, Justin, Rick, Mom, and the people in my life that I loved. Yet I knew that to express all that was going on in my life would cause them even further pain. I had so many demons to confront. Where would I begin?

My first rational thought of this whole process was to deal with Jeff Brown's death. I knew I had to confront Dr.O. Spending thousands of dollars to prostitute the systems, to manipulate the representation of my defense, to mitigate my social punishment was wrong. Simply knowing this difference allowed me to feel at peace. I felt the assurance that deep inside, I still had retained the moral and ethical values of life taught long ago. I still was unwilling to confront my alcoholism at this point. I had far too much pain to medicate. I reasoned that alcohol at least temporarily provided numbness, an equalizer.

Joe, my Attorney called me to his office late in June of 1994, informing me that the District Attorney had called the Brown family and their Attorney, Mr. Ben Feingold. The state wanted to pursue a grand jury indictment charging me with vehicular manslaughter second degree, failure to keep right and reckless driving. I didn't fully understand the ramifications. Joe indicated that the charge is a class D felony considered nonviolent and could carry a state prison sentence of up to two-and-one-half years minimum, to seven years maximum. Joe returned the D.A.'s call in my presence.

The D.A. was very vocal insisting that the Brown family demanded a prison sentence. Mr. King must be punished. But how? They didn't know about Dr. O.'s proposition. I had already made up my mind they would never know. I was taking responsibility.

Joe made it very clear that I would be going to prison. But, he minimized, it would be easy. I would probably do about one year. Usually first time offenders are sent to camps he referred to as "sweet!" Well, four years later I can assure anyone reading this that there is nothing "sweet" about prison time.

As Joe and I talked, I expressed my wishes not to go to trial. I simply had caused enough pain to everyone involved. It was time to stop. We reviewed the facts. I would not testify at the Grand Jury allowing the indictment to stand. There was nothing we could do anyway. The Brown's, M.A.D.D., S.A.D.D., all wanted the maximum penalty. Terry needed to be punished. Well, as I view it today, Terry would indeed be punished, but I would receive so much more. Facing one's demons in life, changing the inner person and finding the love I once knew as a child is more than a blessing today. It is one of my life's greatest gifts.

Leaving Joe's office that day, I began to take back my life...my "being." There was a lot of work to be done, still more confusion, still more feelings to explore. Realizing that my behavior had directly caused Jeff Brown's death was a beginning. But what I didn't yet accept was closure. Closure was beginning on a past, a life style that was so wrong. A lot of work was yet to be done with the inner me. But going to prison didn't scare me as much as the alternative. I just couldn't continue to live my life of lies any longer. Nor would I allow others to control my destiny. Enough.

The Grand Jury issued an indictment. The indictment was straightforward vehicular manslaughter second degree, reckless driving and failure to keep right, a class D felony. Life was changing I knew it and I could no longer run away from my past.

June 30, 1994 I went to Supreme Court, alone, with Joe. The courtroom was full. The Brown family was there along with the media. The arraignment was quick, a formality. The charges read and a "not guilty" plea entered. I was handcuffed and remanded to custody, pending release on $5,000 bail. I was taken to the Erie County Court Holding Cell to wait. I was now a ward of the State, property to be disposed of. Approximately six hours later Angelo pledged the bail and I was released.

Seeing the Browns, their hurt, their tears broke my heart. I so wanted to approach them and tell them something, if nothing more than to say how sorry I was, and plead for forgiveness. Every time I look at Josh and Justin I am so overcome with emotions. The "what ifs" take over. For Mr. and Mrs. Brown this tragic, violent, senseless death all could have been avoided had I only listened.

Today I realize that we cannot change the past. Trying, as many of us do, simply perpetuates this out of sync cycle. Closure is so important. Accepting my life script and taking responsibility for actions was my beginning. A part of me actually felt relief. A feeling of "let's accept whatever happens next and find some good from this." The God I had known as a child, loved and trusted was helping. I was beginning to listen.

Joe had lied as to the meaning or the understanding of plea agreement. Initially, when we met in his office in July of 1994, he told me that under New York State sentencing law I'd qualify for a program called Work Release. Joe brought in his office expert, Frankie, a rising star in the legal defense community from Youngstown State. He made it clear that the state prison system was so over crowded that I'd probably do eight months on a two-year minimum to six year maximum.

Work Release is intended for nonviolent felony offenders. Frankie's quote: "Terry you'll be home for Thanksgiving. Trust us."   He was so wrong.   Joe said I needed $2,500 to get through the sentencing. Angelo and Joe had discussed my insurance license. Joe assured me MetLife couldn't take any action until I was formally convicted.

A most interesting concept, "conviction." In whose eyes are we convicted? Society's...God's...our own? I had convicted myself by accepting the responsibility for my behavior, my choices my actions. No matter what society elects or recommends doing as a punitive punishment, it will never equal the punishment I have inflicted on myself. This memory, this awareness of the power of choice will stay with me for a lifetime...perhaps beyond.

But while I'm alive I shall forever live as testament to the power and consequences of choice. For all who will listen, and will see by my actions and life script today, change is possible. Real change begins by facing our demons from within, recognizing that we need help beyond ourselves, and reaching out to God with Whom all things are possible.

~ Limbo ~

Chapter Seventeen

Although we must put closure on the past, we soon learn that we simply cannot escape its consequences. Judgment day comes.

In August of 1994 I had to appear in court for a procedural hearing where each attorney was allowed an opportunity to present to the court pretrial discovery motions. To the surprise of the court and the District Attorney we (that is I) elected to enter a "guilty" plea. Joe's advice was to end this soon, to demonstrate to the court our remorse and sincere effort to avoid any more public examination of this case. Actually Joe had spoken prior with the D.A. and explored his position. Entering an early plea might possibly result in leniency, hopefully a reduced sentence. Joe's goal was one and one-third years to four. The D.A.'s initial offer was two years to six maximum. I entered to the plea. Life had changed, and I felt it was for the good. I was relieved. It was hard to explain.

Many people were upset that I had accepted a guilty plea. They expressed the feeling that I gave in too early, that I should have forced a trial. I knew in my heart that I had done the right thing. The pain was ending. I was at peace with my decision.

Angelo, Elise, the Judge, conspirators and protectors of their own comfort zones, were upset. Elise screamed at me like a child demanding to know what ever possessed me to make that decision. Angelo was worried about my job with MetLife. "Oh, why didn't you check with me first?" The Judge was angry. "You should have made sure your business affairs were in order first." In other words, protect his comfort zone while away. The fact was, I was done with Elise, the Judge, Angelo, and with the old Terry.

Defense lawyers in general may not be devoid of feelings but mine were. Frankie was very pompous about the whole situation. He didn't care if I was guilty or innocent. His job was to create a reasonable doubt, making accusations, placing blame elsewhere, not caring about the pain he inflicted on an already devastated family. It wasn't until years later that I found out the cold, calculated tactics he used as my representative. It ripped at my gut to think how hateful and vindictive he made me appear to the Brown family. The structure of the judicial system did not allow me to speak for myself or express my feelings. Never would I have agreed to such a defense. But who cares what Terry feels or thinks. They had a job to do, and the better the defense, the longer they could drag it out, making more money along the way. To them, it was just business.

I was in shock, no question. My emotions were in turmoil, but I could not nor would I express them, at least not to those around me. Everyone had an agenda and what was clear to me then is that when tragedy occurs, we each internally run to find our own comfort. Only, I had nowhere to run. Work, the media, friends…everyone had an opinion. Turning to work became a comfort zone. Frankie advised, "Build up a little cash, hide it, you'll need it when you get out. I'll work with Angelo to protect your insurance license. You'll be home before you know it."   It was all a lie.

My brother Rick and I met with Frankie, prior to sentencing.   I thought it odd that Joe no longer met with me. There was no longer money to be made. He left the mop up work to a junior partner. Frankie told us sentencing was set for September, but he would try to delay so I'd be able to work a little longer and make more money. "I don't know what you're worried about," he said, "You'll only be there for eight months then you'll be home for Thanksgiving. In fact, let's just accept the two to six-year term. This way we'll show the D.A. and the Browns that we are cooperating. Then, when you qualify for work release and parole, they'll not oppose you. You've got to trust me, I know how these things work."

As reality will prove out, he did not know how these things work. He didn't have a clue.

During the fall of 1994 I concentrated on securing the Buffalo School contract. I made a deal with another agent, Jack, an ex-restaurateur turned successful sales agent. Eager to protect his interests, he willingly agreed to drive me around everywhere necessary. Jack was a rescuer and codependent. His view of this situation was that "things happen." Oh, how wrong he was! In the end he betrayed my trust. In collaboration with Angelo and Elise, he created a complicated deal to secure the income of commissions excluding me. I didn't know it at the time but would soon discover this sordid cycle.

Angelo was worried about finishing Brant. He knew I needed money and attempted to make a deal. At least he made no pretense about his motives. "Help me finish the apartments before you go away. I'll rent the units and I'll pay you. You'll have the money when you go or I'll give it to you while you're there."

I thought about it. It was a chance to build up a nest egg and do something for others. Plus, if I stayed busy, I could put my feelings on hold. Years later I realized that in the process of shock, denial and depression I had numbly accepted certain aspects of the past and present. My unspoken plan was to isolate, use this time wisely to address my problems and begin to heal as I waited for the future to develop. But this simply wasn't possible yet.

I never did finish Brant. I went there to work on weekends and we did manage to complete three out of four apartments. Other than work, I tried to be there for Josh and Justin.

The boys understood that the reason I was going to prison was the result of consequences of my behavior resulting in a tragic death. This is the least I could do for society to repay my debt. At the time this was the point of view. Recovery was not even considered just yet. At least not until the probation officer was called in to prepare a pre-sentencing report and investigation. Reflecting back, I can see God beginning the process.

The woman from the probation department was most thorough. She asked many, many questions. One area of discussion, which I knew would eventually be examined, was my alcohol use. Seems this women had quite a bit of information. She insisted I begin counseling at Spectrum Human Services. She wanted to know in detail why I stopped going to Dr. O. Where would I begin? Should I tell the truth? Why wasn't I with Jane? Why did I leave? Was I dealing with the crash?

She was sincere, perhaps the first person I met along the process who elicited comment that was meant to help. "Mr. King, as you prepare to possibly go to prison, no matter what length of time, use the time wisely for you. Get yourself right. Start with your God." She was right in all respects.

My relationship with Elise was over. In fact, the relationship was nonexistent, yet I was afraid to reach out to Jane. I don't know if I was perhaps more embarrassed, ashamed, guilt-ridden, or all of the above. The probation officer discussed Josh and Justin and we explored how to continue my parental obligation. The boys needed their Dad!

Spectrum required three visits every week, Monday, Wednesday, and Friday, along with the initial interviews and assessments. "Mr. King, do you think you have a drinking problem?"

"Of course not. All these problems, my chaotic life, these recent consequences are just happenings. Right?"

Wrong! We all have options and we make choices. It's not that we're bad people. But some of us have made wrong choices. And for some of us, we will live with the consequences of our choices for life.

I called Mom and talked with her about my going to prison. We discussed the future, the boys, my career and my alcoholism. She pleaded that I not drink again. I promised her I would stop drinking. I meant that. But I wasn't ready, just yet. There was too much pain to medicate.

Discussing the Browns, "Should I reach out?" The Attorney's were adamant "No!" Reflecting back and knowing today from a family member that the Browns did want to hear something from me, I should have ignored my attorney's counsel. There were just too many unanswered questions for them.

I assured Mom that things would work out. But I was far from convinced that this was true. I was overwhelmed with pain and confusion, trying to hold on. But hold on to what? Perhaps the way of life I had so purposefully re-enforced over much of my life. It was the only way of life I knew.

I had not listened, but deep, deep down inside I knew this way of life must not continue. "Shoulds" and "ought tos" were simply not enough.

Knowing that you've reached the end is frightening yet comforting. It's comforting to know that we have been given the opportunity to end cycles that have led to the existing pain. Paradoxically, confronting these demons means that you will have to choose a new way of thinking, a new support system. That in itself is alarming, as you anticipate how you will cope with the pain of the unknown future. My self-esteem and self-confidence were fragile, inadequate or maybe at this point even nonexistent. I needed to start over with the faith and a value system I had come to know so long ago. For most of my life I had ignored, manipulated, or bastardized my value system simply to get my needs met. But which needs? I did learn that we can't make up for lost time. Living in the past just perpetuates the irrational, delusional world I was desperately attempting to leave.

Needing money and trying, as my attorney said, "to get things right for while your gone," I continued to take on jobs. In fact I took on several large projects renovating homes, bathrooms and so forth. My days were now occupied once again, 18 hours out of 24, seven days a week. The sickness is that I was so tired of this ugly cycle. It seemed that everything I was attempting to solidify in the present and for the future was self-imploding. The more money I made, the more debts I was paying. Working harder and longer, I was just burning myself out. I ran, ran, ran everyday.

Angelo tried to placate me. His behavior was puzzling to me at this point, promising, protecting, and convincing me to trust him. Jack promised that the school contract would be mine when I returned. Angelo agreed. The Judge was very concerned that he would be paid his thirty percent. He called me two weeks before sentencing in September of 1994, insistent that we execute a contract. He was not licensed at MetLife and his vain attempt to secure a sales position at MetLife via a family member fell apart. His year's worth of work was slowly disappearing. He called me daily, but he was the last priority in my life.

Simultaneously, I found myself served with a civil lawsuit filed by the estate of Jeff Brown, for eight million dollars. Meeting the Brown's Private

Investigator in Brant, I was able to speak openly with him, expressing the thoughts and feelings I had so long wanted to communicate. My attorney was livid. "How could you do that? He's on their side." Frankly there are no sides in this. A man's life has been lost and two families are mourning. For me, this meeting was a gift. Morally and ethically I had begun to confront my demons.

The attorneys, Joe and Frankie, approached the presiding Judge and requested a ninety-day sentencing extension that allowed me to, as Frankie arrogantly put it, "Use the time to hide money."

Interestingly enough, I viewed this reprieve as valuable time. It wasn't. The madness and chaos were overpowering me. In retrospect, going to prison was a relief. At this point I was in limbo. Life was going on around me. I was there in body but felt as if I was far removed in spirit. But interestingly, sometime during that month of October I sensed an awakening to the presence of who Terry King really was. I was acknowledging who I had become and I did not like what I saw. Prison time would be invested wisely. But I had to hold on until then. I was trying to hold on by a thread but the thread had snapped long ago.

Selling my mini van, collecting my job payments from final clients promised me a little nest egg of money for my return. Elise placed the money in her account. Although we both realized our relationship was over, she assured me I could trust her with my money. Angelo assured me that he would give Elise the money he owed me from Brant. "Don't worry. You'll have it."

Mom and my sister Carol were upset. They didn't trust her and felt that Mom should have handled my financial affairs. I couldn't allow Mom to be burdened with this. Confronting my demons of life for me meant confronting every part of my existence, fearlessly and honestly. I had to let go of everything, even my finances, and begin to allow God to be in control.

Thanksgiving proved to be a futile holiday attempt. Working alone in Brant, waiting to spend time with the boys, I felt isolated.

Angelo was being Angelo, minimizing, justifying and referring to my time away as "a little vacation." What was it that so deeply bothered Angelo while in my presence? Perhaps he saw glimpses of himself. Could it be that my life mirrored his own. Upon honest reflection, perhaps the issues he was uncomfortable confronting simply said to him, "This could have happened to you." For Angelo certainly drove "under the influence" more than once, if not on a weekly basis. Angelo, like many of my acquaintances, simply said to himself, "thank God it's not me." The behavior of his life was in question. He knew internally how close he had come many times to being exactly were I am. Angelo drove for two years with a suspended license. He simply didn't care. But it hadn't happened to him and he had other concerns. He was obsessed with securing the school contract. Angelo was a lot like me. He couldn't let go. Jack knew there was money to be made and he did not want to lose any of it. The Judge, well, let's say, money and greed ruled his judgment.

In November I had arthroscopic knee surgery in another attempt to repair my damaged cartilage. The day after my surgery I returned to MetLife, and the next week resumed the construction work. I stayed busy to avoid confronting those around me. I was in so much pain, but couldn't let anyone know. I refused to reveal too much of myself. I had an image to protect. Issues were avoided. I was isolating again, withdrawing, medicating the pain.

Angelo, the master manipulator, convinced Elise to become a full-time sales agent. He would run the school contract and she would retain the book of business while receiving the commissions from the school arrangement. She would also pay the Judge. I was confused. Jack was confused as well. This was happening before my very eyes and there was nothing I could do to control it. Not that I didn't want to, certainly the old Terry did. But something was beginning to occur from the very depth of my soul. I was detached from it all. I didn't care. I had determined in a most peaceful way that I couldn't control whatever was unfolding. My fears and worries were most assuredly elsewhere.

~ To Everything There Is A Season ~

Chapter Eighteen

Being raised in the northern hemisphere, I've always been intrigued by the changing seasons. As God designed them, they change slowly and purposefully. The fall gradually prepares one for winter's solitude, a period of rest and stagnation with a purpose. In winter we bear the storms, the cold and isolation. It is a time of inner work, serving a purpose for those willing to invest their time carefully. Winter gradually gives way to spring, a period of cleansing and spiritual rebirth in the promise of blossoming new life. The warmth of summer nurtures growth and development in a celebration of life. Each season has much to teach us as we consider the seasons of our lives.

Autumn is my favorite season…the magnificent colors, the fragrance of fallen leaves, the crisp clean air and refreshing breezes. Because we know winter is coming, autumn is a time of preparation, perhaps indicative of closure. As the fall unfolded, the leaves turned, so did this season of my life. Ever so slowly the process was beginning, although I didn't understand just then the importance of what was occurring.

Working alone at Brant provided me a measure of inner peace. In the solitude of my thoughts, inspired by the beauty of nature around me, I was able to accept my pending imprisonment with calm resignation.

Although she entered my life and left during a short period, a MetLife Agent, Lida Cabballes, from the Philippines inspired me with her wonderful philosophy of life. I will forever be grateful for Lida's listening ear, her frankness, wisdom and spiritual support. She really made a difference in my life. She taught me to listen, at least to begin. She shared stories of others she knew who had made wrong choices and served time in prison. She told me to value this time and invest it wisely as a unique opportunity offered to those that choose to make a new beginning. She assured me that I would find the Terry that really wanted to be. My purpose would unfold and along the way and I would rediscover life's blessings.

I was afraid of change, but after Thanksgiving of 1994, realized that I needed to find whatever life was meant to be for me. What was my God-intended purpose? Jeff Brown's death would not be in vain. I knew that. I was not sure what I'd do, but it was strangely calming to know somehow, the future was not mine to control. Paradoxically, I realized that as I let go of all the issues and events of life over which I had no control, I was able to regain control of me.

Many of us are obsessed with influencing and controlling people and circumstances over which we are really powerless. We can only control our beliefs, taking responsibility for ourselves and our own actions. This is fundamental in the process of "letting go."

So part of me was changing. What was occurring around me was something I could not control. I didn't even care. These people were making promises of support and concern, but their care and concern was really only for themselves. Their lives represented a conscript of money void of values, beliefs or faith. My winter solitude was before me, the autumn of my life was shedding past events. Closure for the very first time in my life was occurring. I liked that.

Needing a change of scenery, I decided to take a trip, a "last hurrah" of sorts. I left Buffalo the first week of December 1994, and headed for Las Vegas. Mom was worried. Would I be back? My attorney knew where I'd be, "The Flamingo Hilton," home of Bugsy Segal, credited with the birth of this city, which knows only one speed...fast! Gambling, drinking, it was a last escape. Never intending to run, I was screaming to be left alone. I was tired of people, of home (what was left of it), the questions, my approaching incarceration. My friends didn't know my intentions for this trip. I certainly didn't either at the time. But there in Las Vegas, something happened to me. Life would never be the same again.

During my stay, walking, thinking, simply being aware of the value of life, I realized that I was not going to run anymore. No...I was confronting my demons. One-by-one I would begin to take back control of my life. Sitting on a park bench watching life happen around me, allowed me for the first time, a chance to step out of the picture and see things from a different vantage point. Life was different that day and would be different from that day forward.

Most significantly, I remember my last drink. That moment alone, setting that drink down on the bar and, of my own free will, walking away, I was overwhelmed with a feeling of awe. It was a sense of "power," a new awareness of life that I could control me. No matter what decisions other people made, I had the power to challenge my beliefs and take responsibility for my life from this day forward.

Returning to Buffalo from Las Vegas allowed me time of reflection. My new determination and self-awareness inspired and strengthened me during the next three weeks through the ordeal of saying, "good by." It was closure of the most important kind, closure of the past…a marker point, the cycle of a futile life script coming to an end.

I believe today that I went to Las Vegas to mourn Terry, to grieve and bid farewell to all that I had been, and all that never would be. A way of life was being laid to rest.

I remember Angelo inviting me to a "going away" gathering. The memory still remains vivid. Between Christmas and New Years we went out to our old restaurant establishments. Angelo left the bar with a glass in his hand full of gin, and attempted to open his car door on the driver's side. He sat the full drink glass down on his BMW 730i console and proceeded to start the car. I asked him what he was doing? To him this was acceptable behavior. He was in his comfort zone, unchallenged, without boundaries. I could no longer be a participant. I left Angelo's car immediately. He was dumbfounded and angry. His moral integrity had been challenged and he didn't like it. I didn't care what he felt or thought. Obviously I knew the consequences. Angelo knew as well, yet his life script had taught him to ignore the consequences. He viewed such circumstances as fate, luck, chance, events of life beyond our control. Oh, how wrong he was. As his life evolved, during 1996, Angelo came face to face with the reality of the consequences of his choices. He would be judged accountable.

The day after our "going away" party, Angelo met me at the MetLife office and asked me how I got home, as if that was the important issue. Transfer the pain, avoid, ignore the issue, push on, and hurt more people. I saw in him so much of the old Terry, the person whose existence I had just begun to acknowledge. Change is painful, as I've so often said. Yet enduring whatever is necessary to bring about positive change, yields rewards that will last a lifetime and beyond. Through this single event, I realized that I was going to be okay with Terry.

Between Christmas and New Years was a very trying time for me. The holidays weren't the same. I felt so lonely. I thought of the Browns. Their holidays and life's activities would never be the same. I grieved for them. I live with this memory as a daily reminder of all that was so wrong and as testament of change that began within me.

Sentencing day, January 6, 1995, was approaching. The phone became my worst enemy. Work colleagues, friends, relatives called to lend support, asking, "Are you okay?" What could I say? I knew they meant well, but it pretty much didn't matter if I was or wasn't okay. The system is not designed to consider my emotional well being. Some people were genuinely concerned about me. Others, whose conversations revolved around their own fears, knowing my fate was a possibility in their own future, exhausted me emotionally. I never mourned the loss of my freedom yet through this process I was grieving many issues. I wasn't prepared to deal with them all, at least not yet. In a strange almost captivating, alluring way, I wanted to go back to the world I was about to leave. I knew I couldn't, yet the pain of not knowing where I was headed left me unsettled and anxious. So many issues were bombarding me...business, personal, family, and of course, concern over all that was involved in paying my debt to society.

As I've studied grieving, mourning alcoholism, what remains a recurring theme, especially for me, is that the loss of one's life script is powerful in deed. The alcoholic will always retain a craving for alcohol but he or she can shed behavior, change a life script and mourn the loss of all they are leaving behind, all the while completing the necessary process of closure.

So often we tend to try to speed the process along, unnaturally. We resolve that we are strong, focused, dealing with these issues of life. Well, although I was demonstrating to those around me that I fit the script, the part that they wanted me to play, inside I was hurting. Hurting for what I was responsible for doing in my life, yet somewhere from deep within knew that there had to be meaning for all that occurred.

The day before sentencing my brother Rick and his wife Sue came to be with me. Angelo stopped by. Angelo promised over and over that he would do everything he could to make sure what I did at MetLife was protected. He promised to visit me and anytime I needed something, to just let him know. Sounded good. But Angelo's promises were broken the moment he made them. He had no intention of following through.

Jack also came to visit. I really wanted to be alone.   I was apprehensive, uncertain, depressed. I looked forward to peace and serenity. What would life be like? Could I return to Buffalo? Would I want to?

The morning of the sentencing brought me face to face with yet another harsh reality of the self-serving agenda of my so-called support system.   I'd received a call from Frankie setting 8:30 a.m. as the time to meet at his office prior to the 10:00 a.m. court time. Frankie insisted that Joe needed to receive another $2,500 in order to represent me in court. I was insulted. Frankie stated, "Well, Joe got you out for the holidays. At least pay for his service. It's the least you can do."

The cycle of my life script came to a screeching halt. "No! No! No!" Frankie said, "Then you'll have to go by yourself."

 What a time to abandon me. Not knowing the criminal justice system I was afraid that I needed representation. What should I do? This attorney who long ago distanced himself from my association now inflicts legal lawyer privilege. Do I have any recourse?

I asked Elise what my account balance was and she became incensed that I'd ask for money. But it was my money! What was she doing? Her response was, "You have no money. It's mine. That's that!"   I couldn't believe it! The day before sentencing!

I had a battle brewing on two fronts. Elise and her broken promises, and an attorney who thought, "I've got him! He has no choice." Yet I realized I did have a choice. And I decided to exercise that choice.

That afternoon I went to Frankie's office, irate. I met with Joe and we argued. He was so proud of his work, my pending sentence. He wanted his reward…more money. But why did he wait timing his request to the very bitter end? What I didn't know of the criminal justice system is, that at this point, I didn't need Joe. Yet I was still vacillating. I thought Joe represented my pending release.

On January 6, 1995, Rick and Sue drove me to Frankie's office. Meeting Frankie at 8:30 a.m., I gave him $500. That was that. There would be no more. Frankie spoke to Rick and Sue making sure they understood what was about to take place. Terry was being sentenced today, accepting societal judgment, being removed from society per the rules long ago established. Rick asked Frankie to review his understanding of the plea agreement. Frankie minimized the time frame of my pending imprisonment. Terry will be sentenced to a two-year minimum term to a maximum term of six years. "Don't worry about the sentence. No one with a nonviolent crime ever does the full sentence in New York State. In fact the prisons are so overcrowded that well, guys like Terry never convicted before, no criminal history, heck they don't want to keep him. Terry qualifies for an early release program anyway. After being upstate six months he's eligible. So best case he comes home in July, worst case November 1995."

I was half-heartedly listening. But I was listening. I was hearing. You'll be home later this year. I wanted desperately to believe this, to hold on.

Driving to court I looked around Buffalo, my comfort zone. Looking up at the Marine Midland Center I knew Jane was there, yet I was so ashamed. Closure was nearer than I knew then. Arriving at the courthouse reality settled in. The courtroom was full of friends, relatives, representatives of Mother's Against Drunk Drivers, Jeff Brown's parents, and, of course, the media. Frankie informed me he didn't want me to speak during sentencing. He would handle that.

Uncertain as to the future, yet at peace with acceptance, a new life had begun. The Judge acknowledged that the court appreciated the plea arrangement, saving the emotional exposure of two families.

Mr. Brown addressed me and Jeff's sister read a poem. The madman, demon stood before the family, guilty. Sentence him, place judgment upon his soul. Make him feel the pain.

I listened intently to the Judge, willingly remembering her words. I also listened to Mr. Brown. The ultimate price had been paid.

As I left the courtroom, hand cuffed, the media surrounded me. The one question that I will never forget was asked by a veteran news reporter Rich Kellman, WIVB, channel Four, "Mr. King how do you feel right now?" The other questions seemed insignificant. I was not angry at the question, I was angry at the insensitivity to the feelings of the family. I was hurting for the Browns. Perhaps Mr. Kellman expected a dramatic display of emotion, a stage show or a rehearsed apology. What could I possibly say or do at that moment that wouldn't be viewed as manipulation for public support or empathy? Nothing! Later I learned that Mr. and Mrs. Brown did expect some form of communication from me. But I am fortunate that I didn't say anything at that time. I was not prepared.

The evening news included a statement of life events in America today. A message was sent to those willing to listen. "Drinking and driving" does kill. Drinking and driving is a choice. We are responsible and most importantly we are accountable to our God, ourselves and to all of humanity. This day, this moment, I was held accountable and most assuredly had begun to confront my demons.

Many men and women have written numerous stories about prison, and all the human degradation that accompanies one's term of incarceration. (As I was to discover first-hand, they are not exaggerated). But, reflecting back to this day, leaving the courtroom, saying good-by to my brother, Rick, I remember my feelings vividly. It wasn't a feeling of sadness or fear, as you would suppose, but a new awareness of "me," a new beginning. Prison meant a refuge from all that was wrong. In a sense, I was grateful to be getting away from all the madness I had caused. I knew that something profound was missing from my life and up to now I had not been able to find it. Amid all the chaos, I was beginning to realize that there was a God, and He was somehow trying to get through to me.

Redeeming Grace

"There is a time for everything, and a season for every activity under heaven... time to search and a time to give up, a time to keep and a time to throw away, a time to tear and a time to mend, a time to be silent...." *(Ecclesiastes 3:6-7).*

~ Behind The Wall~

Chapter Nineteen

Believing that I'd be home in a few short months, I told myself, "This won't be too bad. You can do this! Strength! Remember Baba!" She believed in herself and held on to her faith and values, traveling alone in an unknown world. I decided right then, I would survive in this unknown world, among those whose society, up until today, was foreign to my own.

So there I was, wearing a suit, handcuffed, sitting from 12 o'clock to about 3:00 p.m. in a court holding cell awaiting my fate. Coincidentally, another man, Pat, also in suit and tie, was sentenced at the exact time in the same court area. I looked around at the other occupants of the holding cell, rapping, singing, speaking street lingo. My life, as I had known it, had changed. Would it be for the better or for worse? The choice was mine.

Many of my life choices were taken away from me. For the next several years, the State of New York would decide for me where and when I would sleep, on what and in what I would sleep. The State would also decide what foods I would eat, and the length of time I would have to eat it. My wardrobe as well, socks, underwear, shirts, pants, shoes and a jacket, were chosen for me. All of the basic requirements of life would be provided.

Dr. Abraham Maslow, an existentialist, believed that if man's basic needs are met, such as food, clothing, shelter, he is then freed to focus his objectives to seek self-actualization…to be the best he can be, rationally. Without having to concern ourselves with basic necessities, we refocus our attention in a step-by-step process, culminating in continued personal growth in community and social environment. Well, the State was meeting my needs, at least physically. But an equal component to this equation requires us to have our psychological needs met as well. Psychological needs address our spiritual, emotional and mental stability.

With my physical needs met I was focusing my energy but not in the most positive way. Yes, change internally had already begun. I was clearly accepting responsibility for the crash resulting in the death of Jeff Brown. But I was still remaining in the "old Terry" state, attempting to deny feelings, ignore problems and half-heartedly assume responsibility for occurrences in my life. I was not yet confronting all of my demons of the past and present. Unless these demons are identified, removed or understood, accepting responsibility for my present period of incarceration would mean absolutely nothing.

But January 6, 1995 I saw none of this. Life is about, "Okay, it happened. I accept that so let's move on." My lawyers had promised me work release in September. This time too shall pass. And pass it did with out work release, any release for that matter. But it proved to be very valuable time in deed.

I have often read and heard from men imprisoned that this time can be man's most valuable time. It's true, provided the time is invested wisely, within one's sphere of needs. I wasn't sure what my needs were. I was still attempting to control. But attempting to control from within the walls of confinement simply doesn't work unless of course you're John Gotti. But then again look at the consequences of his behavior simply for the right of power to control from within. I have since learned that "letting go" is power. In fact by letting go you slowly begin to take back control. But on this day I was still trying to hold on to whatever thread of comfort I could. The unknown future was scary, full of uncertainties.

Yet a part of me, a part often hidden, felt an inner peace, a divine feeling of gratitude to be segregated from the influences and reminders of all that was so very wrong with my life.

That very first day segregated from my problems was most interesting. Having spent the major part of the day in a holding cell waiting for my needs to be met, I was rewarded approximately 4:00 p.m. with a shower and an official orange outfit, rather like a surgical shirt and pants.

I received a mattress, toothbrush and instructed to enter a 15' x 15' court holding cell. I was told find a place to set my mattress. Pat followed me having shed his suit and personal identity. We were twenty men, inches apart, one sink, no cups, one toilet and no curtain. The toilet was for all to share. Pat was in shock and visibly upset. I resigned myself to find a spot and take a nap. There was nothing I could do. Dinner arrived, two sausages. I watched a man wrap them in toilet paper light them and burn them. Barbequed, I guess.

Things were changing and I was very well aware. I was the lead story on the evening news that night. For the next several hours I was called, "a movie star," shaking hands all around. How very sad. These men who surrounded me actually viewed this as a jailhouse accomplishment.

Confronted with possibly of spending a weekend or a week in these deplorable conditions, I was elated when at 7:30 p.m. a deputy entered the room and called the names of seven men. Pat's name was called sixth, I was number seven. I picked up my possessions (a mattress and a toothbrush), and followed the deputy. Seven lucky men were moved to a day room. My journey to confront my demons had begun in earnest.

The Delta dorm housed 40 men. The day room double-bunked sixteen men with one private toilet. Pat was my neighbor. At least my basic needs were met: cards, a television, three meals a day and a telephone. There was no one to call just yet. As the month of January passed into February I became comfortable with the daily routine. I met many men, some I'd see again three years later. Dick and Jim were from Buffalo. For Dick, prison was a recurring theme of life. Released, return, released, return. No change other then his prison address.

Pat was a clinging vine. Sentenced to a one-and one-third years to four-year term, he continually lied about his crime to protect his true identity. I would later learn the true nature of his crime. He had reason to be afraid.

In mid February I called Angelo. My anticipated financial arrangements were imploding. I'm not sure exactly what happened. It doesn't matter now, but at the time it meant real frustration…things were beyond my control. Once I let go, honestly and truthfully, it didn't matter at all. Closure will occur as a blessing.

Those who promised to come never came. The events that unfolded remain as testament to all that was so very wrong. Angelo's idea of Elise taking over the school contract backfired. Jack attempted to subterfuge the deal. Angelo called in family favors in order to protect the union arrangements of support. Elise demanded her own deal, which would eliminate the Judge, and me. Angelo promised, "Terry I'll get this back together, you have my word."

Interestingly, the one person I turned to, to help me hold on to the life I knew was, in fact, making a promise he could never fulfill. Angelo, the consummate dealmaker was busy making his deal, which didn't include anyone but Angelo.

Later on I was told that Angelo left Buffalo rather abruptly. Judgment day was unfolding only he didn't know it just yet. During the early part of spring Angelo announced to the staff that he decided to accept a transfer to take over a profitable sales office in Las Vegas. What he didn't tell his staff was that this was effective immediately and he was taking his secretary with him. He sold Brant, took the money (even my money) and ran. More promises broken.

The school contract was open game. I am not sure what happened but everything fell apart sometime in mid-spring. MetLife stepped in, and after auditing all the activity, closed the office. It was easier to place closure than to pick up the pieces. It was a lesson for me as well.

At the time I was angry. I felt abused, but I had to let it go. I must put that chapter of my life behind me. It wasn't long after that I learned Jack lost the school contract, and the Judge was under a formal FBI investigation into alleged loan fraud. I was experiencing a sense of peace unlike anything I'd known.

Each day, Dick, Jim, Pat and I waited patiently, to be transferred to state prison. From my window I could see the world I once knew. I was no longer a part of that world, or was I? Part of me wanted to be. I determined that while I had this unique time apart, I would discover why that world held such attraction for me, and what needed to be changed in me to set me free from its addiction before it was too late.

February 22,1995, at 4:30 a.m., I was informed that I was being transferred to Wende State Prison, a maximum-security prison.

Pat (my extra possession) was coming along. That day was most interesting. We were taken by mini van to Wende, arriving at 11:00 a.m.

We filled out questionnaires, shed our personal clothes, showered, and had our heads shaved. We were issued a pair of pants, shirt, shoes and a jacket. The rest of our clothing needs would follow. The State will provide. We found ourselves in a cellblock tier area. Pat was in cell seven, and I was in cell twenty-seven. I was escorted to the cell at 4:00 p.m.

My first of many profound jailhouse experiences occurred within a half hour of being in my new home. Dinner was served at 4:30 p.m. As I was eating my first official prison meal, an Hispanic inmate in the next cell was screaming, completely out of balance. He was throwing urine and feces all over the walkway outside his cell. The Correction Officer came and beat him repeatedly.

Soon after, I smelled something burning and noticed quite a bit of smoke coming from a cell across the walkway. As I looked into the reflection of the metal heater register directly opposite our cell, I realized the cell was on fire. Not just the cell, but the inmate inside had ignited himself. I'll never forget that gut-wrenching stench. He had wrapped himself in toilet tissue, doused himself in baby oil and deodorant and set himself on fire. The fire, the horrible spectacle, the agonizing screams…life was changing very quickly. The alarm sounded and the officers arrived in complete riot gear. It seemed to me that they just stood there watching as the man screamed in agony. Finally they extinguished the fire…using high-pressure hoses. Dinner set aside, we were taken to the yard. I watched in horror as this man, half dead, with his skin melted away, was hung naked from a wooden pole placed across his burned back, under his arms, with his wrists and ankles chained together behind him, and carried to the infirmary. Welcome to a maximum-security prison.

I'm now number 95B0273. The State simply declares that Terry King who was, does not exist. He is now state property. Up at 5 a.m., recreation, exercise one hour, locked down next 23 hours. We were allowed one shower in 3 maybe 4 days. Some men lose their self-respect in these conditions. They stop caring for their personal hygiene. Life has lost its value anyway. I refused to let that happen to me. I shaved, cleaned, maintained Terry. Even though I was temporarily restricted to a cell 6' x 8' I refused to allow my mind and soul to be imprisoned. I was starting to understand. My basic needs were met. I was finally willing to take care, address, nurture my most basic human psychological needs. I acquired, simply by asking (not paying or promising) a wide assortment of reading material. I developed a schedule of exercise performing 500 sets some days, 1,000 other days in my cell. Exercising, writing, reading, thinking, analyzing, pondering, this was, in fact, becoming very valuable time.

Pat was struggling three days after arriving. Early one morning, approximately three o'clock, six to seven corrections officers visited our cellblock tier. Waking everyone up, turning on the lights these men confronted Pat in his cell. Pat later defended himself explaining that one of the Corrections Officers, the instigator, was a high school acquaintance who simply did not like him. The CO's challenged Pat to leave his cell, screaming at him that he was the Amherst, New York panty sniffer. I did not understand. Pat said he robbed an apartment. Who was this man? The CO's seemed to really know. What did they mean? A rapist...stalker...peeping Tom? As time proves out Pat's hidden past was revealed. Someone discovered his true identity from newspaper clippings. I learned we simply cannot hide from the truth. Pat lied. The men, some lifers, have their own moral code. They simply would not accept his answer. I tried to help him but he continued to lie. His life was only about him. He wanted out, he needed out. This time to him was meaningless.

Although at the time I believed I would be home by fall, this time most definitively had meaning. I listened and learned to do what I was told.

I spoke to the man (or as I learned, child) that was placed in the cell next to me. He was only 17, just one year older than my son Josh. He was sentenced as an adult for 5 to 15 years. How could this happen?

Thirty men were housed on this tier. Two weeks later, March 5, the names of 26 men were called. They were to be transferred to Elmira Correctional Facility reception center to be stamped, marked, evaluated and classified. My name was not called. Later that day I discovered that Pat was left behind as well. The next day the school bus left, then the final four names were called. Terry and Pat were destined to be together again. Now I was getting concerned. It was as if this man had been sentenced or shall I say perhaps I had been sentenced to accompany him. But his antics were humorous. He provided plenty of entertainment.

The next morning, handcuffed, shackled and placed on a bus, we were driven to Elmira, New York, another maximum-security prison. This was the real place about which stories and movies have been written and recorded. I know today what is meant by the expression "behind the wall."

The imposing foreboding structure was built in the 1800's, a stoic, monstrous edifice adorned by the statue of a giant warrior guarding the entrance.

Processing through Elmira reception, I was assigned to "A" block, third floor tier, cell number 12. Well, guess who was assigned cell number 11? Pat and I were side by side. Pat's difficulties again followed him to Elmira.

Josh and Justin were writing regularly. Actually Josh developed a game of tic-tac-toe by mail. I looked forward to mail call. A phone call was still several days away. I was quickly becoming very much aware of the dangers to human life and dignity that pervade this institution. Many were doing terms of incarceration exceeding 300 years without ever a chance of parole or release, "behind the wall." The wall is an intimidating forty feet high. It was as if life did not exist beyond the wall. Here was a world of souls, with its own rules, boundaries and ideologies. Each man had secrets to be kept. They had their own system of justice and retribution, a law unto themselves. During my sojourn at various prisons I witnessed (or was at least painfully aware of) stabbings, mutilations, beatings, rape. One man, retaliating against another, used a metal weightlifting bar to smash open the head of his victim. He literally split his skull in two pieces. I was standing six feet away. Only the grace of God guarded me and kept me safe.

The second day in Elmira I was employed in the school as a teacher's aide. It was my job to present vocational assessment tests, to determine reading and writing level skills. I enjoyed the job. The third day, I was informed by the civilian counselor that she hired Pat to work with me. Enough already!

I truly enjoyed working 8:00 to 11:00 every morning then returning afternoons 12:30 to 3:30 p.m. The days passed quickly. My evenings were spent reading, writing and, of course, exercising. Approximately Day 6 brought a move to "B" block, the general reception tier blocks once again. I was moved to "F" block cell 16. Pat was placed in 18. Pat declares, "Well, it looks like were doing this together!" (Oh, I hope not!)

March 20, I was informed that I was scheduled for a transfer. "Pack up and go to draft." Pat was really upset. He had found a comfort zone. Actually he was informed that he was being transferred to "C" block in Elmira, general population. Could he survive? His secret was now his own. The inmate lifers would not appreciate Pat's secret. He was scared. The next day I was placed on a large bus similar to a tourist bus. Ten hours later I arrived at my destination, Cayuga Correctional Facility, Moravia, New York, a medium security facility. Two fences, no wall, open dormitories, I was grateful. Sitting alone waiting to be cleared to enter the facility, I was praying a prayer of thankfulness.

That evening I found myself in "C" dorm, top bunk 27. We were seventy men, one dorm, three phones, two TVs, a dangerous place. Yet, alone, that evening I met numerous people who offered assistance. I learned early on, "borrow nothing, ask for nothing." If I do not have, I do not need, or the state will provide.

I liked Cayuga, perhaps the openness, the weights, a track, my work, a place to work on one's soul. Change was occurring in me. Peace was coming slowly but definitely.

The third day at Cayuga I was a participant in a Pre-Release Orientation class. Pre-Release is an inmate run organization designed to help men confront their issues and learn how to invest their time wisely. It assists them in preparing for parole, job placement and their return home, a community plan.

The next day counselor Cheryl Lee, hired me as a facilitator in training. I was now working, signed into a program sponsored by the New York State Department of Labor. I became a counseling aide. It was a 2000-hour program. The counselor at Cayuga would assist me in my quest to be approved for work release, but first I would have to complete a six-month alcohol and drug addiction treatment program called A.S.A.T.

Unfortunately, the waiting list to get into the program was over one year. This was devastating news, but there was nothing I could do. I'd have to get busy. The Pre-Release inmate staff welcomed me. I owe a debt of gratitude to men who became my friends: Byron Austin our inmate Coordinator (who had already served 18 year), Rolando Rodriques (5 years), Henry Rivera (20 years), and Leslie Jimenez. They were committed to others in need, heart and soul. This impacted me profoundly. Their advice and discernment helped me mentally and spiritually.

I was at Cayuga now approximately two weeks, when walking to the mess hall for lunch, I heard a most familiar voice behind me. Couldn't be.

No way. I turned to look. Sure enough… it was Pat. He had been transferred to Cayuga. Some cycles of life just don't seem to ever come to an end. So here we were together. (Why me?) I would try to help him, but deep down inside I knew that first he'd have to help himself. It was time to grow up, shed the past self-centered old ways.

~ He Who the Son Sets Free ~

Chapter Twenty

Teaching the lifestyles Pre-Release classes afforded me an opportunity to express my inner most feelings each and everyday to other men in need. I was a salesman who had found a new career counseling. By studying the module material, preparing class research, listening to my elders about life and prison, change was occurring. I was growing ever so slowly and a new Terry was emerging. I was finding new purpose for my life. I was confronting my demons each day, yet still holding on, believing that I just might return to Buffalo as a life insurance agent. I am a salesman. But the gift I will experience that actually began at Cayuga was a kind of sublimation. I was learning how to take my learned behavior and talents, and redirect that energy in behavior more socially and morally acceptable, effecting very different consequences.

Yes, I could sell. Yes, I had empathy. But a good counselor primarily needs to listen. Listen to what's not said as well as what is. That's a process, I had just begun to practice. Learning to listen, I began to hear subtle comments around the compound, affirming that men could come to me for help, comfort and guidance. I was trusted. The greatest reward was when individuals would approach me, shake my hand or offer a word of appreciation after class. Something was at work here. I was feeling at peace with myself. For the present, "Time" became my best friend.

Meeting my Correctional Counselor in April of 1995 was an opportunity not only to confront my demons but also to begin a new life script, this time, reality driven.

I had heard, although I didn't want to listen, that work release for vehicular manslaughter cases was no longer available. I learned that my conviction, by plea agreement to vehicular manslaughter 2nd degree, was no longer legally eligible for participation in work release or any form of temporary release. Prior to leaving office, Governor Cuomo signed a state statute eliminating certain crimes from this special program. My attorneys must have known about this prior to presenting it to me. They had lied to me. I tried contacting them but they refused to accept my calls. They ignored my letters, never responding to even one letter to answer my questions. I felt used, set up, abandoned. I needed to come to terms with this. Mom was upset, Rick was confused, the boys simply didn't understand. As I wrote to Governor Pataki, the facility superintendent, Work Release, whomever, I eventually accepted the fact that I would not qualify. So now what? When will I go home? When would I be eligible for parole? November of 1996? Possibly. In the meantime, what do I do? The audit. How will I invest my time?

The administration building for Pre-release was located next to the library. The law library was an interesting place, in some ways similar to a church. Men went there seeking a new life or at least the hope of a shot at one! The difference was that in the law library their hopes were pinned to the choices of man, and the truth of justice or the manipulation of the judicial system. The church, however, is a place where men seek God Who is able to give them a new life far beyond anything they could hope or dream.

But here I was, struggling to hold on to my life, seeking guidance, as I attempted to confront my lawyer, others, and anyone who may have been able to help. George, the law clerk, was always willing to help me. At night we would walk and talk together. Wherever George walked, he always carried his Bible. I observed and was intrigued by his calm, serenity and his smile. He was at peace. He actually beamed…like a lighthouse, a Beacon of Hope. What an inspiration!

As we walked in the yard, men of all backgrounds would come up to him simply to say hello, seek help, a handshake, even a friendly hug. Thugs, drug dealers, mean men and even nice guys seemed to seek out George. He possessed the serenity that I had longed for and had the light from within that I'd often seen in Ellen but shunned for fear of change.

In 1986, Ellen and Bob had their boat docked next to mine and she would witness to me and ask to pray. Hearing her speak of the Lord, I would listen, see the joy in her face and wonder if I could have the same. She would confront my behavior and challenge me to welcome Christ into my life. But then, I was not ready to leave my comfort zone. I would stand aside and continue to flaunt my behavior at her.

In the prison yard I didn't have my old comfort zone and I was aware that change was necessary. I wasn't quite sure how or when but I knew change was near.

During this time George would listen to me moan and groan and moan and groan. Finally, one day George was done listening! He said "Terry Stop!" Perhaps for the first time in my life, stop meant stop. He said he was tired of my moaning and groaning. He shared that, though he had been incarcerated for 47 years, he was free. The Lord had set him free. He told me to go and read the book of John in the New Testament. Then he told me to begin taking inventory of my life and ask myself why God had blessed me to place me here and keep me safe! He said God has a plan for each of us when we seek Him and surrender to Him and let Him lead. We have to learn to walk by faith. I'm not sure I was ready for all this just yet, but I liked the way he addressed me, firm yet loving. It felt good. He was serious and I knew he meant what he said. I was grateful and took heed. The next day a dorm mate of mine was transferred and left his Bible for me. I still have it today!

I will always remember the night of July 11, 1995, for this night I met God. It was approximately 9:30 p.m. on a beautiful summer night. The sky was clear...magnificent with thousands upon thousands of stars. I was overwhelmed with emotion, realizing the life I once led was over. No more negotiating. Done! I began to weep and shake, crying tears of sorrow, yet, at the same time, tears of joy. As I cried, I fell to my knees looking toward heaven. At that very moment God was right beside me. I felt His presence embracing me, enveloped in a pure, white brightness. It was something I had never experienced before. I surrendered my life to Jesus. Something within me was set free, and I prayed in a language foreign to me. I learned later that this was the baptism of the Holy Spirit. He was cleansing and comforting and somehow I seemed to know exactly what God wanted me to hear. I knew because I knew because I knew that if I died that very moment or from that time on I was going to be with our Lord. I knew that my sins had been forgiven and that I belonged to Him. I did not know what my life would be like. I did not care. I knew that I was forgiven and that I was able to forgave myself. I also accepted that others may never forgive me, but I was called out to walk with our Lord and from that moment on I was His.

I remember walking back to the dorm and having the peace and serenity that I had longed for. That evening I began to read the Bible for the first time, I think, ever in my life. The first book was the Gospel of John. I was moved to tears. I read John 8: 36 *"So if the Son sets you free, you will be free indeed."* Oh, the myriad of emotions, the release and freedom of that experience. I knew that something neat was occurring here. This is why this scripture is so important to me. It's personal and passionate for freedom and deliverance. How wondrous that the very next morning I awoke and had such peace and contentment, a feeling that I longed for and a life reborn that I had never known.

As I progressed in my newfound faith, I was eager to seek the Lord and study. Initially I was not into worship. That was foreign to me and I was mechanical in my biblical research. I had to read everything I could regarding scripture and biblical studies. I eagerly attended Bible studies and began to study the teachings of Christ. I was so touched by the written word of God. As I read each day, I often would think, "Boy, this was written just for me. Wow! This story is all about the old me." Amazing! God provided the text and Jesus came just to save me. I began to diligently study and root myself in the ways of God.

As I began to share with other Christian men in the dorms and express my love of Christ, other miracles occurred. The prison administrators allowed me to address large groups of men regarding salvation and change of behavior. In pre-release I could not refer to God nor pray, yet as I taught, it was clear in my presentations about Whom I spoke.

As the months progressed, an interesting transformation began to occur. That which I had witnessed happening with George was now happening to me. Men were now coming up to me and asking for advice, questions about relationships and about God. I remember clearly that people I met would often comment, "There is something different about you."

Men would say "Terry you always have this peace and serenity about you. What is it?" George would often be asked that question and he would respond, "Let me tell you about Jesus." Well, now I was responding, "Let me tell you about a guy named Jesus." Even the Muslims, Five per-centers, Long House believers, would seek me out for advice and ask me to pray for them or others. Wow. My life had come full circle as I was beginning to take steps in my life as a believer in Jesus Christ. I was in awe of God's mercy and through this journey I loved to testify of His marvelous saving grace. Prayer was now becoming a vital part of my day and my life. I found myself arising at 5:00 a.m. to pray. Even today I arise early to seek our Lord and rest in His love and guidance.

As the madness and chaos of the prison world continued around me I now had a peace and was entering into fellowship with other Christian men and counselors. It seemed everywhere I turned someone was supporting my Christian walk. At each facility I was housed in, the Lord arranged for Christians to either work with me, be my roommates or be near. It was amazing if not miraculous how He orchestrated these Divine interventions.

I was included in groups and the church community yet even in times of aloneness I realized that I was not alone. God was on my side! And...He was making a way! The song I sing today, "God Can Make a Way," is so true. He can! But first we have a choice to make...to seek Him and then surrender to him.

"If...you seek the LORD your God, you will find Him if you look for Him with all your heart and with all your soul" (Deuteronomy 4:24). *"...Seek Him and reach out for Him and find Him, ...He is not far from each one of us"* (Acts 17:27).

~ New Beginnings ~

Chapter Twenty-one

Throughout our lives we search for its meaning. It seems a rather simple process, birth to death. Perhaps we complicate the process just a bit along the way. As we go through the motions, we work, we love, we learn, we teach, and often we stumble. But that which we leave behind, our legacy of life, will last for all eternity. Our faith, and the choices we make, based on our values, all become part of who we are today and that which we will leave tomorrow. How we will be remembered? How will our legacy impact future generations? It's an awesome responsibility.

My prayer is that as you have read this text, and reflected upon your own life, you have gained an awareness of who you are. No matter what your influences or life choices have been to this point, I think we can now agree that with God's help, change is possible.

Isn't it interesting that when we were young and full of questions about life we were told, "Go ask your grandfather, or grandmother," or an elder statesman. Why? Because, experience is a valuable teacher. We are fortunate if we have older people in our lives who love us enough to teach us what they have learned. They have lived through the progressions of life's seasons and perhaps, upon reflection, can see more clearly that which really is important in life. Perhaps they will share with us mistakes they have made along the way, and the long-range consequences of misplaced priorities. Life is precious. How wonderful if we can learn from someone else's mistakes and not have to experience everything the hard way. And also, when we take the time to listen, we are giving their lives value and significance.

When a son, or daughter, lover, partner, or even a stranger takes the time to thank you for helping, guiding, supporting or loving them, take heart. These are the blessings that give our lives purpose.

My alcoholism was my medication, an escape for all that I did not want to deal with...my comfort zone. The fact is, as I've come to realize, I did have the strength to deal with life issues on its own terms once I was willing to be honest with myself. For me, the very sad reality is that it required this tragic event in order for me to come to terms with myself and accept who I had become.

The summer of 1995 brought about an awareness and a peace I had never known since my early childhood. Having surrendered my life to God, I saw life in a brand new way filled with hope for the future. I knew God was working in all areas of my life. I am at peace today with my past. My search for purpose in life wasn't over during this summer of 1995, it was just beginning.

Alcoholics Anonymous has become a way of life. Adopting the twelve steps of AA has not only provided me with the inspiration to stop drinking, but the process has provided me with the tenants step-by-step to find this inner love of my self. No, it wasn't easy. Perhaps it shouldn't be. If it were easy the rewards would not be so appreciated.

During this time I was moved to a new A.S.A.T. dorm (Alcohol, Substance Abuse Treatment.) The dorm is segregated for a six-month alcohol and substance abuse treatment program. Ninety men met three hours every day. The intent of the program was excellent, and the counselors were committed, but the structure was an abhorrent procedure. Over an hour would be spent just trying to take attendance. There would be fights, stabbings, thefts, drugs, normal prison activity. Only a handful of inmates knew why we were there. Tod and I were together again, searching for sobriety, for meaning, committed to change.

Mr. Earl Merritt, the A.S.A.T. Director, took me under his wing. Two weeks into the program he called me into his office and we talked. We prayed together and he spoke as if not from himself but from God. The prophetic words were that "a life would be put to death and a new life would be born." At the time I thought this related to the death of Jeff Brown. But he was speaking of me. It was I, the old Terry King, who was being put to death. *"I have been crucified with Christ and I no longer live, but Christ lives in me. The life I live in the body, I live by faith in the Son of God, who loved me and gave Himself for me"* (Galatians 2:20).

My old way of life was over. My new life in Christ was just beginning. The habits and patterns of a lifetime don't die easily. I needed help. Throughout my prison experience, God placed Christians in my life to help me grow and develop in my newfound faith…people like Mr. Merritt.

Having served 17 years in prison, he understood reality, knew addiction, and could recognize sincerity. We would talk for hours. He knew I wanted sobriety, I just didn't know how. So step-by- step, he guided and nurtured me on my journey. He encouraged me to trust God, believe in myself and to not fear the future. With all my heart I thank God for Mr. Merritt. I owe him a debt of gratitude. I do hope we meet again.

As I progressed through A.S.A.T., Mr. Merritt began to allow me freedom to present workshops. Eventually I was facilitating the workshops each day for weeks at a time. Mr. Merritt asked me if I would be willing to make a commitment, upon my release, to return to Cayuga, to speak, or just to listen, and perhaps guide others who might need a just simple intervention in their lives. I said I was willing.

An issue that continually plagued me was the way I had walked away from my relationship with Jane. I felt I needed to reach out to her. She had been a wonderful friend to me. I had allowed myself to believe that the reason I avoided her was to protect her. I knew that the past required closure, but Jane deserved an honest explanation. I owed her that. Having committed my life to Christ, I wanted to make things right.

Over the course of the July 4th week of 1995, I began writing her a letter. I wrote it and rewrote it over several times. I sent the letter the first of August. I wanted the opportunity to meet, to explain. I prayed to my God for guidance, for the right words. I knew my behavior had hurt her.

When I wrote the letter I hoped that she'd write back, though I could understand if she didn't. Being honest with myself, I needed her forgiveness. I prayed for her understanding as well as her friendship. Correspondingly, I wrote to Jane's Mom, Rita. I needed to be honest. She had been my friend. Whether Jane wrote back or not I felt a sense of ownership of responsibility. Getting honest from within rewards us with the knowledge that we do have meaning in our life. I prayed for God's will!

Working out, programming, I became contented, even comfortable on a day-to-day basis. I was accepting that which I couldn't control. I was taking responsibility for me.

Mom, Carol, Rick, Aunt Margaret, Cheryl, Uncle Ed, and Aunt Helen, all came to visit. It was a time of renewal of family spirit. Issues that once may have caused strain between us were no longer important.

August turned to September. Each day I waited and waited for the mail. Concentrating on work, I was committed to completing the New York State Labor Department contract of 2000 hours of various kinds of instruction by year's end. This accomplishment was met as well as several others.

AIDS is very prevalent within the inmate population. I presented the health education material and actively assisted those in need of advocacy. Becoming a Certified AIDS Educator solidified my counseling foundation.

Rolando Rodriquez, director of Prison Group Ministries, assisted me each evening for many months, to become a facilitator/trainer of a program called Life Without Violence. Teaching, administering program needs and counseling were now a part of my life. Seeking me out, strangers seemed compelled to express their life's innermost secrets. Men were reaching out for help, strangers yet brothers. I was trusted. This virtue was most inspirational to the inner Terry that I was getting to know. God was really working a change in me and I liked it. My life had come full circle and I was beginning to walk the steps in my life with God as a believer in Jesus Christ.

I had surrendered myself to God, and that included all the talents and skills the old Terry used to use to manipulate my own agenda. I realized that all I have, all my abilities, my interests, my personality, everything, has been given to me by God, and that He had a plan in mind for me from the beginning.

"We are His workmanship created in Christ Jesus for good works, which God prepared beforehand, that we should walk in them" (Ephesians 2:10.)

Positive consequences were naturally evolving as my new life's script unfolded. I'd found a way of life helping others. Counselors, fellow inmates all encouraged me, supported my speaking, group work and counseling career.

It was fascinating to me to realize that the more I gave of me, the more I received back the greatest gifts in life…peace, a deep inner joy and a purpose in life that I had never known before. All of my striving to acquire never brought me the satisfaction that I received from giving. It was a simple tenet of life I was just beginning to learn. I was starting to listen.

The process of shedding the old ways was continuing. The difference was I was letting go, closing the past. Accepting the present and taking responsibility is the first of many steps I shall take on a daily basis.

I was still eagerly pursuing my release from prison. I was still unwilling to accept the idea that I might be incarcerated for longer than expected. I prayed that some way, upon completion of A.S.A.T. that something would break to allow my release. But this was not so simple.

My parole board was November 1996 and that seemed so far away. The older men, who had served the State of New York for upwards of 15, 20 years kept these thoughts in perspective. I was no different than anyone else. I was responsible for the taking of life. I'd better focus on me and the changes God was making, and use this time to turn my life around. For the probability existed that I might not make parole.

My Attorney assured me I'd make it. I had nothing to worry about. But He was not in control. God was. There were still a few things I had to let go.

My workout partners, Harry Bowles and Nate Packer, were supportive friends, encouraging and helping me deal with life. I had a lot of days like this. Working out became a therapy session (a routine that is still a part of my life.)

I realized, perhaps for the first time, that there were many men, literally thousands upon thousands who had stories, life situations far more confusing and problematic than my own. I knew that God loved each one of them, and could help them, if they would just call out to Him.

Summer ended and gave way to fall. One beautiful "Indian summer" day, mail call delivered a letter from Jane. She had written back! I was almost too nervous to open it. It had been so long.   Reading the letter brought tears of joy, pain, and sorrow. Not for myself, but for Jane. She chastised me, expressing all her anger and hurt. I deserved that, no doubt! The old Terry expected what? That everything would be all right? All is forgiven? Perhaps, but the new Terry prayed to God and asked Him for His guidance. I took time to reflect. For Jane to write back told me she was a friend in pain. I understood that this process of venting and grieving was necessary.

As I reflect upon my past, I had so often tried to manipulate and effect change in areas over which I had no control. Stress and anxiety would ensue. I would drink, medicate, and forge ahead, a vicious continuing life script. This script had changed. The cycle had stopped. I would write back, not to defend myself, but to help a friend. I did write honestly answering every question. Several days later she wrote back.

As fall evolved Jane came to visit. We talked. Jane was able to express her feelings and I was listening…really listening. I felt that our relationship had a chance to grow if we could be completely honest with each other. She wrote back about Thanksgiving time saying that she was willing to work things out. I was happy. But this time, I was not manipulating or forcing things to happen. I was simply being Terry, God's child, allowing His will to unfold in my life. Whatever His will, I would accept it.

I've come to believe through experience that men, God's creatures, all of His creation, have a meaning purpose for being. See, many of us travel through life living in a delusional reality, projecting, contracting with ourselves creating our own goals and boundaries, leaving God completely out of the equation. The mystery of life in its simplicity is not in the magnitude of what we accomplish, it's in recognizing God's purpose and meaning for our lives. *"For what is a man profited, if he shall gain the whole world, and lose his own soul? Or what shall a man give in exchange for his soul?"* (Matthew 16:26)

Cayuga imprisonment was the greatest gift of my life. I had choices. I could follow the formula for failure: blame, make excuses, feel self-pity, express a sense of entitlement, ("life owes me"), deny my past. But the future results would be more of the same. Or, I had the choice to change, change to who I really am. *"If any man is in Christ Jesus, he is a new creation. The old has gone and, the new has come"* (2Corinthians 5:17).

The foundation of my recovery was being laid. A life of sobriety was new to me. I liked what was occurring. I questioned whether I deserved these blessings. How long would I punish myself? Letting go of the past and looking to the future, I realized these rewards of change were, in fact, a testament to the new life script that was evolving. While men around me practiced the formula for failure, my inspiration remained the choice I made, with God's help, to change.

I met men who were incarcerated for upwards of ten to twenty years, who yet refused to give up hope. As Byron Austin so aptly said to me, "They may have me behind a fence but I'm free in soul and spirit."

I know how I return to society, balanced or the same old self, will in fact be the foundation of my future life being.

Winter had settled in and Christmas time was approaching. I was feeling the results of God's blessings in my life. Jane was planning to visit, and I was feeling blessed with a sense of peace.

From the beginning of December, although I was not aware of it, I was being observed, watched from afar. For about two weeks, the new evening shift C.O. would ask me questions about where I was from, why I was here, what I was doing with my time. Then one Friday night (I still remember the call), "Mr. King how are you tonight?" "Good sir!"

He was very cold, hostile. "Mr. King do you know who I am?" "No Sir, I do not!" "Well, look at the name tag. C.O. Brown! Sound familiar?" Realization hit me like a ton of bricks. I was speechless.

"Mr. King, I hate your guts. I am Jeff Brown's first cousin, pallbearer at his funeral. His father is my Godfather. Do you know what you did to our family?"

What could I possibly say? How could I respond? Returning to my bunk I was confused. I so wanted to speak to him. Then the cold reality struck me. This man had the power to place me in grave danger if he chose to do so. What should I do? I told Tod Davis what occurred, and expressed my concerns. About 6:00 p.m. I was called to the front desk. The sergeant said, "C.O. Brown wants to talk with you tonight in the chapel building."

I went to work. I told Byron and Les. They were very concerned for my safety. Stories, experiences of prison life...anything could happen. They had been in the system long enough to know I needed to report the incident and request protective custody. I didn't want to do that. I remained steadfast. I would speak from my heart. As much as I wish I could, I cannot change the past. My prayer was that we could move forward where we could find common ground.

I went back to my bunk and read. I waited. Seven o'clock arrived. We met. He shouted, expressing his anger and pain. He cried. I listened, empathized. I understood his anguish. There were no excuses, blaming, self-pity or justification. I explained the facts of the night, perhaps the facts of my life. I took responsibility, expressed my sorrow and regret. "What can I do? How may I assist?"

"Jeff's family, our family, has to grieve, to heal, and carry the message. But why haven't you written? Mr. Brown expected to hear from you long ago. The perception from your lawyer was you'd buy your way out of this!"

I assured him I had no intention of doing that. (I knew that I had to let go of Frankie, Joe, the promises.) Two families were hurting, grieving their losses. This is about honesty, human compassion, and accountability. We do have choices to make. I was making choices right then and there.

December 22, 1995 I was transferred. There would not be a Christmas at Cayuga. As I understand, C.O. Brown reported to his superiors that he knew me and explained the relationship. He was a man of integrity.

A two-hour trip by mini van brought me to Oneida Correctional Facility. I realized that I'd need to find a balance once again.

Christmas was spent in a reception-processing dorm. I was starting all over. Jane and Mom had hoped I would be moved closer to Buffalo, but that was not to be just yet.

"But I trust in you, O LORD; I say, 'You are my God. My times are in your hands...'" (Psalm 31:14,15).

~ A Solid Foundation ~

Chapter Twenty-two

On December 28, 1995 I was interviewed and hired as a facilitator for the Oneida Pre-Release center. I used the mornings, afternoon and weeknights to work out. Before I knew it I was in "C" dorm, general population. It wasn't long before men were coming to me with legal questions, for counseling, more secrets being revealed. Again, I had found a purpose for my life.

By mid January I had met several Jamaican men who soon became my friends, Jungu, Desmond, and Rasta. They brought about an inner strength and determination that I can be okay with me.

The stories, the laughter, and oh yes, the food! We cooked in the dorms using food products purchased at the prison commissary or items supplied in a monthly package from relatives or friends. Jungu often made the famous jailhouse sautéed Octopus in ink oil (delicious), and mushroom, onion, and pepperoni sandwiches with melted cheese.

Using can tops, folded and sharpened, we became experts at slicing, chopping and dicing our food for cooking. The irony was that knives or cutting instruments were not allowed in the prison, yet there we were with 3 inch (or larger) can lids, folded and sharpened. That was perfectly acceptable. A well sharpened can top was highly prized and kept as personal property. (Believe me, those lids in the wrong hands are as deadly as any knife.) Along the way I managed to amass a collection of cooking utensils and pots. Cut off Clorox bottles were excellent for boiling water in the microwave. We used them for cooking pasta. A plastic bottle, with holes punctured in the bottom, served as a pasta strainer. Or perhaps the best pot was my foot basin. (I told you, I had learned to be resourceful.) We used it for everything from cooking rice dinners, macaroni and cheese to spaghetti sauce.

During our bonding time, Desmond, mocking out the music I listened to, shared his Jamaican tapes, taught me rap songs and street lingo, (not that I'll ever use these words again.)

Jungu helped me master the "pull-up bar" and taught me that life's balance must be practiced every day in all our affairs. So as I followed his commitment, I worked at it every day, never giving up until the spring of 1997, the bar was mine. I can do twenty sets of pull-ups at ten pull-ups per set.

These friends were a blessing and inspiration to me. I am thankful to Rasta for not forgetting, we are friends for life. They taught me the value of commitment. Promises generally will be broken. Commitments are made from the soul.

Jane and I had now visited numerous times, were corresponding weekly, as well as speaking by phone. It seemed that our relationship was blossoming. She said we were "kindred spirits." I felt that we were building a foundation for the future.

My focus was now to present myself to the November 1996 Parole Board and hope to be released on January 6, 1997.

After arriving in Oneida, my determination to stay on the path to recovery was reinforced many times over as I reacquainted myself with men that I had said "good-by" to at Cayuga. When it was just one person I thought, "gosh, how unfortunate," the second, "well, people make mistakes," the third, the twentieth…I really better take a harder deeper look at what was going on. Witnessing many lost souls, criminals, violent people, or people who simply made a mistake, I saw a common theme reoccurring. "The Formula for failure" seems to begin and end with excuses, self-justification without regard for the value of other fellow human beings, transferring blame, refusing to take responsibility for one's own actions.

Working in Pre-Release, confronting these attitudes of failure, and antisocial behaviors, the pattern was obvious. Men with a life script continually reinforced and reaffirmed by other men who are just as sick and lost as they are, resulted in unprecedented return rates. Men being released and then in two months, three months, one year returning to prison. Why? Something wasn't working here. (I soon learned that each prison seems to develop its own life script as well.)

I soon met Mrs. Z., a counselor at Oneida, who was very anti-inmate. She didn't believe any one could really change and pretty much felt that all self-help programs were worthless. I remember hearing that Mrs. Z. was transferred to another prison and felt relieved that I could now write and develop programming to facilitate change, giving hope for a better future. Much of the material I wrote is still taught in the Pre-Release classes.

At Oneida, I immediately sought permission to participate in the AA program only to learn that the AA meetings had a waiting list. Only twenty men were allowed to participate at a time. Security, you see, is the first concern in prison.

The incarceration experience is punitive, no question about that. But restricting a proven program of recovery for those that seek help? Well, I'm not going to argue that point here, but it is difficult to understand a system that would limit a voluntary recovery program with a proven record. Through the years this program has demonstrated a self-help path to stop drinking, change behavior and aid society.

The Twelve Step Program is a device that allows us to internalize and understand who we really are, to give us the courage to confront that which we have become, and help us develop a game plan for changes that need to be made. Many have experienced profound life changes as a result of this guidance. This Twelve Step program is a ladder to change, with manageable little steps we can take, one-by-one.

Funny, but as I adapted the AA way of life, I always envision a ladder. I understand the purpose of rungs. Yes, maybe a twelve-foot ladder only requires a first step and a final step at the end. Some could make the distance but others cannot make it "in their stride." They will fail. Not because they did not try, but because the steps were too big, spread too far apart, unmanageable. But as rungs are inserted, steps provided, equally spaced, it enables us to climb, step-by-step, rung-by-rung, ever so slowly.

Some of us will attempt to skip some steps, to get there faster. Why take them all? Some of us even forget to establish a firm foundation for our ladder. No matter how sturdy our ladder, without a solid foundation…you can well imagine the consequences.

I remember all too well the consequences of climbing a ladder without paying attention to the foundation. Years ago, while building an addition to a home, in Niles Ohio, I had placed a ladder through a garage attic opening in an attempt to reach the peak of the roof. The ladder was resting on the ledge of the opening, but, unfortunately, the feet of the ladder were not firmly attached. As I climbed higher and higher up the steps, proceeding toward my goal, reaching, climbing, stretching, the ladder slipped. Out of balance, I came crashing down, sixteen feet, face first, flat onto a concrete garage floor. My hand, extended as a shock absorber, was pinned under the ladder. Permanent scars remain as testament to this feeble attempt to climb a ladder without regard for its foundation. Only then I wasn't listening nor appreciating the necessity for balance in my life. Today my permanently dislocated finger and misshapen thumb serve as a reminder to the necessity of foundation and remain a witness to the very basics of a step program. One-at-a-time, purposefully, honestly, ever so slowly, anchored on a solid foundation.

So AA, like a ladder, is a process for developing a new life script. Sometimes I find it a bit annoying that there are so many twelve-step programs in existence. Seems to me that there must be a 12 step program for every ill of humanity from alcoholism, to sex addiction, to chocoholics, the list goes on and on. But twelve steps it is. And, my testimony is that it works. At least it worked for me.

Working, for me, meant making some changes. I had to begin by being honest, acknowledging who I had become, fearlessly confronting my demons of life and executing the will to practice these AA principles in all my affairs. And my foundation was my faith in Jesus Christ. Remember, your foundation is all-important. *"God's solid foundation stands firm, sealed with this inscription: 'The Lord knows those who are his...'"* (2 Timothy 2:19).

Beginning at Cayuga, I started to climb my ladder. It seemed that as I enjoined each step in my life script, the circumstances and consequences of my life began to change as well. The first blessing was a feeling, an awareness of life. "Spiritual," I believe, is the best way to describe my being. So often as I progressed through life I went through the motions of "being," acting and reacting to circumstances, wants, needs. All the while what was lacking was the very first step, a foundation, a balance. Was my life script destiny, fate? No, I believe the choices we make in life bring with them their own consequences. I was here because of my choices. But as winter was gradually melting away to spring, so our Creator was melting away those old ways of dealing with life. Something new was reborn in me and emerging as the birth of Spring.

~A Life Under Construction ~

Chapter Twenty-three

Receiving my final divorce documents from Elise brought comfort. Little by little parts of my life were returning to me. My identity of "who I had become," "who I wanted to be" evolved ever so very slowly.

For the first time in my life, I began to notice that I was surrounded by many friends. As the days progressed, I felt an inner strength being in the presence of so many men who demonstrated genuine care and concern. Whether it was at work, in the classroom, in the dorm, on the weight court, handball, or moments when I was walking in the yard, I was never alone for long. Whether I was approached to answer questions about parole, work release, legal questions, or men simply wanting to talk and share thoughts about life, my life was evolving with a purpose.

I was aware that I was free to be "me." There was no one to please, no one to impress. I had only one goal, and that was to live my life with purpose, allowing God to guide me. See, I had never gotten this straight before. I was so busy running, hiding, trying to prove myself, that the formula for failure seemed easier to let happen than the reality of finding and pursuing my life's real purpose.

Mom and Carol visited, as well as my brother Rick, Aunt Helen, Uncle Ed. I began to notice subtleties about their visits and the letters I was receiving from them. Something was happening here. Unique for me, certainly, was that I was actually communicating with my family. We were talking and listening, back and forth and (could it be?) I was listening! I was listening to what was said as well as what wasn't.

Letters from my family members contained little remarks, subtly referring to the changes they saw in me, my reactions, my expressions. They commented on the new person they were visiting.

Mom remained supportive in my new walk. My brother was less supportive. His wife, Sue, shared that Rick was changing for the better because of the events in my life. Yet she prayed for Rick to surrender his life to Christ. I reminded them that my life was now in God's hands.

My sister said that she was scared of me. At least she knew what to expect from the old me. That's the person she knew. The new person concerned her. Could she trust me? Could I be for real? As I think about this now I understand that people remembered me as I was. They knew the man that left them. Though they loved me, they remembered the pain, the lies, the broken promises. Could be this just another facade?

Jane would question, "Is that what you think? Oh do you?" "Really?" "Are you sure you feel that way?" Initially I thought, "Heck, look at me I've changed. I've got it! See…I'm different."

Funny isn't it, how we so often want people to remember only the good. As if one good deed, one act of human commitment should over shadow, three, four, five acts of dishonesty or every other action incongruent with societal expectations. As time passes, I will understand and appreciate the full extent of societal expectations.

Well, let me share with you something I'm learning. It would take time for wounds to heal. See, all the bad things I did, the past indiscretions, perhaps my entire life script, far outweighed the good that I was doing now.

I have learned that though the process of "change" in your life is real and precious to you, and even welcomed by those who knew us and were involved with us in the past, we still may be viewed with a skeptical eye. Some may be critical, judgmental, and unconvinced. They have every right to be. Be patient.

At this point I knew beyond the shadow of a doubt that changes were taking place in my life. However, at this point, no one else could really know for sure. They heard what I said, read my letters, but would I practice it? I had not been put to the test. Well, they had not seen this side of Terry nor would they for several more years.

One issue that I had to accept is that not every one in life will like me nor do they have to. The same will be true for you. We have no control over that. Accept that your life is precious today. Know that God loves you just the way you are...but loves you too much to let you stay as you are. He is committed to helping you. Know your value and focus on the purpose that you serve on this earth. And remember: *"He who has begun a good work in you will be faithful to complete it"* (Philippians 1:6).

Redeeming Grace

As time passed and the healing of my family relationships progressed, I can say that today is different. Today I feel from Mom, Josh and Justin an awareness of respect and trust. The test of time will continue on, but my day of proof has already begun.

The time came to prepare for parole, my opportunity to return home. As I met with my counselor, he spent a considerable amount of time discussing the events leading up to the accident. He indicated that it was his professional opinion that I was beginning to accept responsibility, demonstrating change of attitude and a willingness to live my life as a contributing member of society.

Although I had progressed or as I believed "changed" enough to warrant returning home, the counselor made it very clear, "Mr. King, your chances of making parole are very slim. This crime, your circumstances…well, society just doesn't accept this behavior. Releasing you early sends the wrong message." Releasing me early? What was this man saying?

"Mr. King, how do you feel about possibly staying an additional two years?"

I could not comprehend what he was saying. So much of my work, my efforts had revolved around going home. This prospect was slimming, and reality was beginning to dawn on me, for the very first time, that I might be incarcerated until November 1998. The listening part was finally beginning to work. From the deepest part within me, I realized that this time was in fact "a time out" not from life …only the life I had left.

"'For I know the plans I have for you,' declares the LORD, 'plans to prosper you and not to harm you, plans to give you hope and a future'" (Jeremiah 29:11).

As I always affirm, this prison time was precious, a gift of life. I must practice the "change in me" here…in prison…while I have this gift. I must live one day at a time. I could no longer live my life according to the expectations of others. I had found peace in knowing my Savior. I had found purpose in life through my study of His Word, the Bible. It was the solid foundation on which I could build a new life.

Believe me, it's easy to go back to our old ways…our familiar comfort zones. But as time continues, a new script based on newly acquired or renewed values emerges. Living a new life supported by faith in God, yourself and your spiritual convictions, gifts of life (blessings I call them), suddenly appear without even asking.

After two years of letting go of my past, I realized that I still had unfinished business. I knew I needed to communicate with Mr. and Mrs. Brown. Several people asked me if my purpose was to convey an affirmative message to parole. My answer was, "No." I knew that some would perceive it this way, but I knew what God was prompting me to do. Since early 1995 I had a definite need emotionally, mentally, and spiritually, to reach out to Mr. and Mrs. Brown. I really didn't know how. I wasn't dealing with the real me, how could I convey my true feelings to Mr. and Mrs. Brown. Writing the letter required several weeks. Well, actually I wrote the letter in one evening, the editing required several weeks and numerous rewrites. Communicating with Alan McCarty, an old attorney acquaintance, I was convinced that it was time for some explanation of "why," and "how." I needed to express my feelings.

Change was abruptly forced upon this family and their lives will never be the same. Why? My actions alone. This letter helped me take the step of responsibility that I had so purported to know internally. No, I certainly was not looking to be affirmed, accepted or acknowledged by Mr. and Mrs. Brown. My intent was simply that I wanted to convey my feelings to them. I am deeply sorry. I realize the magnitude of what has occurred. I pray for them for God's comfort and healing.

Mr. Brown had requested that I consider funding $1.00 per week to a scholarship fund in memory of his son, Jeff Brown, for the rest of my life. He also wanted to see physical evidence of this commitment. Understanding life today, appreciating the meaning of commitment, I am committed to change. My intent is to live life sober, different. Time will tell. Today I live each day as if it's the last, with purpose and meaning. Life is precious indeed.

Yes, Mr. Brown, I will make a commitment in my life for different reasons today. Day-by-day, step-by-step the commitments shall evolve. Living this life script, maintaining a balance in and of itself shall be testament to the God that I have come to understand, love, and once again believe in.

The counseling staff at Oneida had selected me to participate in a Victim Awareness Program. Through the office of the New York State Unified Court System, I was requested to meet face to face with Mr. and Mrs. Brown. Tom Christian received my letter to the Browns, forwarded the letter for presentation to them by their attorney. Accordingly, their attorney reported back that they received the letter. I was at peace with this communication. I honestly did not expect a response from the Browns, simply writing was a blessing to me. It helped me admit my responsibility, express my feelings and heal.

Taking back control of my life has proven that blessings, gifts of life that we receive, have nothing to do with money, power or control. But they do have a fundamental premise in faith, beliefs and values, as those instilled in me so long ago.

Writing that letter brought a comfort deep within my soul. Being asked to meet Mr. and Mrs. Brown also brought a feeling of healing.

As you begin to change, to heal, begin living a new way of life, don't fear the future. Take each day for its value, whether imprisoned or free. Every one of us on this earth retain that "right of choice," an internal freedom to value one's life. Life is a precious gift from Someone far greater than ourselves. Realizing that this time on earth is so brief, we should begin to value each moment, for it will never come again.

During this period, spring turning to summer, I found life was beginning all over again. This awareness, I'll never forget for even moments in the prison yard, either running, walking, working out, life happening around me took on new meaning. Birds singing, leaves emerging from buds, the clear nighttime sky, evoked feelings from within me that I was at one spiritually with my Creator and His creation. I was beginning to comprehend this vast world around me, the intricacies of design. I knew that the Master designer had a plan and design for my life, too.

As I prepared to present myself to the November 1996 parole board I felt that I would assemble documentation testifying to the changes in me. Receiving copies of letters from family, Jane, Rita, and my boys were very encouraging to me. To read these letters of support, expressions of faith reinforced my conviction that my life, a new life was before me. Prison was a unique time to get things right...right with society, right with God, right with my family, right with me.

Many of us may never be imprisoned as guests of the state in our societal penal systems, yet we may find ourselves captives in our own self-made prisons. For many, these vicious cycles, life scripts of failure are in fact an internal torment from which we believe there is no way out. But step-by-step, we can find our way out from these living hells. Relationships, behaviors, habits of life all can be changed if we first start with us...acknowledging our need of God's grace and mercy. That's why John 8: 36 is such a powerful promise. *"If the Son sets you free, you will be free indeed."*

~ A Better Plan ~

Chapter Twenty-four

The summer at Oneida provided me with a new comfort zone, a time of reflection. It was so different from Cayuga a year prior. See, the year before, I was trying to control, influence, to hold on. But this year I was holding on to my God and trusting Him for what He had planned for me.

I made many friends at Oneida, men reaching out without regard for anything in return but friendship.

On August 4, 1996, my counselor called me in and informed me that I was scheduled to be transferred soon. Transferred again? Where? Gowanda Correctional Facility. The State of New York had authorized a new DWI Program. The computer shows it as a 90-day treatment program.

"Mr. King, only good can come from this. At least you'll be close to home."

Eighteen miles from Jane's to be exact. As I sat there, I realized I was headed home, home to Buffalo, and home with a change of heart, change of soul and change of being.

My period of incarceration had taken me to many prisons, Attica, Auburn, Elmira, Wyoming, visits to Southport, Camp Pharsalia, Camp Georgetown, Cayuga, Oneida, Wende. I had witnessed a lot, learned a lot. Perhaps closure was evolving again.

That night I called Jane and told her. She was pleased. Josh and Justin were very excited. Mom and Carol were happy that I would be closer to home which would make more visits possible. We would have time to get reacquainted and find common ground.

That night a thought came to mind, "Gowanda is next to Brant, New York. Gosh, that's approximately eight miles from the accident site." The Browns were neighbors of Gowanda. Terry could run no more. The new Terry was coming home. Would I be ready? Would I be able to handle life in practice the way in which I knew so deeply in theory that I must?

Going into the Pre-Release office the next morning brought sadness from many of my new found friends. I was moved, touched by their sincere expression of loss, hugs, handshakes, expressions of gratefulness. These emotions, feelings of appreciation I was counting as special gifts from God. The greatest gift for me was that I was able to feel and express real emotion without embarrassment or hesitation. I was aware of what was happening around me.

Taking the walkway from work to the dorm, I walked slowly, knowing the Oneida, the physical place, I would see no more. But Oneida the growth, the teachings, the awareness that developed there, will never leave me. This too, is a gift.

Packing up to draft, with all my worldly prison possessions packed for travel, produced a profound feeling hard to describe. I had one last night to say good-by. My friends surprised me with a farewell dinner they had prepared. They provided cups, coffee, plates, utensils and food, the works! I was truly astounded. Men were sharing and expressing appreciation and thankfulness with other men. These moments of pure emotion, without pretense or self-consciousness, I simply had never known. Not because they weren't available, but more than likely, because I wasn't open to listen, receive or comprehend the spiritual significance of these events.

The morning of my departure was hard. Several men had tears. I left behind men that shared their stories and demonstrated faith in me. I am richer because of knowing them. I am glad that we had that opportunity to meet. I was saddened by the circumstances under which we had come to meet, but rewarded in the knowledge that fundamental life changes were occurring and insight to this new life was being shared, carried to others in need. The peace and serenity I experienced traveling back home was a gift, a blessing from a God, my Creator.

Leaving Oneida by mini van, traveling toward Buffalo, I realized change was and is a natural evolutionary process. See, the old Terry would take risks, push, and create new boundaries. I had to be in control. This Terry was simply going along for the ride.

What I could control I did, and that was what I thought about, what I felt and how I responded. Remembering that the most basic needs of life were provided, I had the opportunity to absorb all that was occurring around me. Traveling west on route 90, I was heading home. I knew where, but why? For what purpose, exactly?

Our mini van stopped along the way, picking up others, DWI, vehicular assault, vehicular manslaughter. As the mini van traveled south of Buffalo, the sights, sounds and memories flooded back. Approaching the 190 North turn off, seeing the Marine Midland tower, home was near at hand. Looking south toward Abbott road, The Pony Post...chapters closed, time was healing, progressing.

Turning on to the Hamburg exit, through which I had traveled hundreds of times before, memories of events were vivid. Passing on Route 62 south, I was within one block of Josh and Justin, the prospect of which was exciting. Being closer for however longer could only aid the building of our relationship.

Gowanda is a most interesting facility. It had been an old psychiatric hospital. Patients were returning for treatment only this time a different New York State Department was in control. Yes, health and human services were involved but security was the number one priority.

Arriving August 5, 1996, brought together many men I met years before. Eric and I had been dorm mates in Oneida. Again I was adjusting to change. As I processed in, I found that although my basic necessities were provided by the state, I had accumulated quite an inventory of goods. Actually I was directed to send 55 pounds of excess personal clothing and property home. Seems I was overly concerned about clothing. I had 46 pairs of sox, 38 pairs of underwear. So there I was shrinking down to basic necessities. I'm not exactly sure why I had accumulated so much. The officers on duty received quite a chuckle out of seeing all my "luggage."

Knowing parole was near and my term of incarceration was nearing its halfway point, retaining my balance was my first priority.

Arriving at the dorm that night, no one had any clue what was occurring. Counselors simply said, "We do not know anything at all. All we know is that the building next door is being remodeled to house the men selected for a new DWI treatment facility."

I remember the very first day I was transferred back to Gowanda. I went into the day room and turned on the television. It was after five o'clock and there on the screen was Ellen, my neighbor from my former boating days. She was advertising her Tax Company and recruiting people to prepare tax returns. I remembered her witness for the Lord and was touched and moved to tears. I immediately wrote to her and she wrote back. The very next week she and her husband Bob came to visit.

She was so excited that I had written and so happy that I had accepted Christ into my life. We shared the stories of our past trials and tribulations and agreed that it is only by the grace of God that we are saved. We prayed together. That meeting was a moment of healing.

August 6, 1996, I thought I'd venture to the recreation yard and begin the process of assimilation. The yard had no weights but they did have a pull up bar and dip bar. I could certainly continue my work out just as Jungu had taught me. I began my routine. Within minutes several other men had joined me. Names were exchanged and I was welcomed. I was invited to return later that day. I now had workout partners.

Walking around the yard I was amazed at how many men I knew. Adrian from Cayuga, Joe from Wyoming, and on and on it went. As the days progressed, men continually arrived from around the State. It was surprising how many of them I knew.

August 8, 1996 was our first meeting. A correctional counselor came to see me. My initial Gowanda interview was with Mr. Paul Gray, a Christian psychologist, college professor, mentor and ex-offender. Paul, having served 18 years in state prison, understands antisocial behavior. After Paul surrendered his life to the Lord, he went to school and is now on staff at University at Buffalo as a professor in the Social Science Program. He also maintains a private counseling practice in Orchard Park. Over the years, Paul and I have developed a personal friendship.

After approximately 15 minutes of discussion Mr. Gray stated, "Well as the coordinator for the Pre-Release program, why don't you come to work for me?" "When?" "Today, as a Pre-Release facilitator." He added, "By the way, my current inmate coordinator is leaving in September or October so why don't you take his spot."

That afternoon, less than three days being at Gowanda, I was re-employed. Well, actually back in my new comfort zone, in the classroom helping and sharing what I have learned with others in need.

Mr. Gray allowed me to create a program and made sure I had access to the resources necessary to make the program a success. In less than one year, the Pre-Release Department grew from a staff of three to thirty-five trained facilitators running nine classes daily from 8:00 a.m. to 9:00 p.m. The program was a success. The classes are about life skills and behavior, teaching men and confronting them concerning the real life issues they will face upon return home. I wrote all the class programming. The job also allowed me time to write the book and to counsel other men.

The DWI program is an admirable attempt at treatment. Many of the men had now resigned themselves to not making parole. Conditional Release, a Contingent Release, returning to your community before your maximum period of incarceration, one-third off for good behavior, is a gift from society, so to speak.

Many of these men simply viewed this mysterious program as another mandated program that, if refused, would jeopardize their conditional release date. Anyway, from their perspective, it's a "no win" situation. The program participants (hundreds of them) are sent to Gowanda to sleep, to remain incarcerated, with no program, no counselors. Though the concept sounds admirable, if the public really knew, it would be questionable.

I would like to think that I am beyond the use of this program's "nonexistence" as a reason to further justify all that is so wrong with the system. Long ago I had realized that this precious time was about change.

What I did with this time was up to me. Change had to come from the desire within me, no one else.

Josh and Justin came that weekend. Returning to the area renewed an awareness that, yes, my day too will arrive when I will leave here. Putting all that I learned, evaluated, discarded or accepted into practice had begun in earnest.

Jane visited that weekend also. A gnawing suspicion was becoming increasingly clear. We were not as much "kindred spirits" as we thought. I was beginning to see that I could not have a relationship with Jane as God intends a relationship to be. I prayed that she would accept Christ into her life and that we could move on, but that did not seem to be what she had in mind. It seemed that she wanted things to be just as they were before. I could never go back. Jane offered money. Working for Marine Midland Bank she had established financial security. She insisted that I could move to Florida after my release. She was the recipient of a large estate that gave her a sizable bank account, and I do mean sizable. Her aunt in Florida has a mansion with all the trimmings and a summer villa in the South of France. Jane was offered the house in Florida, complete with gardener and house staff. We could have it, with one stipulation. I was asked to change my name.

All of this was most unsettling. I shared this with Mr. Gray. He teased me and said, "Take the money and run." Well, running is what I did all my life. I was not running and it was not to be joked about!

I wrote Jane and asked her to define her understanding of God. I had shared my conversion and she indicated that it was "rubbish." I knew it was far from rubbish. She responded that church and spiritual life had never and will not ever be part of her home or her life.

She stated, "You will not pray with me or for me. You will go to Florida, change your name and live life just as you did before."

I knew this wasn't going to work. We no longer had anything in common. I wrote back and shared my feelings regarding the present and the fact that we didn't share the same values and beliefs. I knew that this relationship was over and it was time to move on.

It was then I understood the deep underlying reason why I had wanted to reestablish our relationship. Initially, when I wrote to Jane, perhaps I did need to explain my motives and set things right. But more than any motivation of love or friendship, I think contacting her was a vain attempt to hold on to the last vestige of my past…the old lifestyle that we had shared, the Terry that she knew. But that Terry was dead. This was a startling revelation to me. I had come this far by faith. I was never turning back.

Part of the call of Christ is knowing when to walk forward, to walk by faith. God did speak very clearly to me. Ministry and prison would somehow be intertwined. I still did not know what or when, I just knew that He had a plan. I was witnessing all of the happenings around me, from those intervening and holding me up in prayer. I knew that this, too, was God.

Meeting Mr. Gray renewed a realization that things in life happen for a reason. God always has a plan. Seventeen years of incarceration, an anti-social, violent criminal history, 30 plus arrests, the taking of life, sober for over 20 years, I needed to listen to this man. I am so thankful for Mr. Gray and his consistent counsel. He provided me with the tools I needed and I have taken heed. Arriving at Pre-Release, meeting him, becoming friends, is a gift for which I am truly grateful.

The center was going through a transformation. Mr. Gray allowed me the chance to place into practice all that I've learned. He asked me if I would be committed to counseling?

"Yes, I am. I am committed to making it a way of life."

Mr. Gray asked, "What's your release plan? So you think you're ready for parole release? How are you demonstrating to the Board evidence of this professed change?"

"Well, I'll tell them of course! Look at all the letters of support people have written."

"Not enough. You see, Terry, your sentence is for six years. Parole is a gift, a blessing. Right now, politically you're not a favorable candidate for Parole Board Release."

"So what can we do?"

"Plan for your release. Demonstrate a life of change. Put it on paper and share this plan with those you love. See, this time, this change is not for parole, it's for you, to find your purpose on this earth."

This man pushed me. No excuses, no blaming, insisting on full ownership of my responsibility for my actions, my feelings, my thoughts, my behavior and subsequent consequences.

Mr. Gray was so right. For many of us seeking change, we plan a new life script, but aren't really ready to follow through. It's important that we don't change or rewrite our script for the wrong reasons. It's not a temporary solution. It has to be a "for the rest of your life" change. I was truly beginning to value how precious this time was.

Simply knowing that I was changing and able to listen, others were beginning to acknowledge that my new chosen path was well founded. But my goal was not. I am grateful to Mr. Gray for working with me, for our talks and all his support.

As you go through the process of finding your new way of life, remember, it's a slow gradual process. Don't push, don't force, just take one day at a time. As you progress, things just aren't always going to work out the way you'd like. That's the way life is. But don't give up. Assimilate to people, places and things that empower you to be your best, to help you find your balance. Don't be afraid to seek help climbing your ladder.

Mr. Gray suggested that as a facilitator, I should I read a textbook, a psychotherapy book each week, write a report, maintain a journal of what and how it applies to me. This process has been very therapeutic.

Mr. Gray allowed me to rewrite the program curriculum applying my newfound tenets of life, a weekly itinerary. AA is not enough. It's a vital part but a solid foundation must be built.

As I wrote my plan, I learned a simple process in problem solving. Take a moment to identify three to five major problem areas of your life. An example: I am alcoholic. I do not have a job. My goal: maintain sobriety, then later find and maintain employment. The inverse of one's problem is always the goal. Some of us never acknowledge the real problem.

Once you establish your goal, next identify five to six objectives. Objectives are like sub steps on our ladder. As I was taught and as I have come to appreciate, these objectives must be specific, measurable, and realistic. Identifying problems, Mr. Gray would challenge me to my very core. Why is this a problem? Are you sure that's the problem?

See, he knew differently. We continued week after week, challenging, disputing providing me a unique opportunity to take personal inventory. I never got frustrated but I did, however, get confused. I asked questions. Mr. Gray would lead but not feed. He would tell me what book to read, suggesting what to study next and so step-by-step, rung-by-rung we climbed toward our goal, based on a solid foundation. This foundation is a very precious part of life. For without this we will miss the valuable meaning and purpose of our lives.

You see, I had searched so long and hard for answers when, in fact, they lay within my being. See, this very foundation was laid a long time ago. Building blocks were being laid in place by Mom, Dad, Baba, Grandma

Rose, and all my forefathers and mothers before me. I could build on the courage of my Grandmother (Baba) who had left her comfort zone, all that she knew and loved, to make a better life for herself and her family, in a strange new world. I could build on her faith. It was so precious to her that she was willing to risk everything for the freedom to exercise that faith rather than submit to the domination of an atheistic dictatorship. I could build on the example of my ancestors from Hungary and Czechoslovakia who knew the meaning of hard work and sacrifice for a higher objective…a better life for every generation that would follow. I could build on the tenacity of my father who went to work everyday, to a dead-end job that he hated, to support his family financially. I could build on the unconditional love demonstrated by my mother, who sacrificed her wants and even her needs all her life, to create a loving, secure, nurturing home for her children. I could build on the rich heritage of family ties, love and loyalty and the security of belonging to something greater than myself.

Yes, there was the other side. I saw that, too. Alcohol had been a "staple" in the family for social gatherings, holidays, family celebrations, even religious observances. It was a common part of every day life, for forgetting, for medicating pain (sometimes physical, but mostly emotional, when facing life was too frustrating and confusing.) I saw what it did to good, loving people. The fights, the cruel words…the pain inflicted on the innocent. I saw the remorse, the shame, the isolation and the vicious cycle of medicating that pain so as not to have to deal with it.

But all that aside, the building blocks were there. And my solid foundation was the grace, love and mercy of our Lord Jesus Christ. There was a Master Plan for my life and I would not be building it alone.

Yes, God's intention for my life, His fundamental purpose, is the core of my new foundation of life. Spiritual awareness, emotional well-being mental stability and physical wellness are necessary components to achieve balance in order to build upon a foundation. When we're right with us, when we take time to get right with God, every thing else in this world follows in a natural progression. When we try to build, as I did so long ago, upon a shaky, weak and crumbling foundation, as with a house of cards, the outcome is predicted long before we start.

Preparing for the parole appearance I assembled all the plans, documents I could. Mr. Gray would often laugh and ask, "Do you plan to be released or do you want to live a released life?" Thinking, pondering, I began to understand. This process of introspection I was being mentored to do, had nothing to do with parole. This was about me, and all that was precious to me in life. This was about now, from this day forward. The past was closed. It was time to move on.

"'For my thoughts are not your thoughts, neither are your ways my ways'
declares the LORD. 'As the heavens are higher than the earth, so are my
ways higher than your ways and my thoughts than your thoughts'"
(Isaiah 55:8,9).

~ It Began With A Burden~

Chapter Twenty-five

Meanwhile, I was beginning the DWI program, a residential treatment facility, a beginning with no end. You see, recovery is a lifetime process. So many issues, for so many years my life I had gone down the wrong path. Seeing the difference today, and knowing all that took me most of my life to become, it would now require another lifetime to rewrite, chapter by chapter, a new life script. Not only will my new life require faith, but also strength and moral conviction of all I knew could evolve, as well as that which I have not yet even envisioned. A big job, yes, but I am not in this alone. *"I can do all things through Christ Who gives me strength"* (Philippians 4:13).

Moving into the DWI dorm facility brought me face to face with the reality of denial. A novel program and full of promise, but like many bureaucratically managed programs, it opened without any infrastructure, no counselor, no outlines, no direction. As one of the initial counselors stated, "At least we have an opportunity to draft the program curriculum as we go along." The only question was, "Where were we going?"

As October arrived, Mr. Gray and I discussed a desire of mine to write. Ten years earlier someone commented, "Terry, you ought to write a book." Well, I laughed off the idea at the time, but over the years, the thought lingered on and the feeling grew into a passion. Ten years ago the time was not right. I was living for Terry…a greedy, self-centered person. Today my life has changed. The saddest most gnawing awareness is that the warning signs were all in place then, if only I had paid attention. Instead, as a result of my choices, I was responsible for taking a precious life, a child of God, from this earth.

Could this have been different? Yes, without question. But based on the choices I made, who I had become and the paths I traveled, the resultant consequences were inevitable. If by my mistakes, and ultimately the lessons I have learned in life, I can prevent anyone from experiencing tragic consequences such as mine, this project will be well worth the effort. My objective for writing is to share my innermost feelings and the journey I have taken to wholeness and healing. I know that change is possible for anyone who is willing to admit his need and call out to God for help. Together, on the foundation of His love and forgiveness, a new life can be built, one step at a time.

As the writing progressed a pattern began to unfold. I was writing, by hand, each weekend twenty pages per day, some days a little more. Typing the manuscript was a problem because there was no typewriter in the dorm.

My first meeting with the newly appointed Director of the DWI, Reverend Ernest Kellner, was hilarious. I wanted access to a typewriter, a simple request. Access denied! He threw me out of his office. He thought I was one of the users and abusers. We have become friends and we laugh about this today.

Mr. Gray made arrangements to get me the typewriter. I knew it was Divine intervention! I used thirty-seven typewriter ribbons and the state provided them all on the orders of my Heavenly Father.

I spent half of my days at DWI, and the balance of the day working for Mr. Gray. Having traveled through the prison system I've met men of every imaginable background, life script, beliefs and learned behaviors. But now I was housed with 480 other predominately white inmates who were here for one basic premise…they drove drunk. Some of them, repeatedly and some had progressed to accidents, even to the point of being directly responsible for the taking of life.

During the first several weeks of "Group," (a most interesting interactive dimension of human behavior,) I was astonished to see how many men were still holding on to all that was so wrong. The theme was the formula for failure: blame others, ("it's the politicians,") make excuses, ("it's his fault,") self-pity, ("it was only an accident,") a sense of entitlement, ("we're owed parole.") I was confronted face to face with what I had worked so hard to leave. Listening to these men, who were just as sick as I was, was a startling confrontation to the perverseness of alcoholism. Men stereotyping, justifying, "Look I'm white, I work, pay taxes. So I drink a little? I don't belong here."

Being forced to listen to this predominant theme was disheartening. Yet I was blessed, for I realized that being able to see the difference, feel the emotional difference, I knew change from within had occurred. Not all of these men were so obstinate as to deny the disease of alcoholism. But when one's life has deteriorated to the point of bringing you to a state prison, this is more than a mistake.

For each one of us the profiles were horrifyingly similar. Why? Because if we honestly view each and every one of our life scripts, the reoccurring confession was that this was not our first time breaking the boundaries of society or our communities. Some of us were here because we finally got caught enough times. For others, the ultimate sacrifice was paid.

I was bothered by the initial negativity and denial. The common rationale was, "If only I didn't drive." How absurd. These men needed help, primarily in facing the truth. The societal danger was driving, but the primary cause was the disease of alcoholism. But the blame was placed on dysfunctional families, divorces, issues of abandonment, isolation, loss, hopelessness, a sense of uselessness. It was every one else's fault, someone else's responsibility.

My ex-roommate, a vehicular manslaughter case, justified himself by stating, "It was their time, accidents happen." An all night party, drinking, drugs, 110 mph car race, this was no accident. Choices were made. The wrong choices were made, not just that night but many nights over a long period of time. Take responsibility!

See, if we don't take responsibility for our actions, we delude ourselves into thinking that we don't have to change. But I knew differently. I know paramount to change is a conviction, an awareness, an admission of who we really are, and a willingness to do something about it.

Preparing for the parole appearance I assembled all the plans and documents I could. Attending "Group" reconfirmed my conviction to change. Seeing my old self face-to-face told me how perverse my life had become. I'm grateful as to how our system of law and order work. We needed to be here. Society was in fact, for the most part, being protected from our life script. While everyone's focus seemed only to be on getting out, very few men were actually committed to doing whatever needed to be done to stay out. I began to understand, in greater depth, my mentor's spirit. This time was a unique opportunity to look around, observe, feel, experience life and day-by-day place closure on the past.

Finding several other men who were seeking change, having found a new life script, we were growing as we shared together. We were living our lives, not for parole, but for the right reasons.

Well, guess who transferred to Gowanda and became Paul Gray's immediate supervisor? Mrs. Z. was now overseeing the expanding Pre-release Department and was my immediate supervisor. One day she called me in. She had studied the Pre-Release Department and stated bluntly that we were having too great an impact on the viability of men remaining free. That could not be. She stated that we had to tone down our material and presentations. She said, "Mr. King, you are a fool. If you think these men can change, you are as sick as they are. I thought you were different. Look, you are now playing with my retirement system and my paycheck. Stay out and leave this alone. The only thing you are to worry about is getting yourself out of here."

Then she asked me if I thought I could do that? I said "No. I know men can change through the grace of God." She responded, "God has no place for these men!"

Wow! I was in shock. I shared this with Reverend Kellner and Paul Gray. From that moment on I knew because I knew that something had to be done. Mrs. Z. is not alone in her thinking. Most of the state employees, who work within the system and do not know the Lord, are of like thinking. I am now very much aware of the recidivism rate (the fact that men return.) I am now painfully aware that not only do they return but in 90 days or less. Startling. During my period of incarceration alone, I could write story after story of men returning. Something has to change.

God was birthing in me a burden and vision for a ministry of intervention, a lifeline to extend to those seeking change. "Grace House" was necessary.

In the fall of 1996, after prayer and discussion with Paul Gray, I began writing a business plan and outline for Saving Grace Ministries. Paul would challenge me and encourage me in thought and in prayer.

I began to compile all the data and information I could collect and forward out for future use. Then as I began to view life through my Christian perspective and understand Biblical truths, I realized that God was guiding me in this mission field. What a precious gift He gave me to bring me into the center of the storm so I could feel the pain, see the need, empathize with others and live a saved life, preserved and protected by His grace. I was able to live my salvation, not just know about it in theory, but experiencing it and share it. What good is salvation if we keep it a secret? As Christians we need to be the light showing direction in this dark world. Jesus said, *"Let your light shine before men, that they may see your good deeds and praise your Father in heaven"* (Matthew 5:16). God was using me there during this cocoon time and He was rebuilding me for use in His Kingdom for His eternal glory.

His calling was upon my life. I had no doubt that. He was already assembling everything necessary to fulfill that calling.

"The one who calls you is faithful and He will do it"

(1 Thessalonians 5:24).

~ Blessed Is The Man ~

Chapter Twenty-six

Bob and Ellen's visit were a gift and a joy. To be able to share the love of our Lord and the gift of friendship was a blessing. I was a living testament of God's grace and was beginning to experience the miracles He performs in our lives daily once we surrender to Him.

The first visit and numerous phone calls were filled with emotions and sharing. Ellen wanted to hear all the details of prison life. I do mean the details. All we read and hear from press, media, movies, can never quite equal the horrors and pain which occur routinely within the confines of prison.

I have not shared with many people, but because she wanted to know, I told her some of the harsh realities of prison life. Bob was not too interested though he dutifully listened.

We shared our stories concerning our past, about business, the kids and Bob's struggle the past few years with issues that affected their marriage and their sustaining will to continue as man and wife.

After I separated from my first wife Elaine, Ellen hired her as her assistant. So Elaine and Bob were keeping tabs on me from the outside. I once thought with prejudicial eyes, but they were witnessing the real me during that period. The person who was blind was I.

Ellen and Bob said that they knew God had performed a miracle in my life and they were so glad to be there to witness my conversion. Together we shed many tears of joy.

During their visit in August, Ellen asked me if I was interested in meeting a fine outstanding Christian woman named Sheryl. They gave me a little of her background, telling me about the time they went with her to Russia and several other missions trips. Now this is what was soooooo neat how God had planned this long ago! I asked Ellen what church Sheryl attended. She said, "Evangel." "Evangel! Wow," I responded. "I'm studying church theology and doctrine with Rev. Ernest Kellner who was one of the initial members who founded Evangel on Maple Road." I gave Ellen the history of the church from when it was in Buffalo, before they moved to Williamsville. She was shocked that I knew all that.

I was overwhelmed by Ellen's willingness to introduce me to Sheryl. My immediate response was that I would pray about this. I wanted to seek God's guidance and know that it was right. She was surprised at my response and teased me. She said the old Terry would have jumped at the chance.

I shared with Ellen and Bob my cares and concerns, which I needed to give to Christ and deal with first. I didn't know if I was ready for a relationship. I explained what had happened with Jane. I wanted God's will in my life more than anything else. I would pray and then perhaps entertain the possibility of corresponding with Sheryl and see where God would lead.

At the same time Ellen was talking to me about Sheryl, she was talking to Sheryl about me, asking her to consider writing to me. Sheryl tells the story of Ellen calling her in the fall of 1997 and saying, "Sheryl, we have a friend of ours we want to introduce you to. His name is Terry and we knew him long ago."

Sheryl said, "Tell me about him." Ellen proceeded to tell her all about my business career, which was now nonexistent, and then she told her, "Now he is a new man."

She shared my conversion experience. Listening, Sheryl picked up on the situation and asked, "Ellen, he's where? Where?"

Ellen then explained that I was in prison and told her the background.

Now for over two years previous to this, Ellen and Bob had been attempting to fix Sheryl up with someone. To Sheryl's credit and faithful walk with the Lord, she knew that the people introduced to her just would not work. But now this was really unexpected.

Sheryl's response to Ellen was, "He has baggage Ellen, I mean baggage! A full suitcase. Like, he is a heavy load. You want me to do what??? Wow, are you nuts???"

It is funny to hear the two of them share this story.

Ellen gave Sheryl my address and numbers. Bob and Ellen, Sheryl and Sheryl's Dad, Jim, traveled to Washington, D.C., and the Promise Keeper's Convention. Though I was not there, I was! Bob tells me that each night at dinner Sheryl continued to ask them all about me. They answered all her questions and finally and she told Ellen she would write to me. This was September of 1997.

Sheryl wrote her first letter in October 1997. I never received the letter. We just do not know where it went. Anyway, Ellen and Bob came to visit and asked permission to bring Sheryl to visit me the next time they came. I wrote a letter to Sheryl and she received it several days later. I placed everything in God's hands…and tried to leave it there.

Well, several days before New Years, December 28, 1997, Sheryl came to visit with Ellen and Bob. As Sheryl was waiting in the visitor's room for me to come out, Bob and Ellen teased her, telling her to look for the man weighing 300 pounds.

(Actually, I did, once. I lost over 100 pounds and now maintain my weight through a disciplined program of exercise. We cannot forsake our responsibility to maintain our bodies. We offer them to God to use to do His work.)

The visit room was packed. I was excited! All of the roommates, Tod, Jessie, Dave, Jeff, were just as excited for me. I remember when I returned from the visit room all the men were lined up at my cube area teasing me that I beamed like a spot light. Tod said, "I've never seen you like this." We had been together since 1995. That's another story.

Sheryl and I met and shared that very first day. I was nervous. Funny, I can speak to thousands and share my life but that day I was so nervous. I think she was too.

I think of the courageous step Sheryl took, coming to the prison, entering the pit of society and walking by faith to seek out the will of God. We both knew from the very first letters that God's hand was upon this relationship.

There was Sheryl alone, in the worldly sense, with no support, except for Ellen and Bob. I knew how difficult this must have been for her.

Yet by the grace of God she came and she walked with Jesus into the life He had called her to. I believe that all of her spiritual training and life experience, both in education and in the church, have prepared her for this chapter of her life.

Not many can handle the sights and sounds of the prison. Sheryl looked beyond the confines of the prison fence and saw through the eyes of our Lord.

Bob and Ellen were concerned what I would do with my life once I was released. I told them that God had spoken to my heart and I would be in ministry. Ellen said, "Why not come to work for me preparing taxes? At least you'll have income and a career."

The facility superintendent did something unusual. He approved me to take the tax course. Over the next six months I took every tax course while sending my homework out to be graded. Only God can ordain these events. So by June 1998, I had completed all the course material and was now ready to manage a tax office. (If God would so choose.)

After Ellen and Bob left the first day, Sheryl stayed about another hour and a half until the guards asked her to leave because of overcrowding.

Sheryl returned to the prison on New Years Day, and that was our first full day alone.

Sheryl and I knew during the second visit and our prayer time together, that God had given us a gift. We began to explore our feelings. I felt so comfortable sharing my heart with her. We wrote daily. What a gift. I would write five to six pages daily, six days a week. All the letters are chronicled. Sheryl would write back and share her life with me.

Sheryl would arrive at 6:00 a.m. to get in at 7:45. If she arrived later she would have to wait until 11:00 a.m., which meant a four to five-hour wait for a one to two hour visit. I knew this was hard on her. I often asked her to come just once a weekend or every other week. She was insistent that there was no other way.

As we visited for one hundred and eleven visiting days, we would sit for six hours at a time, with no physical contact other than to hold hands and pray. (Try sitting at the kitchen table for six hours with your mate.) The only book we were allowed was the Bible. All food was dispensed from a vending machine, and only the civilian could acquire the food. We had to ask permission to go to the bathroom.

During this time of sharing, the "table talk" time, we often received comments from the security staff like, "Man, what do you two talk about?" I'd respond, "Christ!" God was using the time we were there together, mightily. Others were noticing the fellowship and love. I was grateful that the staff and others were touched as well.

We would someday like to lead a Couples Retreat. One of the exercises will be the "table talk." To have couples sit for just two hours, and then using an interactive questionnaire, examine the two-hour dialogue, I think they will begin to understand and appreciate the importance of communication. So many seminars teach and outline the steps necessary for good communication, but very few couples ever go home and actually put those steps into everyday practice.

But from other couples I have worked with, the "table talk" exercise has an immediate impact. The outcomes are generally similar. One partner becomes fidgety, the other quiet. They have nothing to talk about. They're bored. Then the reality of the intimacy of their relationship becomes apparent. With the Bible present, the power of God takes over. The experience is neat.

Sheryl and I grew in friendship first, expressing our common love for Jesus, and sharing our pasts. When Sheryl would ask me a question about my past, I would answer. Sometimes I wish she hadn't asked, but I had to answer honestly. I'd wait for her response. Usually it was, "You did what?" Anyway, I had nothing to hide. I was free. I knew that this woman had taken a step of faith and she needed to know the whole story. There could be no lies, no secrets if we were to have a future together. The past is now used as living testimony to God's Saving Grace.

I share this thought and message regarding the past. I would often enter relationships with others to get a need met. I always had an ulterior motive, to fulfill a want, or to make money. When I married Elaine I was 19 and she was 26. When I went out with the Big Guys and tried to be important, Elaine was an ornament to show off. She also took care of the daily drudgery of life that I didn't want to deal with. How could I get to my goal of making money if I had to wash clothes or take care of a house? So she met a need.

Elise and I met while out drinking very late one evening. The relationship emerged around the ability to drink and to lie. The fact that she came from a wealthy family wasn't bad either and I could figure out a way to put this to my advantage. Or so I thought. Anyway, I always had to be the one creating the persona and presenting the image I wanted you to see. If I wanted you to think I was rich, I'd create that image. A family man, I could do that too. A mobster, I was good at playing that role. I certainly had enough training.

But here I am in prison, broken and humbled. What strikes me is that Sheryl saw me for the man I really am. I did not have to create an image. (Boy, would that have been a neat trick!! Here I am in green prison attire.) I did not have to lie, I did not have to manipulate. I simply had to be who I am. I was grateful for Sheryl's comforting ways, her tenderness. She knows how to listen, and share, and even cry. Our times together for hours were glorious. For we grew and understood that the time in the desert that God ordained for us was good. He was uniting us as one in Him.

Sheryl and I started as friends sharing the stories of God's grace and very soon we realized that God had blessed us with the most precious gift of all. Love in the truest form, agape love, the willingness to love unconditionally and to surrender all wants and needs to simply serve the other.

"Blessed is the man who makes the LORD his trust.... Many, O LORD my God, are the wonders you have done. The things you planned for us no one can recount to you; were I to speak and tell of them, they would be too many to declare" (Psalm 40:4,5).

~ The START Program~

Chapter Twenty-seven

Writing the START manual was a labor of love an represented and exhaustive study of the human condition. This is the six-month program of recovery currently being taught in several prisons and the homosexual community as a program of change. It is also being offered as part of the curriculum of Elim Bible College. Pastor Mazzella often remarks about the program's value and the significance it will play as a vital part of the discipleship program of Grace House and the Christian community at large.

During this period of time I was working directly with Ernie Kellner and Deacon Gainey. I transferred to the Chapel office and was listed as a Chaplain's aid. I had access to a new computer, with Windows 95. Wow! It was exciting. Deacon Gainey provided me with paper and the research material to begin writing a program for Pre-release. The real gift was when Ernie Kellner's office was moved next to mine. I saw him on a daily basis and was able to share my research. He began to do the edit work helping me add the salvation message of Christ. After having spent the last year and a half with Paul Gray, studying the psychological component as to why man does what he does, and sharing this weekly with Sheryl, we began examining scriptures relating to "dying to self" and the emergence of a new man in Christ.

For Sheryl and I this examination took on a personal meaning, for we began to examine the chains of the past that would preclude us from entering into daily communion with God and personal revival. The scripts of life, including old behaviors had to be surrendered. Some Christian men would continue to blame others, eliciting a sense of entitlement, (I'm owed because I did my time) and hide in his church denominational affiliation so as to avoid the real sharing of his feelings.

As we shared and examined the material we interwove scriptural principles into the context of the classroom material. As Sheryl and I were visiting and writing we would often write six to ten pages daily.

I had explicit instructions from security that "God" and identification to "Christ" must be avoided or I risked further imprisonment in isolation.

When I mean isolation in prison I mean "the box," solitary confinement. Usually a man is sent there for violating a prison rule. The cell is 6 foot by 8 foot and on average, the man stays in there for six months to one year. You are not allowed out for any purpose. The recreation area is a dog run outside the cell. It's a connected cage 4ft. wide by 8 ft. long in which a man can go out one hour a day and walk back and forth.

Yet in the construction of over 50 classroom-teaching modules, Christ is evident and the message of salvation is clear. Yet the specific use of His name is avoided. I had fun with the Muslim and Jewish participants.

As I began to write and relate my personal walk with the Lord, and as I listened to Ernie Kellner and so many other brothers in Christ share their testimony, the concept of "dying to self" was becoming more and more clear to me. This is where the freedom lies. Unless we die to self and our old ways of life, we can never freely walk with our Lord. I believe surrendering everything to the Lord is necessary for me to experience an intimate relationship with Jesus, and to receive the spiritual gifts that are evident in the book of Acts.

I was now praying daily with Ernie and Deacon Gainey. As I explored my prayer life and church relationship, Sheryl provided me with the Statement of Faith and Bylaws of Evangel Assembly of God. God is an economist! I begin to study the various relationships between church doctrine and my own salvation and need to worship.

Several occurrences happened during times of prayer and during my sleep. The utterances were God's prophetic touch upon my life and direction. I knew at that point that I would be involved in church life but just didn't know what. I knew I was called out to do God's work.

Mr. Gray shared with me that he dreamed I would be speaking to great multitudes and Ernie Kellner said over and over, "Brother, God is going to use you mightily." Well, I did not know how or when, but after hearing Him directly and the prophetic utterances, I knew my life would never be the same.

Being raised Catholic and separating myself from the ritualistic worship was a time of processing. I challenged Reverend Kellner and he challenged me by bringing in books all about the Pentecostal doctrine and the church. I read feverishly and would bring him my questions daily. Now Sheryl was guiding and Reverend Kellner was praying and teaching and Deacon Gainey was hoping I'd remain a Catholic. Then one day, I ask Reverend Kellner a question on baby baptism and salvation compared to the Catholic theology and the Protestant view. The next question was regarding the gifts of the Spirit and my own personal experience. Well, Reverend Kellner and I met Deacon Gainey at 9:00 a.m. at 11:00 a.m. we were still in a deep doctrinal discussion. At two o'clock that afternoon Deacon Gainey conceded that I was one of them…as he joked, "a non-catholic." I was growing and free and it felt good. Peaceful.

I considered being baptized in prison but knew that I would return home soon. Reverend Kellner advised against it and strongly suggested that I wait to share the moment with Sheryl and family. And so it was.

Anxiously awaiting the November parole appearance, I began to consider what I would be asked. What will they consider? Do I even have the right to want to go home? Am I ready? So many questions. What I was beginning to understand was what Mr. Gray so profusely impressed upon me. It's not about getting out, it's about staying out. Staying out was directly related to my conviction and passion to change, for I was beginning to discover who I really was.

Mr. Gray informed me, "Terry the early evening class was approved. You're now approved to supervise the Pre-Release cycle." So another gift was granted, to work each night for a program we had fought to implement. Our facilitators, Randy Luce, Roy Montour, talented men, were mentoring under me, learning about behavior, attitudes, beliefs. So it was that a new inmate program was enlarged to carry the message.

Our purpose was simple. Many men leaving prison are scared, apprehensive and in need. For those facing release, the Pre-Release program would provide them with a two-week cycle of health education, life skills, understanding their obligations of parole, instruction on how to fill out employment applications and other basic forms, to help them reprocess into society.

But our evening program was uniquely different. We gathered as a group of men, assured of going home with a definitive date three to four weeks away. The purpose was to express feelings and discuss issues common to one another. These men were frustrated at being confronted with one program after another. Yet as I've experienced over and over, when the steps are followed module by module, slowly, passionately, the rewards were worth the effort.

Men have difficulty sharing their feelings. So often we were taught as children that we should not share or express ourselves. Some remember a father who would repeatedly predict, "You will never amount to anything." The memory of past failed relationships, hurtful words from of a parent, spouse, or friend can remain vividly painful. Self-esteem can be wounded. But we can find healing if we will leave these painful memories at the cross.

We wrote the program allowing a man or woman to see the person they really are when no one else is looking, and the person God wants them to be. The group consciousness was forming and barriers were being broken. Our mission was to provide the men a safe environment for introspection and self-evaluation to face honestly who they have become. The goal, to help them process their feeling, to appreciate life and see its possibilities. It is possible to break vicious cycle of irrational thinking that results in self-defeating reactions. As we grow in the Lord we will be confronted by daily struggles and memories of the past. What can we do? We must walk by faith. We won't always have the answers, but as we put our trust in Christ, read and study His Word and live in obedience to that Word, He has promised to be with us, giving us strength for each new day.

Standing outside the classroom one evening, the third week into the program, I observed men who were one week away from leaving state imprisonment. These men were sitting silently, all diligently completing their worksheets. I was touched and deeply moved. My feelings were overwhelming. The fact that I felt these emotions was testament (to me) that my life had changed 180 degrees. I had found my purpose and I was at peace. The gift of life was simply knowing that maybe I could make a positive difference in someone's life.

Perhaps these men may come back. I realize that I cannot control the actions of others, yet I feel so much compassion for these men. They are a part of my life now. I want them to succeed, not just to stay out of prison, but to go back as productive members of society. Even more than that, I want them to find their balance as God our Savior provides.

I know that this vicious cycle of events, negative consequences can be broken and new life from God with His rewards of life can be experienced by anyone who calls upon Him.

"He is able to save completely those who come to God through Him, because He always lives to intercede for them" (Hebrews 7:25).

~ Called To Freedom ~

Chapter Twenty-eight

As Sheryl and I began to share and grow, the issues of the START manual were part and parcel to our own walk. So often when we first submit our life to Jesus, we begin to praise Him and follow Him gladly. We delight to study His Word, relishing His promises. But when we are asked to shed the past and become one with Him, forsaking the old ways of the world, some times we back up and some quietly rebel. We begin to negotiate our Christian walk. It's not negotiable. The Christian life involves surrendering our whole life, taking up a cross and following only Him. Jesus said, *"Anyone who does not take his cross and follow me is not worthy of me. "Whoever finds his life will lose it, and whoever loses his life for my sake will find it"* (Matthew 10:39).

As the months turned into a year, we focused on my release and the building of our family. Sheryl was right. I came with baggage. But I came with a contrite heart and willingness to share. I prayed a prayer of thanksgiving for God gifting me with His beautiful angel. She had a difficult road. I was so grateful she was willing to walk it.

She often shared about her church family, their love and support. But as the year unfolded the challenges grew. She was hurt by the abandonment of friends who did not support this relationship nor care to take the time to pray with her or seek for themselves if this could be by God's design. Perhaps they were genuinely concerned or simply it was their own immaturity prompting some of those who had been so close to her to walk away. It was painful for me to see her hurting.

She told me how she asked numerous people to write me. Several did, most would not. She asked others to come and visit and meet me for themselves. One couple did. The others would not. There was one who wrote to encourage me and extend himself. That was Pastor Mazzella. I am grateful to this man of God for taking the time to reach out and include me in his life. Meeting him the first day of my release, I knew because I knew that this man and I would walk together in the call God had placed upon me. I believe I journaled these thoughts.

For me, having walked this road, I am painfully aware that we as Christian are called to leave our Christian comfort zones and walk among the broken and wounded that Christ so loves, to do the work of evangelism.

Jesus identified with them when He said, *"For I was hungry and you gave me something to eat, I was thirsty and you gave me something to drink, I was a stranger and you invited me in, I needed clothes and you clothed me, I was sick and you looked after me, I was in prison and you came to visit me.' Then the righteous will answer him, `Lord, when did we see you hungry and feed you, or thirsty and give you something to drink? When did we see you a stranger and invite you in, or needing clothes and clothe you? When did we see you sick or in prison and go to visit you?' The King will reply, `I* *tell you the truth, whatever you did for one of the least of these brothers of mine, you did for me"* (Matthew 25: 35-40).

Being a follower of Jesus Christ is not simply about church attendance nor is it about revival services. It's about a way of life. We are the church, "the called out ones" representing Jesus every day in spirit and love. To be in revival daily walking by faith, bringing the Good News of God's love to everyone is our mandate.

Having lived the dark side of life and being on the precipice of hell I realize that this life is not negotiable or at times comfortable. When we try to make it comfortable are we doing the work God has called us to? Perhaps not.

"You, my brothers, were called to be free. But do not use your freedom to indulge the sinful nature; rather, serve one another in love" (Galatians 5:13).

I love church and the beauty of corporate worship, prayer and the encouragement, instruction and correction we receive through the preaching of His Word. I appreciate the desire for a spiritual revival. I know that these times are a blessing and encouragement in our walk with the Lord. But the call upon our lives to a relationship with Christ is not relegated to the church alone. We must live it everyday.

"Therefore, I urge you, brothers, in view of God's mercy, to offer your bodies as living sacrifices, holy and pleasing to God--this is your spiritual act of worship" (Romans 12:1).

Yes, we may struggle with trial and tribulations of life. God does not promise this life will always be comfortable. He simply promises that if we rest in Him, He will be with us, our needs will be met and we will have purpose and meaning in this life and the assurance of eternal life.

While we remain here and heed His call on our life our comfort zones may be challenged and changed. And then the question remains. Will we as brothers and sisters in Christ walk by faith? Will we be judgmental of those who do? Will we attempt to circumvent the call God placed upon us?

When I think about all God allowed Sheryl and me to see during the prison experience, I thank Him. The witness to staff, officers and other men and their families was a gift. There are so many blessing from this time. The time was necessary, preparing us for our mission field, the work of evangelism that we now find ourselves called to do.

To be invited into churches weekly and share the gift of God's saving grace is a privilege and honor. We are humbled. Yet the season of life that we processed through was required for both of us to comprehend what God had in store for our lives.

I remember one day a C.O. asked which church Sheryl belonged to. When she told him, he said, "You two don't belong here." I often heard that from staff. I responded, Yes, I do and I have been blessed to be here." In reality, I had been sentenced to death before I ever went to prison and I didn't even know it. The Bible says, *"The cost of sin is death, but the gift of God is eternal life, through Christ our Lord"* (Romans 3:23). It was in prison where I actually came to life. This time was a loving gift from our Lord and Savior. Prison had become my "Grace House," the place where my life was changed forever because of God's redeeming transforming grace.

Other officers would come to my dorm area and ask me to pray for them. Several would share their innermost feelings and here I was, an inmate, counseling them. Only God could orchestrate that! God is amazing!

It was at Gowanda that I was able to start the first Promise Keepers group ever inside the prison. The superintendent insisted we have an outside facilitator come in to run the group. The volunteer was my friend Bob and Jim Wheaton, Sheryl's Dad. To this day, Jim goes into Gowanda every Thursday night to witness and pray with the Promise Keepers men's group. It is a blessing from the Lord to the broken and wounded.

I began to express to Sheryl, my concerns and for the men in pre-lease and their need for a strong discipleship program on the outside. I shared the vision God had given me for a home, a haven where men could come upon release and be slowly acclimated back into society. Yes, many had genuine conversions in prison, but they needed the support of other Christians. Returning home to the same influences that helped put them on the road to prison life in the first place was setting them up for failure. I had witnessed it too many times.

There was also the need for the families of inmates to understand the changes that had occurred in them while "away." I knew all too well how difficult it was for loved ones, who had not experienced God's amazing grace, to understand the changes that had happened in me. As we talked and prayed, it became more than just my burden. "Grace House," as Sheryl named it, became our mission. We both knew God was calling us to this ministry.

Sheryl and I walk by faith. We are amazed daily by the wonderful people He has brought into our lives. They are His gifts. These people have most assuredly, left comfort zones, taking risks, to reach out and walk with Jesus in a new adventure. So often, in our humanness, we want to see the outcome of events before we decide to get involved. We want to know the risks, the rewards, "what's in it for me." We want guarantees. Society teaches this and rewards this kind of thinking.

Yet Jesus breaks tradition. He says, *"Take up your cross and follow me."* We don't need to know where we are going, or how we will be used, or whose life He has appointed for us to impact. But He invites us to walk with Him in faith. Wow! It is so simple. Yet it is man who complicates the equation. No matter what has happened in the past, Jesus forgives and restores. He wants us to live today by faith and obedience looking forward to the reward that awaits His faithful servants.

"Forgetting what is behind and straining toward what is ahead, I press on toward the goal to win the prize for which God has called me heavenward in Christ Jesus" (Philippians 3:13,14).

Being released from prison on January 5, 1999 brought a sense of renewal and intimacy with Christ. The cocoon was opening. I had been changed and a new season in Christ was unfolding around me.

I remember the day I was released from Butler Correctional Facility. I signed out and the officer handed me my personal property, the American Flag my uncle had sent me, and my accumulated prison money, $100.

The officer said nothing, turned and walked away. I wasn't sure what to expect. I was alone in the prison entrance foyer and unsure where to go or what to do next. I asked the secretary at the front desk. She said, "Just leave. You are free to go."

Free! Yes, she was right, I was free! *"If the Son sets you free, you are free indeed"* (John 8:36). I am free by the blood of Christ and I will go wherever He leads.

Epilogue

"Take up Your Cross and follow me!"

So often in life I anticipated events and contracted with life for the outcomes. Much of my old life depended on knowing the secure future or the orderly progression of life. From birth to death, contracting, projecting, always resulting in madness and chaos.

The call of Christ upon my life is testimony of the miraculous healing power of God's saving grace. Through the grace of God I understand the power of prayer and repentance. My repentance to Christ is more than just being sorry for my sin, it's about dying to self, allowing the Holy Spirit to bring about change in me. Repentance is a precious gift from our Lord that opens the door to a brand new life. It is possible because *"God so loved the world that He gave His one and only Son, that whoever believes in Him shall not perish but have eternal life"* (John 3:16).

As I walked out the door and turned toward the drive entrance I saw the new van pull in. Sheryl and Justin had arrived to bring me home. Justin drove, Sheryl prayed and God guided our journey.

Arriving in Buffalo, our first stop was Evangel Assembly of God to meet Pastor Mazzella. Prayer began the journey and remains the center of life in all we do.

That first night home I spent at Bob and Ellen's aware of my parole restrictions and the obligations. All I was asked to do for parole was to report to my parole officer. I considered that another gift.

Each day brought about a new awareness of the struggles of life. Yet, through God's grace and sharing my struggles with others and the discipleship of so many loving friends, life as Christ had planned long ago was unfolding.

I never doubted that God would use us in ministry. I was not sure how or when. I do know that one week after release a counselor suggested to me that I consider ministry as a career. Well, a career, no, but a calling, a life commitment to Christ. Yes! I rest in the comfort that He is in control and not man. The ministry call and all that God had blessed us with is testament to His will and His grace upon our life.

Saving Grace Ministries was conceived as a vision from God and birthed in His love. On April 20, 1999, the ministry began to formalize and express its vital need upon the community. As we have witnessed the growth and development of the ministry, we have witnessed miracle after miracle. We are in awe of God's touch upon the lives of so many as He prepares the way.

Though the ministry was official born on this date, the missionary journey is not complete. God had chosen a partner to bless and enrich my life and share in this ministry. On May 22, 1999, I married my best friend, my partner, my equal, my precious gift from our Lord and Savior. Sheryl Wheaton became my wife. Pastor Mazzella performed the ceremony as many of our family and friends witnessed this union that Christ had brought together.

Today Sheryl and I are in the mission field together. We are challenged daily by the demands of life, yet we are comforted by the blessings we receive doing the work God has called us to do each day. We have learned that God does not present us with any request, job, or task for which He has not already prepared us.

"Faithful is He Who called you, Who also will do it" (1 Thessalonians 5:24). "His calling is His enabling." He knows if we walk by faith, and it is by faith, that He prepares the way. And... prepare the way He did.

Returning home from prison, I was blessed with housing, employment, transportation and discipleship. God has brought people into my life who have encouraged and supported me, providing me opportunities to share my testimony. Not every one is as fortunate.

I am painfully aware of the recidivism rate and the continual return of men to prison. I was staggered as I studied the statistics. Each year 22,500 men are released to parole supervision from New York State prisons and within 60 to 90 days, 40% of them have violated parole and are back in the penal system. Within three years, 85% of them will be reincarcerated. Each parole violation means another victim, another family in pain, more lives in chaos. God has laid on my heart a ministry to provide support for men who truly want their lives to be different, giving them the tools they need to succeed.

The ministry is preparing to open "Grace House" in the Buffalo area. Our Mission Statement is simple: To provide a smooth transition to community life for men recently released from a correctional facility, providing a highly structured program based on Christian principles, while evangelizing the Gospel of Jesus Christ.

Grace House represents hope to the broken and wounded, receiving men who have committed their lives to the Lord and desire to grow in their new life with Him.

This is a voluntary program. These men could, in fact, live independently on parole, yet must choose to submit to the ministry rules and accountability for up to one year, in a sincere effort to become productive for the Kingdom of God, their families and their community.

The Ministry services include: twenty-four hour on site program management, meals and lodging, employment opportunities, Christian counseling, family reconciliation counseling, life skills training, Bible Study, discipleship training, recreation, community involvement, neighborhood support projects.

To the Glory of God, this ministry has been miraculous. A network of churches throughout the Buffalo area is joining together to support this ministry. The Pastors Planning Board meets monthly and represents a wide variety of denominations. They are a living testimony to the power of God working through the Body of Christ. It's inspiring to witness the coming together of so many from various churches in the community, laying aside denominational differences to simply serve the will of God as Christ teaches.

The needs of the ministry are many, from staffing to prayer partners. Yet as we walk in faith the daily gifts and blessings we receive are amazing. There are so many stories to share about the miracles.

It is a miracle how the actual building for Grace House was presented to us by God. It was a miracle how the property, 1924-1932 Bailey Avenue, Buffalo, New York, was kept safe just for God's purpose. It was a miracle how we were given the gift of office furniture for Grace House, down to the envelopes that arrived with love offerings from someone touched by the healing power of Christ. We prayed for stationery, requesting five hundred sheets. God answered with the arrival of six thousand four hundred sheets. Someone, inspired after hearing our testimony asked, "Do you need envelopes? The next day ten thousand envelopes were delivered. We have been given an IBM lap top computer, copiers, a church organ and a freezer. The donations continue to amass.

The ministry has been given free radio and television airtime to present our testimony and the vision of Grace House. Many costly hours of legal services have been donated, without cost or obligation. Doors have been opened from churches to political institutions, to share our testimony and present our burden for Grace House. Men and women have donated hours of volunteer work. Area churches have given generous financial gifts and have pledged continuing support.

The miracles continue and remind us that none of this is possible through man. It is *"Not by might nor by power, but by my Spirit,' says the LORD"* (Zechariah 4:6).

God loves the people He wants us to reach and He is making the way possible. It is by His amazing, saving, redeeming grace and we give Him all the glory!

The Challenge

As a nation, subject to the wrath of God, to the changing world and all the struggles from within, many of us gladly received the blessings and privilege of being born into the family of God. Will we accept His call to pick up our cross and follow Him? As we grow in the Lord, our service is much more than gratitude for the grace he has lavished on us, it's an obligation. Let us rise up, take up our cross and walk with Christ! Being renewed through our intimacy with Christ, let us leave the comfort of our relationships within the confines of the church building and walk with Him as He directs, not as we want but as He wills in our lives. I pray that when God speaks to you in the intimacy of prayer, that you, having heard the call, will rise up and walk. Whatever your call to ministry, heed the call and never turn back. The choice is yours. His blessings are free and His promises are eternal.